praise for You're with Stupid

"A story of passion and perseverance with a soundtrack that echoes from the pages. . . . Dedicated fans of '90s alt rock will find inspiration and lessons."

—*Publishers Weekly*

"[*You're with Stupid*] succeeds as both a memoir and a cultural history of a brief wrinkle in time when a few Chicago neighborhoods seemed to comprise the center of a then-flourishing underground rock universe."

—*Aquarium Drunkard*

"*You're with Stupid* abounds with interesting insights about musical and cultural niches that deserve more attention and, more importantly, it reveals the inner workings of one of history's greatest record companies. . . . [This book] is every self-described Gen X music nerd's dream come true."

—*The Stranger*

"*You're with Stupid* nurtures our sense of nostalgia for a tremendous decade of music, especially in kranky's pursuit to 'release music that transcended the moment,' and reminds us of simpler, pre-Internet times where radio airplay, touring, and fanzines heavily influenced the success of music's breakout stars."

—*SPIN*, "Best Music Books of 2022"

"Independent music from Chicago was absolutely essential to my developing sensibilities. My teenage mind was blown away by labels like Touch & Go, Drag City, and Thrill Jockey, but as I dug deeper, I zeroed in on the magical, shadowy kranky. It was pre-Internet, and I didn't get all the scene connections or timelines, I just happily listened in my shitty apartment and felt my world shift. *You're with Stupid* does something equally remarkable: It tells the history of that time and place without making any of that early, optimistic magic disappear."

—Brandon Stosuy, cofounder, The Creative Independent

"*You're with Stupid* serves as a primer on the independent record label boom of the late 1980s, the documenting of a city's diverse scene, and the quiet explosion of a new kind of music via kranky. Most importantly, it offers the backstories of some of your favorite bands and albums of the last thirty years."

—Mac McCaughan, coauthor of *Our Noise: The Story of Merge Records, the Indie Label That Got Big and Stayed Small*

you're with stupid

AMERICAN MUSIC SERIES

Jessica Hopper & Charles L. Hughes, Editors

Recent Titles

Franz Nicolay, *Band People: Life and Work in Popular Music*

Tara Martin López, *Chuco Punk: Sonic Insurgency in El Paso*

Alex Pappademas and Joan LeMay, *Quantum Criminals: Ramblers, Wild Gamblers, and Other Sole Survivors from the Songs of Steely Dan*

Margo Price, *Maybe We'll Make It: A Memoir*

Francesca Royster, *Black Country Music: Listening for Revolutions*

Lynn Melnick, *I've Had to Think Up a Way to Survive: On Trauma, Persistence, and Dolly Parton*

Lance Scott Walker, *DJ Screw: A Life in Slow Revolution*

Eddie Huffman, *John Prine: In Spite of Himself*

David Cantwell, *The Running Kind: Listening to Merle Haggard*

Stephen Deusner, *Where the Devil Don't Stay: Traveling the South with the Drive-By Truckers*

Eric Harvey, *Who Got the Camera? A History of Rap and Reality*

Kristin Hersh, *Seeing Sideways: A Memoir of Music and Motherhood*

Hannah Ewens, *Fangirls: Scenes from Modern Music Culture*

Sasha Geffen, *Glitter Up the Dark: How Pop Music Broke the Binary*

Hanif Abdurraqib, *Go Ahead in the Rain: Notes to A Tribe Called Quest*

PETER BLACKSTOCK & DAVID MENCONI,
FOUNDING EDITORS

you're with stupid

kranky, Chicago, and the Reinvention of Indie Music

BRUCE ADAMS

University of Texas Press

Austin

Printed in the United States of America
First paperback edition, 2024

♾ The paper used in this book meets the minimum requirements of ANSI/NISO Z39.48-1992 (R1997) (Permanence of Paper).

Library of Congress Cataloging-in-Publication Data
Names: Adams, Bruce (Record label founder), author.
Title: You're with Stupid : kranky, Chicago, and the reinvention of indie music / Bruce Adams.
Other titles: You are with Stupid | American music series (Austin, Tex.)
Description: First edition. | Austin : University of Texas Press, 2022. | Series: American music series | Includes index.
Identifiers: LCCN 2021060196 (print) | LCCN 2021060197 (ebook)
ISBN 978-1-4773-3072-2 (paperback)
ISBN 978-1-4773-2120-1 (hardcover)
ISBN 978-1-4773-2616-9 (PDF ebook)
ISBN 978-1-4773-2617-6 (ePub ebook)
Subjects: LCSH: Kranky (Record label)—History. | Adams, Bruce (Record label founder) | Record labels—Illinois—Chicago—History. | Alternative rock music—Illinois—Chicago—History and criticism. | Underground music—Illinois—Chicago—History and criticism.
Classification: LCC ML3792.K73 A32 2022 (print) | LCC ML3792.K73 (ebook) | DDC 780.26/6—dc23
LC record available at https://lccn.loc.gov/2021060196
LC ebook record available at https://lccn.loc.gov/2021060197

doi:10.7560/321201

For Annie

contents

introduction

> I'm not sure which makes you more Post-Rock, having played on a Tortoise record, or having eaten at Jim's Grill.
>
> —*Matt Lux*

It must have been late in the fall of 1991 when I had my first meal at Jim's Grill. I started working at Cargo Distribution in September that year, and sometime after that the domestic buyer Joel Leoschke and I stepped out for lunch. Joel took us on a short drive to Irving Park Road by Lincoln Park High School to a diner. The chef, Bill Choi, had introduced Korean dishes like Bi Bim Bop, cabbage soup, and vegetable pancakes into the grill's standard greasy spoon menu. There was an autographed Smashing Pumpkins *Gish* poster on the wall. The Pumpkins were the up-and-coming Chicago band, clearly aiming for bigger things and gaining momentum. I came to discover that many musicians in town frequented Jim's. After we placed our orders at the counter and sat down, Joel grabbed a section of the newspaper, opened it up, and started reading. Later, more than a few people told me they found that habit to be irritating. I took another section and did the same. I squirted some of the red chili paste onto my zucchini and kimchi pancakes and chowed down. It was the first of many lunches together, some of which would evolve into "if I had a label" conversations. Joel had a reputation as a curmudgeon and, to a certain extent, cultivated it. One of the jokers, and there were many, who worked in the Cargo warehouse had written "Honk if You Hate People, Too" on the dusty back of Joel's car.

You could say that Joel and I had metaphysically met years before at the cutout bin. If you frequented record stores in the 1980s and '90s, you know what I'm referring to: the place where you'd find discontinued and overstocked LPs and cassettes for half price or less. These bins were full of oddities and outliers that hinted of secret histories and hidden paths outside of the loud underground rock music that took up most of my listening time. I knew that the predecessors of the distorted guitar rock I loved, the Stooges, Velvet Underground, and Captain Beefheart, were relatively unknown in their time. What I discovered among the cutouts were even more obscure musical strains from the '70s that not only ran counter to the Beatles-Stones-Zep-Floyd narrative of mainstream rock music but also pointed to wider parameters indie guitar bands were not touching. Money was often tight. I had developed the habit of visiting the record store weekly, and the cutouts offered an affordable and intriguing island to explore. The low prices there meant you could buy on impulse and take risks.

An early cutout-bin find for me was *Evening Star* by Robert Fripp and Brian Eno. The cover art was appealing: a misty island on the horizon, glowing in the twilight. So was Fripp's guitar, stretched out and cycling across each track. Some of *Evening Star* was soothing; some tracks were appealingly named "An Index of Metal" and struck me as discordant and unsettling. The mix intrigued me, and as an instrumental album it was well suited for late-night or early morning listening. I ventured further into a group of artists aligned with Brian Eno and the Editions EG label, picking up Jon Hassell's *Dream Theory in Malaya* LP and the Brian Eno-Harold Budd LP *The Plateaux of Mirrors* for a couple of bucks apiece. I stumbled across *Psalm*, by the Paul Motian Band, again lured by the cover art, which featured a smeared photo of a fire cutting through a patch of meadow. The blurry jazz of the album presented the evocative, lonesome tones of Bill Frisell as a variant on the potential of the electric guitar. I was prompted to investigate the ECM label that released it. Over lunch, Joel and I would share impressions of particular albums and how we discovered them thumbing through a cutout bin. Every day it seemed to us that indie rock was getting more and more calcified, aiming for nonexistent brass rings in the wake of the grunge explosion. More formulaic and "tight-assed." Those old EG and ECM records represented a set of less-constrained possibilities.

When people asked Joel how things were going at Cargo, he often replied, "We'd be dangerous if we had a brain." Working there was a case study in what not to do. By 1992 the conversations Joel and I had about how we would run a record label had moved to how we could start a record label, impelled by hearing a duo from Richmond, Virginia, called Labradford. Joel told me that he had put some money aside, without mentioning a sum. Whatever it was, I knew it would be sufficient, providing our prospective label operated within its means. Joel wouldn't have proposed it otherwise.

1 hey chicago

The story of kranky is a Chicago story. In the early eighties, as a global music underground was developing, a network of wholesale music distributors, independent record labels, clubs, recording studios, college radio stations, and DIY publications established themselves in Chicago. The city had been a center of the recorded music business since 1913, when the Brunswick Company started making phonograph machines and pressing vinyl. Chicago had been home to jazz pioneers Jelly Roll Morton, King Oliver, and Louis Armstrong for a brief, impactful time. In the 1950s Chess Records was a force in the blues and R&B scenes. Alligator Records was an independent blues label started in 1971. But the founding of the Association for the Advancement of Creative Musicians (or AACM) in 1965 is what created the precedent and working model for independent organization and avant-garde music in the city that eventually was reflected in house music and underground rock. AACM's self-reliance and the border-crossing devotion of related musicians who incorporated ancient African music into the creation of future-facing music put Chicago on the map of innovative and independent music centers.

It was possible to get cheap apartments to live in or practice space for your band or even a storefront to open a distributor or store. The hollowing of the city's industrial base had left empty warehouses and business spaces that were ideal for multiple activities, especially for anyone willing to live near a highway, train line, or in a low-income or overlooked neighborhood. One point of origin for house music was an underground club called "The Warehouse."

The people behind the bars or record store counters, or piling the boxes up in warehouses, were often musicians, or artists, or both. Well-stocked record stores and distributors brought records into the city, giving people opportunities to listen to and process music. The radio provided access to multiple college stations playing a dizzying variety of music. Rent was cheap enough that people didn't need full-time jobs and could pursue their enthusiasms. David Sims of The Jesus Lizard moved to Chicago in 1989 and recalled in the free weekly the *Chicago Reader* in 2017 that the band's landlord "raised the rent on the apartment five dollars a month every year. When we moved in it was $625 a month, and when I left 11 years later it was $675 a month." My experience was similar.

If you were a music lover but not a musician, you could work for a music-related business or start your own. Self-published fanzines popped up, and people had workspaces where they could screen print posters and T-shirts for bands. The major labels and national media were located on the coasts, lessening the temptation for bands to angle for the attention of the star-maker machinery. The circuitous impact of all the above was meaningful in shaping how and why Chicago would become the fertile center of the American indie rock scene, and why it produced so much music that broke the stylistic molds of that scene.

I moved to Chicago from Ann Arbor, Michigan, in the summer of 1987. I shared a house with a roommate from Michigan in a northside neighborhood called Bowmanville and started work in a suburb called Des Plaines, right by O'Hare. It was at a distributor called Kaleidoscope, run by the unforgettable Nick Hadjis, whom everybody called Nick the Greek. His brother Dmitri had a store in Athens and promoted shows for American bands like LA's industrial/tribal/psychedelic outfit Savage Republic. Kaleidoscope was a common starting point for enterprising young music folks seeking to enter the grassroots music business within Chicago. People came in from downstate Illinois or Louisville, Kentucky, or Austin, Texas, and worked there before they went off into the city to work at the growing Wax Trax! and Touch & Go operations. Bands were starting their own labels to record and release their music, following the pattern established by the SST and Dischord labels. In those pre-Internet times, scenes grew up around successful bands who distributed their singles via touring the country, getting fanzine coverage, and garnering college radio airplay. The seven-inch single, LP, and tape cassette were the preferred formats for these bands and labels.

Two guys named Dan (Koretzky and Osborn, respectively) who worked at Kaleidoscope had been impressed, and rightly so, by a self-released, self-titled album by the duo Royal Trux that Kaleidoscope stocked. A little later, I had a single called "Slay Tracks 1933:1969" self-released by the band Pavement firmly pressed into my hands by one or another Dan and was informed that only a thousand were pressed. I bought it that day. Dan Koretzky and Dan Osborn each worked at the distributor, had experience at Northwestern's WNUR radio station, and were strategically placed to discover and make contact with new bands. They reached out to Royal Trux and Pavement, started a label called Drag City in 1988, and began releasing records in 1989. In a similar process, Joel Leoschke and I would start kranky after hearing the first single from an unknown ambient duo from Richmond called Labradford four years later.

In the economic sense and at the label level, independent or "indie" refers to a means of production and distribution. Independent labels operated outside the fiscal control of major labels and multinationals that owned them; the so-called "Big Six" of the Warner Music Group, EMI, Sony Music, BMG,

PolyGram, and Universal that operated from 1988 to 1999. Indie labels arranged and paid for manufacturing themselves and were distributed at least in part by independent distributors like Chicago-based Cargo, or Mordam Records in San Francisco, who sourced records from hundreds of labels around the world and got them into record shops domestically.

The levels of economic independence labels exercised were on a spectrum. So, for example, hardcore punk records on the Washington, DC, Dischord label were manufactured by the British independent distributor Southern Records, which also provided European manufacturing and distribution for a consortium of mostly British labels. Although Chicago-based Touch & Go Records were also distributed by Southern in Europe, the label arranged and financed its own manufacturing. By necessity, most labels had to interact with multinationals, and those interactions also existed along a spectrum. The psych pop Creation label, home to My Bloody Valentine and Oasis, and grindcore pioneers Earache Records with Napalm Death and Godflesh started out as independents in England and were eventually manufactured and distributed in North America by Sony. RED, originally an independent distributor called Important, was eventually acquired by Sony. Virgin/EMI Records opened Caroline Records and Distribution in 1983 in New York. Touch & Go was distributed by both of these distributors.

Labels turned artists' recordings and artwork into LPs, singles, cassettes, and compact discs. Parts were shepherded through the manufacturing process, and finished products were received and warehoused somewhere, be it someone's closet, basement, or a wholesale distributor, and then scheduled for shipment to record stores and mail-order customers. Stores needed to know what was arriving when in order to predictably stock their shelves, and so release schedules had to be created, coordinated, and adhered to. Likewise, fanzines, the magazines created by dedicated fans/amateur writers, and radio stations had to be serviced with promotional or "play" copies of releases so that reviews were run and music was played on air when records arrived in stores or as close to that time as possible. If there was enough money available, advertising would accompany the release. Some labels had paid staff or volunteers who promoted records; others hired agencies. If bands were touring, stock had to be ready for them to sell on the road. And if a label wanted to export releases or had a European distributor, the schedule had to be aligned with the logistics of overseas shipping and sales. At any step in the process of releasing music—manufacturing, shipping, or distribution—a label could easily find itself doing business with a multinational. Complete self-sufficiency and independence for record labels was virtually impossible in practice. It's fair to say that the greater the degree of economic independence a label possessed, the more aesthetic leeway it had to operate with.

As a musical genre, "indie rock" is much more difficult to define with precision. The use of it often tells you more about the person using it than about any band or piece of music. "Indie rock" could be used in 1992 to describe a band or dismiss it, or to do both at the same time. As a pejorative, it worked really well: "indie rock" meant watered-down and weak if you liked loud rock music, and it meant boring and predictable if you were inclined toward more open-ended musical structures or approaches. If you considered yourself to be "with it," listening to someone use "indie rock" sincerely in conversation (as opposed to in an ironic or self-deprecating way) was a sure sign of hopeless squareness, topped only by "alternative" on the Open-Ended Scale of Uncoolness. If "punk rock" was used as praise for righteous motivation or self-reliance, "indie rock" was directed at a lack of wherewithal or poor organizational skills. In the widest aesthetic sense, and for the purposes of this book, indie rock means guitar bands who released music on independent labels, utilizing the song structures and dynamics encoded by '60s garage bands and the Velvet Underground.

Many artists and records you will read about here are described as being "experimental." The musicologist Joanna Demers defines the general understanding of experimental as "any music that rejects tradition and takes risk through running counter to musical conventions." It's close in the horseshoes and atomic bombs sense, which I think is as good as you can expect for the constantly evolving and moving location of convention in popular music. As with "indie rock," "experimental" often reveals more about the person deploying it than it does about any particular piece of music.

Touch & Go Records was unquestionably the lodestone of the Chicago independent rock scene. Touch & Go began in 1979 as an acidic fanzine in East Lansing, Michigan, by Tesco Vee and Dave Stimson and eventually began releasing hardcore punk rock singles by bands from Michigan and Ohio. The bass player in one of those bands, the Necros, Corey Rusk, a distinctly less extroverted person than Mr. Vee, took on label tasks in 1983, began releasing LPs from Scratch Acid, Butthole Surfers, and Killdozer, and moved with his wife, Lisa, to Chicago in 1987. By that time, you couldn't really call most of the bands on the label hardcore punk, though many of the musicians involved had begun playing hardcore. They took the volume, aggression, and distortion of punk rock, played at mostly slower-than-punk tempos, often with a blues-inspired lurch, and used a wider set of guitar textures. There wasn't really a genre name for this "post-punk" tendril until "grunge" came along, although the latter term became associated with Seattle bands. The term "éminence grise" describes Corey Rusk's role in Chicago, and the role of Touch & Go in the city grew almost in proportion to his desire to avoid the spotlight.

The other magnetic pole in Chicago was Wax Trax! Records. Jim Nash and Dannie Flesher opened a record store in the northside Lincoln Park neighborhood in 1978 after selling a Denver store by the same name. The store was well stocked with domestic and imported vinyl, located close to train and bus lines, and quickly became a go-to spot for shoppers. In 1980 the Wax Trax! record label began with the release of a seven-inch single from the Chicago hardcore band Strike Under, followed by the drag artist and John Waters associate Divine's "Born to be Cheap" single. The label's third release was a reissue of the local Chicago band Ministry's self-released "Cold Life" twelve-inch single. That got the label going seriously as Ministry's sound hardened from synth-centric new wave into the blend of harsh electronics and assertive dance beats that became known as "industrial" in the United States. Another twelve-inch, from the Belgian group Front 242, was licensed, and the growth became exponential. Kids wanted to dance, and the heady mixture of clang and menace Wax Trax! dished out resonated with those already enamored with English goth and New Romantic bands. If you knew anyone who worked at the store or label, eventually you would meet Jim and Dannie. They had great parties with a welcoming aura for all kinds of freaks, outcasts, and the curious. The establishment of label offices at the corner of Damen and Wabansia was one of the key events in the development of the Wicker Park neighborhood as a locale for musicians and artists in Chicago.

There was no rivalry or friction between Touch & Go and Wax Trax!, just a healthy respect. Each label had its own lane and stuck to it, and the role of the Wax Trax! store in supporting all kinds of underground music engendered an affection and respect among those who worked at T&G and musicians on the label. This attitude would come to infuse the Chicago music scene in the years to come.

Meanwhile in Seattle, Bruce Pavitt took on Jonathan Poneman as a partner in his infant Sub Pop venture and released the initial twelve-inch EP recordings by Green River and Soundgarden in 1987. The word "grunge" was used in the Green River release sheet and a small snowball was pushed down a hill. In

1988, Sub Pop released the debut Mudhoney single in a limited, numbered edition of eight hundred. A genre was named, and a strategy to stoke demand was implemented. In November 1988 Sub Pop started a monthly Singles Club subscription series with a seven-inch from a trio called Nirvana. The singles flew out, it seemed, each on colored vinyl by a new band.

The trio Halo of Flies had debuted in 1986 with the influential "Rubber Room" seven-inch pressed in a limited, numbered edition, and singer/guitarist Tom Hazelmeyer had the Amphetamine Reptile label releasing more, including the "Dope, Guns & Fucking in the Streets" seven-inch compilation singles series. Hazelmeyer settled in Minneapolis and started releasing records from bands like Vertigo, Cows, God Bullies, and Tar that lived up to the "Noise" motto on the label logo. In Olympia, Washington, Calvin Johnson and Candace Pedersen's K imprint ultimately released more than 130 editions of singles, cassettes, and compilations in the International Pop Underground series, with a highly visible level of participation by women.

LOCATION, LOCATION, LOCATION

Chicago had something that Seattle, Olympia, and Minneapolis couldn't match—the combination of wholesale distribution and infrastructure to support and power the indie rock boom. The import bin was the first stop at the record store for many obsessives, and British records were at the top of the agenda for record store buyers.

Chicago had O'Hare Airport, where freight companies, customs brokers, and a large UPS facility made bringing import goods from London or sending orders to anyplace in the world possible. The Wax Trax! store took advantage of this, bringing in the newest records from England directly. This geographic placement is what powered Kaleidoscope's success. Labels could take advantage of this too. Imports from the United Kingdom and Europe would arrive, and brokers would process them through customs. Consolidating freight shipments to overseas customers was a way several labels could batch relatively small orders together so that one big order could be sent affordably to Europe. Recordings from Chicago got to London or Berlin quickly, while records from Seattle or Olympia or Minneapolis often had to make the trip via Los Angeles, San Francisco, or New York. Bands from all over the United States and Canada were coming through town, giving savvy distributors and labels the chance to build relationships and get access to the newest recordings and maybe keep a step ahead of the competition. The Wax Trax! and House music scenes each pumped vinyl into the distribution channels and garnered attention in the United Kingdom and Europe, ensuring that Chicago was not seen from the outside as a one-dimensional indie rock town.

When I arrived, Kaleidoscope was an "out-of-the-box" distributor. Records and CDs came in, and the sales staff endeavored to make calls to stores to sell them and ship them out. Most of the stores we contacted were independent operations, many of which had started in the sixties and seventies as head shops or small storefronts. A few did well enough to open multiple locations. Most were located in big cities or college towns. Kaleidoscope was a midlevel player at best, a rag-tag operation that didn't have any associated or "exclusive" labels like RED, Dutch East India, and Caroline in New York. Those larger distributors could offer stores exclusive new releases and had in-house promotional people to get radio play, reviews, and book ads so that those albums or singles entered the stores with some level of consumer awareness. We had to hustle, work old connections and make new ones with DIY bands and established labels, and bring in unusual items from Europe and the United Kingdom. The bigger indie distributors could ship relatively large orders to national and regional chain stores like Musicland, Wherehouse,

Camelot Music, Coconuts, Peaches, Strawberries, Rainbow Records, Sam Goody, the expanding Tower Records group, Barnes and Noble bookstores, and (to be noted later) the appliance chain Best Buy. The success of Kaleidoscope rested on the ability of the buyers to find sellable records and CDs, or magazines, fanzines, and even posters, and the sales skill of the staff. And pulling every order quickly, and "packing it up, nice and tight," as the owner Nick put it, to ship to Madison or Houston.

Phillip Hertz was the super salesman at Kaleidoscope, and he bolstered business with connections to independent labels. He'd gone to Evergreen State College in Olympia, Washington, where he befriended Sub Pop founder Bruce Pavitt, Simpsons creator Matt Groenig, and K Records honcho/Beat Happening "front man" Calvin Johnson. Phillip spent some time working at one focal point of the international independent network, Rough Trade Distribution in London, drummed for Aussie proto-grunge heavyweights the Scientists, and hung out with the dub reggae producer Adrian Sherwood of On-U Sound fame. In addition to possessing incredible sales skill, Phil had a talent for spotting interesting trends and record labels and talking people into sending records to Des Plaines for him to distribute. Reputation and trust were everything in a small, tight-knit network of individuals in every city who all knew each other. Word got out quickly when a check bounced, or an order didn't show up.

Kaleidoscope shipped American records to Nick's brother's store in Athens—sometimes in violation of labels' export restrictions, and always taking great care to value shipments as low as we dared to save Dmitri Hadjis money on duties. Likewise, Dmitri helped Kaleidoscope get Greek pressings of much-wanted UK releases—some of which were of questionable legality and even worse audio quality. Dmitri came to visit on one memorable occasion, and I packed up the parts of a vintage '60s Cadillac he bought and sent them in increments to Greece over the course of months. It was reminiscent of the Johnny Cash song "One

Piece at a Time," where an auto worker smuggles a car out of the plant bit by bit.

Nick came complete with a set of entertaining catch phrases. If we had a good week, the next Monday he would walk around the office pointing at individuals to say, "Whole new attitude!" If we had a bad week, the next Monday he would walk around the office pointing at individuals while proclaiming, "Whole new attitude!" Or he would put his big, hairy, Popeye arm over your shoulder and tell you, "I taught you everything you know. I didn't teach you everything I know." It made me wonder if Interpol or the FBI might be interested in everything Nick knew.

The company did well enough to move into a former dry-cleaning plant down the street. More people got hired, including two Texans: one named John Dennett, who became a label manager at Wax Trax!; the other named Patrick Monaghan, who eventually started Carrot Top Records and released albums by the Coctails and Handsome Family. I was nominally shipping manager, and also worked nights at the Touch & Go compound assembling singles and packing mail orders and promo packages. Musicians from bands like David Sims from Rapeman and Rick Rizzo from Eleventh Dream Day worked in the Kaleidoscope warehouse. Sims later told the *Chicago Reader*, "Everything of value I learned about the music industry I learned while riding Kaleidoscope down the drain."

Kaleidoscope always walked a knife's edge but somehow stayed in business from week to week. Bigger East Coast distributors were a competitive threat, the cash flow varied, and often smaller labels had to wait for checks beyond their sixty-day credit terms. Wax Trax! releases were selling tons with the success of Ministry, Revolting Cocks, and Front 242. The Wax Trax! 1987 partnership with Belgium's Play It Again Sam Records brought in releases from artists that would eventually build an aggressive variant of dance music known as Electronic Body Music, or EBM. With the competition edging in on Kaleidoscope's core accounts and able to sell exclusive labels of their own, each week was a battle. The owner very much wanted to secure some exclusive labels himself, and his attempts to do so were poorly executed enough to threaten whatever financial health Kaleidoscope had eked out.

Within a year I had arranged to leave Kaleidoscope, worried about its continually precipitous financial state. I had an offer to work full-time at Touch & Go doing promotional work and took it. My time at Kaleidoscope had provided me with invaluable experience in the logistics side of independent distribution, a new set of contacts at labels and stores, and a lot of insight into how things could go wrong. Other coworkers had moved on to the Wax Trax! store and a new store called Reckless in Lincoln Park. I got my first apartment of my own, in the nondescript northside neighborhood I first moved to. I was a ten-minute drive from T&G world headquarters.

I had been working part-time for the label and observed how Touch & Go operated. Corey Rusk kept a close watch on the finances. I have a vivid memory of him handing me a check from a distributor one day, instructing me to drop whatever I was doing and get it to the bank immediately. The company in question had bounced checks before, and the earlier the check was processed by the bank, the better the odds it would clear. I called magazines to get coverage, worked with fanzines, and sent out promos to college radio and posters to concert promoters. Each town had its scene, with a few people who might work a record store, have a radio show, book shows at a church or VFW Hall, put out a fanzine, or do freelance writing for national publications. It was my job to understand the tastes of each person and direct records to them accordingly. I worked in a converted pantry with a desk, phone, and record shelves. I had a rolodex on my desk, and I added cards as I expanded my contacts list. At the end of every day, I covered the desk with a garbage bag. The cats liked to pee there at night.

Now and then, being a guy with strongly held opinions, I would recommend bands for the label to consider signing. T&G got quite a few unsolicited demos, usually on cassette. Bands that had released their own singles would mail them as well. The label's P.O. box was always full of padded envelopes from hopeful bands near and far. I got a tip that a new band from New York called Helmet was mailing a cassette. I grabbed the cassette when it arrived, listened, and enjoyed it. I passed it along to Corey, who was less impressed than I was. Tom Hazelmeyer signed Helmet to Amphetamine Reptile shortly thereafter. I had envied the guys at Drag City, who were both working day jobs but kept their new label going. I was keenly aware of the financial resilience needed to keep a label operational after an initial release. That was money I didn't have.

I did have enough money to see shows. Miscellaneous glass vials and metal objects crunched under my steel-toed boots when I went to Wicker Park to Club Dreamerz or the Czar Bar. A Kaleidoscope coworker was booking bands in a theater space in the south loop called Edge of the Looking Glass. Sue Miller was organizing shows at a club by Wrigley Field called the Cubby Bear, and in 1989 she joined Julia Adams at Lounge Ax across the street from the Wax Trax! store. On Balboa right off Lakeshore Drive downtown I would see jazz and world music shows at Hot House. A radio show on the public station WBEZ called *Blues Before Sunrise* ran from midnight to 5 a.m. covering rhythm-and-blues, gospel, sermons, comedy, swing, and electric and acoustic blues. I spent many a late night or early morning driving home after a show listening to Jimmy Lunceford, Pigmeat Markham, or Pinetop Perkins. On Sunday mornings Dick Buckley nursed me through hangovers playing jazz from the '30s and '40s on WBEZ while elucidating on their details in a rich baritone voice.

I could get on the guest list to see Touch & Go bands, who played often in Chicago and accompanied bands coming through town. A new group made up of veterans from two Texas T&G

bands had formed called the Jesus Lizard. The group's first EP in 1988 featured a drum machine, and David Yow, David Sims, and Duane Denison were joined by drummer Mac McNeilly in July 1989. The full lineup played their first show in a Thai restaurant on Irving Park, in front of a small audience. The three instrumentalists were locked in a steely embrace, with vocalist Yow reeling out from the stage into crowds like a thrashing tuna hooked onto a cable. The Jesus Lizard quickly undertook national touring, and their audience grew quickly. Urge Overkill was the band on the label aiming for a greater commercial profile, and it became painfully clear to me that they watched those bands that had jumped from independent labels to majors with an eye toward doing the same.

The label moved operations to the second floor of a warehouse on the northside, near the intersection of Irving Park and Western Avenue. I was joined by a direct salesperson and shipping clerk. Every now and then a stoic-looking guy with a flat-top haircut would stop by from the new Cargo distribution company to pick up an order. I might have exchanged brief pleasantries with him, or more likely nodded in his direction. Later someone told me his name was Joel.

One of the aftereffects of Chicago's punk rock scene was the growth of reliable venues available to bands. The fly-by-night clubs that hosted shows in the early '80s were gradually replaced by more professionally run venues. The growth of the national touring network paralleled the development of clubs devoted to showcasing underground bands. Lounge Ax became a magnet for local and touring acts as Sue Miller worked her contacts and Julia Adams managed the day-to-day. In 1993, the Ukrainian Village bar the Empty Bottle moved to a location large enough to accommodate a stage and began booking bands. The Cabaret Metro concert hall was in action beginning in 1982, with a subterranean club called the Smart Bar that hosted DJs and was crucial to later interactions between audiences and musicians. Metro's owner, Joe Shanahan, managed bands as well, including Smashing Pumpkins. The museums, cultural institutions, and universities hosted performances and offered opportunities for those so inclined to see musicians from outside the indie rock corridor that ran from Lincoln Park to Wicker Park. Hyde Park seemed to be an island unto itself, unconnected to the CTA train lines, but with cool record stores, a great radio station in WHPK, performances on the campus of the University of Chicago and the spectacular setting of Rockefeller Chapel, or the chance to see AACM members and groups play. Saxophonist Ken Vandermark, who moved to Chicago in 1989, remembers, "After visiting the city and taking a look at the concert listing in *The Reader*, I was stunned by the amount of music—jazz and otherwise—that was taking place here, and that clinched my decision to make the move."

David Grubbs of Gastr del Sol, a Kentucky immigrant to the city in 1991, explained how his roommate and bandmate Bundy Brown and others exposed him to many recordings. It's a story that happened quite a bit in a city where many musicians worked in record stores and distributors. "It didn't hurt that Bundy worked at Reckless Records and there was a steady stream of vinyl making its way into the apartment daily: experimental rock, jazz, contemporary classical, dub reggae, the Nonesuch Explorer Series, etc., etc.," Grubbs said. "When you added Jim O'Rourke's record collection as well as the total omnivore John Corbett (I used to hang out at his Radio Dada show on WHPK)—that's many lifetimes of listening, and I needed to get cracking. It totally reinvigorated my sense of the culture of records—which had first crested for me in high school, in the thick of hardcore punk."

THE NICE LABEL

I like to think that I worked at Touch & Go during its Golden Age. The Butthole Surfers' catalog on the label provided a secure sales base in the tens of thousands, as did records by Big Black and Steve Albini's new band at the time, the grimly monikered Rapeman. I promoted a label roster that consisted of ferocious live rock bands, Midwest mainstays all, like Laughing Hyenas, Killdozer, Didjits, and Die Kreuzen, who had stretched and then broken the American hardcore punk template without giving up its volume or intensity. I shared my promo mailing list with Jennifer Hartman, who had started a record label to release the debut album from a Louisville quartet called Slint. Slint members Britt Walford and Brian McMahan had been in a band called Squirrel Bait with David Grubbs. I would have a chance to work on the second Slint album, *Spiderland*, which Touch & Go released in 1991.

Having roadied for Laughing Hyenas and through building on my own connections from working at a record store and college radio in Ann Arbor and writing for *Your Flesh* fanzine, it was easy for me to reach out to writers, fanzines, radio stations, and store buyers. Touch & Go had been around long enough at that point to be operationally tight. Releases were scheduled out well in advance, with all the pieces needed to promote them like ads and posters in place. The label operated in an environment filled with what the musician John Forbes describes as "third rate shit heels." Watching the scrupulous integrity Corey Rusk used in dealing with bands and his commitment to independence for the label, and getting a view of the underhanded ways distributors dealt with labels financially, gave invaluable insights that would help me at kranky and provide guideposts for how that label operated.

In early 1990, Southern Records in London opened a warehouse a few floors above Touch & Go. The second album from Washington, DC's Fugazi was due, and it was determined that an American office was needed to efficiently fulfill North American sales orders. I had seen an early Fugazi show shortly after Ian MacKaye of the seminal hardcore band Minor Threat had started playing with members of Rites of Spring. Laughing Hyenas had opened for the band in DC. There was no doubt in my mind then that Fugazi would be popular based on more than the players' collective pedigree. What I didn't expect was the truck that pulled into the alley by the warehouse with a shipping container on its trailer: a shipping container full of Fugazi *Repeater* CDs manufactured in France, sent across the ocean, and then trucked to our nondescript warehouse on Chicago's northside. The tonnage sent my mind reeling. First with how dominant the CD format had become in the marketplace. Secondly with the thought that an equal or greater number of CDs were arriving in London to supply Europe. Thirdly with calculations of manufacturing and shipping costs and how a profit margin still existed for Southern as the distributor, Dischord as the label, and Fugazi as the band. I asked Corey Rusk if any Touch & Go bands sold that many albums, and he told me it represented roughly the number of CDs shipped for the first Jesus Lizard CD, vinyl EP, and full-length LP combined. The scales fell from my eyes as I got a physical understanding of what success as an independent band or record label could mean.

Before I left Touch & Go, Corey started manufacturing and distributing records for two other labels, Austin-based Trance Syndicate and the new Chicago industrial label Invisible Records. He realized that distributors needed to be kept interested in new records between Touch & Go releases. By the mid-1990s, Touch & Go would make similar arrangements for Drag City, the North Carolina-based Merge, and a New York City transplant to Chicago called Thrill Jockey Records, providing important support for those labels as they got on their feet and built catalogues.

By 1990 you could venture to Club Dreamerz in Wicker Park to see touring bands, or to the Exit, an almost comically punk rock club outfitted with a rebar dome over the dance floor in Old Town on the northside, where local hardcore punk bands like Bhopal Stiffs or the Effigies would play, along with the occasional Touch & Go band. The punk rock loyalists and holdovers frequented the bar, where they got the straight stuff without the mixture of other genres that was slowly working its way into other clubs. My Touch & Go coworker Matthew Taylor and I switched off DJ nights at a Lincoln Park bar called the Crash Palace. We had free reign to play what we liked, and we both liked a wide array of music, old and new. Al Jourgenson of Ministry would be behind the bar working the turntables, too. When Jon Langford of the Mekons moved to Chicago, he began playing classic country records there with Rob Miller, who went on to cofound the "insurgent country" label Bloodshot Records. Tuesday nights were dedicated to B movies presented by a group calling themselves the Psychotronic Film Society. Many of the people you would see out at shows would be at the Crash Palace, along with a supply of regulars. On one of my nights off from DJing, Matthew called me and urged me to stop by. Nirvana were playing in town, with the Jesus Lizard opening, and David Yow was bringing Kurt Cobain by the bar after the show. Matthew had to yank "Smells Like Teen Spirit" off the turntable when the two entered. Courtney Love from the band Hole walked through the doors shortly thereafter. I don't recall witnessing the fabled event, even though I was there in that narrow room. I must have been talking with someone about music.

I had an incentive to acquaint myself with people who had radio shows or fanzines, or who booked shows or worked at record stores. Knowledge, skills, and connections were passed through and across this network. I recognized familiar faces wherever I went. There were superfans, the people you could count on when certain bands came through town. I met Dan Grzeca and Greg Dunlap via Touch & Go. As college students at Northern Illinois University in Dekalb they published a fanzine called *This* and booked shows, including an early Jesus Lizard appearance. After graduating and moving to Chicago, each became involved in the music scene. Dan Grzeca had an art degree and began silk-screening posters for bands. Grzeca and another poster artist trained at Screwball Press under Steve Walters, who was making posters and T-shirts for Lounge Ax and various bands. Bruno Johnson was an imposing six-foot-plus skinhead, hard to miss behind a record store register, bar, or the door of a rock club. I remember a shambolic show at a Wicker Park dump called the Czar Bar where Bruno had to pull the plug on Royal Trux. Nobody tried to tell him he couldn't.

By 1993, the punk rock touring circuit was less than a decade old. It had expanded to include a wider variety of bands, many of which were playing guitar-centric rock that broke the loud-fast hardcore mold. In Chicago a variety of venues from theater spaces to the twelve-hundred-capacity Cabaret Metro hosted shows every night of the week. Record stores often hosted performances, which meant you could check a band out on a Saturday afternoon if you couldn't make the show that night. Likewise, WNUR in Evanston and WHPK in Hyde Park each had radio programs where local or touring bands could play live on air. The same was true for other big cities and some college towns. If bands couldn't get paying gigs, there were possibilities to at least perform and promote their music.

Fanzines provided an information conduit to the network of musicians and listeners. The punk rock ur-guide and fanzine *Maximum Rocknroll* was known for its Scene Reports, in which locals would update the readership on the happenings in their city or state. In addition to spreading the news on music, many fanzines served as a forum for the airing of grievances. Aside from allowing readers to complain about or praise any publication's coverage, letters to the editor were also a way to expose shady business practices on the part of labels, mail-order companies, and venues. Many bands were not afraid to use interviews to share their experiences, good and bad, with the individuals and entities they interacted with. It was happening within a closed circuit, and as writers and publications aspired to a greater visibility and professionalism, this dissipated as the decade progressed.

The Touch & Go bands I worked with saw Chicago as an oasis on their tour schedule. Most of them were based nearby in Madison, Milwaukee, Champaign, or Ann Arbor. They could count on a good show and being hosted in an all-night party by Corey and Lisa Rusk afterward. The same applied to bands on other labels I would speak with, who often stayed an extra night or two in town to recharge before moving on. Those bands would go back to Iowa City or St. Louis or Austin talking about what was happening in Chicago. The city had always had an attraction to suburban kids, and as the '90s proceeded, musicians from farther afield in places like Oberlin, Ohio, Louisville, Kentucky, Austin, Texas, and Washington, DC, moved to Chicago. The strong improvisational jazz tradition of the AACM brought the guitarist Jeff Parker and saxophonist Ken Vandermark to Chicago. In 1992, I met the latter at Tower Records, where he handed me a cassette recorded in a sixth-floor loft space called SouthEnd MusicWorks near the fish market west of downtown. Vandermark invited me to watch a performance in the basement of Lower Links a few blocks south of Wrigley Field. The performance I witnessed was a tribute to the iconic free-jazz saxophonist Jimmy Lyons. The duo of Vandermark and drummer Curt Newton were raw, throwing out sparks and then cohering back together. I would see Vandermark at rock shows and came to understand how he was attracted to the energy of the music and the independent ethos of labels like Touch & Go.

Vandermark was playing alongside the veteran Hal Russell in a screwball bebop band called NRG Ensemble. Russell catalyzed a young music obsessive who went by the name of Weasel Walter in forming a "Punk Jazz/No Wave/Brutal Prog" outfit named the Flying Luttenbachers after Russel's birth name. Young Master Walter once schooled me on death metal at a party and could see at a molecular level how extreme metal, free jazz, and the no wave music of early '80s New York City could be linked together in short, sharp blows; hence the title of the Luttenbachers' first single, "546 Seconds of Noise." Rob Syers and Mark Fischer brought their Skin Graft label to Chicago from St. Louis in 1992, marrying their self-published comics to a hybrid of complex, aggressive, and often humorous music from bands like Dazzling Killmen, Mount Shasta, and the Flying Luttenbachers. As a recovering Marvel comics nerd, I saw the crackling energy of Jack Kirby's '60s artwork and Stan Lee's promotional bombast at work. The label made ties across the Pacific, working with Japanese bands like Space Streakings, Melt-Banana, and the heaviest of heavy metal bands, Zeni Geva. The bands were decidedly more chaotic than those on Touch & Go, but equally devoted to performance. With Weasel Walter as the omnipresent connector, links were made to a no wave/improv/free-form scene running out of Milk of Burgundy and other ephemeral spaces in the city. From the outside, it often looked like a fifty-car pileup on the Dan Ryan Freeway, but there was no denying the energy and the commitment by those involved in working things out musically in public. Indie rock had become increasingly predictable. The jolts of surprise were few and far between. As outside interest in the Chicago indie rock scene grew, the infusion of daredevil antics by bands like Scissor Girls or U.S. Maple kept things lively and unpredictable. As was the case with free jazz, when these bands connected, all their misses were quickly forgiven.

The famed Wicker Park scene of the '90s was beginning to seed itself. It had been slowly infiltrated by artists and musicians in the late '80s looking for cheap rent and rehearsal space. When Wax Trax! established a label office and warehouse on Damen Avenue, Urbis Orbis coffeehouse opened and the Around the Coyote art festival at the intersection of Damen, Milwaukee, and North Avenues began to look a lot like Chicago's bohemian quarter. In 1988, Brian Deck, Brad Wood, and Dan Sonis, a trio of musician/producers, built Idful Studios in a former grocery store across from the park itself. As Wood puts it, "We were cheap and fast and located close to where musicians lived, which was the basis for our success." Producer David Trumfio was running his own studio, Kingsize Soundlabs. He remembers, "Wicker Park felt like the Wild West to me. We all were just making shit up as we went. Idful had several engineers working out of it, so when it was booked with one of them the others would book with us here. A lot of the musicians were playing in several bands, and playing on each other's records, so the scene was super strong that way."

The punk rock Underdog Records collective moved into the second floor of a furniture warehouse on Elston Avenue. Their space took up 6,250 square feet devoted to live/workspaces and eventually rehearsal space and a studio. Musicians cycled in and out, most notably those revolving around the Joan of Arc band with its flexible recording and touring lineups. There were performances, and Drag City held one memorable New Year's Eve party. Or so I was told.

Touch & Go's upwardly aiming trio Urge Overkill took their white jeans and medallions from the northside to Wicker Park. Was it after they were called "Ravenswood assholes" by fans of Chicago hardcore pioneers the Effigies during a show at the Exit? The trio built an infamous party palace within spitting distance from the Rainbo, then still a local working-class bar, not yet a place to see and be seen. They were laying the groundwork for Wicker Park to become the scene hub.

The gentrification of Wicker Park and the ongoing displacement of the Puerto Rican and Polish communities who had been living in the neighborhood for decades has been well documented. The demographic would shift from those original working-class denizens to a primarily white, post-collegiate community of artists and musicians. The low costs of living allowed musicians to work fewer hours and spend more time rehearsing, playing, and recording. The result, for these new settlers, was a musically diverse and productive scene. As David Grubbs, who was then forming the band Gastr del Sol, explains, "Folks were talented and generous with their time, and often productively underemployed. It was a shock when I moved to New York in 1999 and all of the musicians I knew had full time jobs or were touring like mad." According to Patrick Monaghan, the cusp between the '80s and '90s was a catalytic time for the Chicago scene; in the late '80s "punk, indie rock, industrial dance, house music, country, and jazz were largely segregated into their own separate scenes and venues. In the '90s those scenes began to collaborate and merge."

A critical mass of music makers and eager audience was building by 1990. Kurt Kellison and his then wife Paula Froehle had moved the nascent Atavistic label to the city from Columbus, Ohio, in 1988, and they would end up working with Ken Vandermark and Eleventh Dream Day and sponsoring the Unheard Music Series of jazz reissues. The Jesus Lizard were a full-fledged local band, settled into the city in a house behind a grocery store they called "The Ranch" with two full-length albums under their collective belt. Seam had moved to Chicago from Chapel Hill, North Carolina, recorded their second album, *The Problem with Me*, with Brad Wood at Idful, and released it on Touch & Go. After visiting Chicago and watching Jesus Lizard, Jenny White moved in 1991 from Atlanta to a two-bedroom garden apartment a few blocks from the Rainbo. Rent was $750 a month, and "it got really cold in the winter." Musicians could find one-room apartments for $400 a month, like the one Casey Rice had across the street from the Rainbo.

After being dropped from Columbia Records, Frank Orral moved to Chicago from Austin in 1992, bringing his Poi Dog Pondering project with him, eager to work at the source of house music. A phalanx of Chicago musicians joined (including two of my Cargo colleagues), adding instrumental, electronic, and orchestral flavors. The band quickly became a major draw in town, showing an audience existed at the mainstream level for a category-stretching ensemble. Much as Wilco did later, Poi Dog musically nodded in the direction of underground currents while appealing to condo-dwellers, mid-managers, and Chicago's equivalent of the bridge-and-tunnel crowd from the suburbs they called "Chicagoland."

Moving into the neighborhoods along the Damen-North-Milwaukee corridor was not risk-free. My college pal Ned Schwartz moved into an apartment overlooking Wicker Park with Phil Hertz. One day the steel back door was torn off the hinges by burglars. Ned bought longer screws to bolster the door back into the frame. The apartment was just too cheap to give up.

I was surprised when the Mekons, an English band whose records I had faithfully bought as imports, set up operations in the city. Drummer Steve Goulding had moved to Chicago to get married in 1990, and guitarist-singer Jon Langford and singer Sally Timms followed in 1991. Having been chewed up and spit out by major labels, the band itself was in limbo but soon reconstituted itself to record an album for the Touch & Go spinoff label Quarterstick Records. Langford showed his paintings in galleries and at clubs, joined a band called the Waco Brothers, and began forming numerous bands around town with names like the Pine Valley Cosmonauts and Skull Orchard. At some point I opened up a copy of the *Chicago Reader* over lunch at Jim's, took a look at the music listings, and saw at least three Langford-related projects playing that week in venues from Lounge Ax to the Americana/roots club Fitzgerald's in suburban Berwyn. Somehow, some way, Jon Langford was making a living making music in Chicago.

By 1989 Phil Hertz had left Kaleidoscope and, as Patrick Monaghan details, "with the help of Bruno Johnson and John

Dennett, before John left for Wax Trax! in the wake of Kaleidoscope's predictable meltdown," hooked up with some Canadians to open a branch of the Montreal-based Cargo Distribution. He refurbished an old gas station and got into business. The Canadian Cargo office had exclusive distribution rights to a lot of high-profile American indie labels like Epitaph, SST, Caroline, Ninja Tune, and Sub Pop, as well as with notable Canadian labels. In turn, they started their own in-house label, signed a Toronto instrumental surf band called Shadowy Men on a Shadowy Planet, and immediately profited when the TV show *Kids in the Hall* used a Shadowy Men song for its theme. Cargo also had an office in San Diego, and their Headhunter imprint signed a raucous band with a rising profile called Rocket from the Crypt. The Chicago office operated as their American distribution hub, and things hummed along. In 1991 I sat down with Phil Hertz, who by then had moved Cargo into a bigger former garage, and talked my way into a job.

2

honk if you hate people, too

I was put in the domestic buyer's office at Cargo, alongside Mark Southon and Joel Leoschke. Our desks consisted of waist-high plywood shelving that ran the length of the wall. Each of us had a stool to sit on. Mark dealt with West Coast labels, Cargo San Diego, and the Mordam Records distributor, where he had a number of connections. Joel handled releases from another San Francisco–based distributor called Revolver and picked up other labels. I was given a grab bag of assignments that included coordinating retail promo and some production with the Cargo Montreal and San Diego operations. A key buyers' function was writing brief descriptions of new releases for the fax that went out to stores each Friday. I had experience and ability for the task, and pretty soon Joel started handing me records or CDs to play on the office stereo and write up. The work had to be quick, as the stack of incoming promotional records from labels or submissions from bands never seemed to get smaller. The descriptions also had to be written with sales in mind; there was no "their first record was better." This process naturally led to discussions and debates about the merits or failings of the record(s) being examined.

Above Joel's workspace was a handwritten "Curmudgeon Records" sign. This reputation was belied as I overheard his phone conversations. Speaking with people at a distance in the time and place of his choice, he's a charmer. His honesty, directness, and a sniper-level-accurate sense of humor helps him build relationships. Like Corey Rusk, Joel has an inherent ability to understand inventory control and bookkeeping skills that many people interested in the independent music business lacked. Patrick Monaghan offers one example that kranky and his label Carrot Top both learned from: "The unguided Wax Trax! juggernaut taught me that you can't make up for a negative cash flow with volume, and that I needed to learn a lot more about managing said cash flow before I could successfully run my own business." Or as I recently read, "Volume is vanity, profit is sanity."

Joel was the main domestic buyer at Cargo. As such he had insight into the Cargo books and saw how money flowed out to big and small labels. He had access to the newest singles from new bands, the latest fanzines, and lots of contacts at labels. He was plugged in. The people working at Cargo were, in the words of my coworker Lisa Bralts-Kelly, "adjacent to all that was super good."

Joel and I shared a lot of musical interests. Just as importantly, as we looked around where we worked and the underground music scene in general, *we agreed on what we saw.* Cargo was a microcosm of the indie rock world around it: the relative success Shadowy Men and Rocket from the Crypt had prompted the San Diego and Montreal offices to start a number of offshoot labels and load up their release schedules. The major label Interscope had signed Rocket from the Crypt and the allied Drive Like Jehu, with Cargo's Headhunter Records subdivision getting billing on new pressings by Interscope as stipulated in Cargo's original contract with the band. Chain stores were placing large orders for the Shadowy Men and Rocket from the Crypt titles, but were notoriously slow to pay on the poor sales levels they achieved. Phil Hertz had a Cargo-financed label, Fist

Puppet Records, that was releasing great records from the Ex and Tom Cora and reissues from weird and obscure bands like Jon Wayne, Toiling Midgets, and the ahead-of-their-time Canadian band Simply Saucer. The Canadian branch pumped records into the warehouse, too.

Whatever financial bonus accrued to Cargo from the Interscope-Rocket from the Crypt connection dissipated. Releases got lost in the sauce of a huge release schedule. A crowded release schedule is like a crowded menu at a restaurant; it confuses customers and hides popular selections amidst unpopular ones. Staff time was spent promoting and selling a phalanx of releases, minimizing the ability to continually push successful releases. Worst of all, putting out more releases costs money and diverts resources from successful titles. The money that should go to artist royalties for best-selling releases gets diverted toward production costs for new releases. Those releases may not be best-sellers, which in turn prompts resentful bands who see their popular records garnering paltry royalty checks, or no royalties at all, to look toward larger indies or majors for better treatment. As Corey Rusk described it to me when Touch & Go's best-selling band Butthole Surfers signed with the in-house label at Rough Trade Distribution, CDs and LPs of their new Rough Trade album would be paid for out of the sales at the distributor that included Touch & Go products. Money owed to independent labels was being diverted from distributors to manufacture CDs and LPs. The labels would have to wait for payment on invoices. There were exceptions to this inherently exploitative structure in well-run operations from Ruth Schwartz at Mordam Records and Gary Held at Revolver Distribution.

As with Wax Trax!, success at Cargo paradoxically led to money troubles. The company's organizational tangles, with offices in Chicago, Montreal, and San Diego each hosting their own labels with their own agendas, didn't help. The Chicago office was pursuing manufacturing and distribution agreements with still more indie labels like K Records, Simple Machines, and Doghouse Records that increased the strain on cash flow.

As a distributor, Cargo Chicago was also in the business of selling accessories. Magazines, fanzines, posters, and calendars were all on the shelves. As the decade progressed, Cargo carried the newest music, design, and fashion magazines like *Option*, *Mojo*, *iD*, *Émigré*, *The Face*, and *Raygun*. Sometimes comic books by underground artists like Dan Clowes and Peter Bagge came in, as did books from ReSearch Publications with titles like *Industrial Culture Handbook*, *Incredibly Strange Music*, and *Incredibly Strange Films*. They were all part and parcel of a wider sphere of interest around music that drew in the low-brow vitality of B movies, comics, and pulp and hard-boiled fiction. The subculture fed off its predecessors. Fanzines followed the enthusiasm of their makers, many of whom prowled thrift stores in pursuit of obsession, be it bowling shirts or old records. As the decade wore on you could see artwork from comics artists Dan Clowes and Peter Bagge on record covers, or reissues of the albums covered in *Incredibly Strange Music*. For a lot of fans, the local independent music store was the only place to get these magazines and books.

CUE THE GOLD RUSH

In the wider music ecosystem, by the late '80s, reps for major-label A&R, or Artist & Repertoire—the company divisions responsible for finding and guiding bands through the corporate maze—had started prospecting for bands from the independent underground. A few bands with the potential, or who thought they had the potential, to reach wide audiences put their names on the dotted line. The Replacements and Husker Du had signed with Warner Music labels in 1986 and 1987, respectively. In 1988 Sonic Youth released *Daydream Nation* on Enigma Records, a label distributed by Capitol Records and then transitioned to Geffen Records, a proper major label then riding high on the success of Guns n' Roses. Eleventh Dream Day, a Chicago band specializing in wide-screen guitar psych, had signed with Atlantic Records in 1989. The first two EDD records had been released on a small California label and could be hard to find. People in the know could hardly blame the band for looking elsewhere. Other bands like Dinosaur, Jr., Meat Puppets, Soundgarden, Screaming Trees, Mudhoney, the Fluid, and Melvins had all left indies for majors by 1993. A Los Angeles band called Jane's Addiction had put out one independent record and then signed with Warner Brothers in 1988, quickly moving to the front of what came to be called "alternative rock."

The high visibility of the Sub Pop bands, especially in the hype-minded English weekly press, drew attention to Seattle. Sonic Youth's Thurston Moore directed Geffen's attention to Nirvana. We all know how that went.

Independence for record labels had always existed along a spectrum. Dischord Records, held up as a standard bearer, had their releases manufactured by Southern Records in England. Caroline Records was an American distributor owned by the British major label Virgin and released the first Smashing Pumpkins album. Indie labels could have a limited number of releases manufactured by independent distributors, they could be partly financed by major labels, or they could band together collectively to share costs. By the mid-1990s major labels were directly involved in the independent marketplace on a scale beyond signing the odd band or two.

The meteoric success of Nirvana's *Nevermind* in 1991 created an all-out Gold Rush across the map. Trent Reznor had extricated his Nine Inch Nails project from a dissatisfactory contract with an independent, moved to the major label Interscope, and proceeded to cement his synth–new wave–goth crossover into stadium status powered by live appearances at the first

Lollapalooza festival. Some bands had experienced slow royalty payments from their indie labels; others were interested in the possibilities for larger recording budgets. Ostensibly punk rock bands like Jawbreaker and Seaweed took the plunge. Even resolute Dischord experienced this when Jawbox and Shudder to Think each moved to major labels. Musicians saw others make the move and figured their band could do it as well. Appearances in Lollapalooza by current and former indie bands like Butthole Surfers, Rollins Band, and Soundgarden appeared to be proof of concept to some. Or maybe the mostly male bands had residual fantasies, fed by tales of '70s rock star excess, that the decadent lifestyles of Led Zeppelin or the Rolling Stones were available to them.

Warner Brothers started their own distributor, Alternative Distribution Alliance, aimed at the burgeoning American underground and began luring independent labels via the promise of chain-store sales to reach and capitalize on the new, vast, grunge-teen overground. Bands, labels, and distributors had all seen how Nirvana had put out a successful debut album on Sub Pop and then became omnipresent powered by one video on MTV. Indie labels had their videos played on MTV at 4 A.M., so why couldn't Urge Overkill follow their pals Nirvana with the right video with the right promo push behind it? Bands asked labels why their album wasn't on display at Tower Records or in the bins in the Coconuts store in the mall. They opened for formerly independent bands that had signed to major labels and wondered if they too couldn't step up a rung on the ladder.

The entrance of ADA into the marketplace began eating into Cargo's sales. In 1992, the English 4AD Records had signed a distribution deal with Warners that complicated the importation of a very popular catalog for Cargo. In Chicago, the phenomenal rise of Smashing Pumpkins, aided by the release of a single on Sub Pop and Lollapalooza, lured major-label scouts to Chicago with their mix of heavy metal, goth, and bubblegum psychedelia. In 1993 Jim Powers and Anthony Musiala started the Minty Fresh label, releasing the debut singles from locals Liz Phair and Veruca Salt, whose catchy single "Seether" became all but inescapable. Liz Phair released *Exile in Guyville* on the Matador label in 1993, and its references to the Wicker Park music and social scene drew even more attention to the city.

Phair had signed with Matador Records after the release of a tape of her home recordings called *Girly-Sound*. It was not a straightforward process. Phair's living situation in Chicago began with her sharing an apartment with John Henderson, whose label Feel Good All Over was manufactured and distributed by Cargo. Henderson played the cassette for Brad Wood and some recording began at Idful. After shedding herself of the would-be Svengali Henderson and his utterly unrealistic ambition of directing her career, Phair moved into her parents' house in Winnetka. By January of 1992 Wood and Phair were driving between Wicker Park in Chicago and the suburbs, recording at Idful, with Wood and Casey Rice providing instrumental backing to Phair's vocals and guitar. A tape of those recordings was enough to persuade Matador Records to offer Phair a contract. With some recording around Wood's daytime sessions, the double LP *Exile in Guyville* was completed.

Once the album was released, a backup band was formed with Wood on percussion, Rice on guitars, and Leroy Bach on bass guitar, and touring began. Casey Rice recalls the English tour in 1993 and an encounter at a university show in Manchester with the opening act, an up-and-coming local band called Oasis: "They weren't like we were in Chicago, where we'd say 'Hi my name is Liam. What's your name?' Their attitude was 'fuck these people, they're the competition.' They were drunk and had their company of tracksuit-wearing dudes. They were saying things to Liz like 'nice tits.' I stepped up and said, 'What's your problem?' and they say, 'Oh yeah, you want to have a fucking go?' I said, 'I think we should get out of here.' On the way out there was a shipping pallet over wet concrete in the sidewalk. Leroy lifted it up and wrote 'FUCK OASIS' and put the pallet back down. We were told that after Oasis got popular, they paid to jackhammer that part of the sidewalk out."

Nielsen Soundscan changed everything in the music business when the *Billboard* charts started using the sales figures it supplied in 1991. Based on scans of the new UPC codes printed on CDs, Soundscan allowed the measurement of actual sales in stores. Prior to 1991, *Billboard* magazine called record stores weekly to get their sales figures. Any old store manager or clerk could report sales levels for any old reason. Record label reps could put their thumbs on the scale and bribe reporting stores with free records, T-shirts, concert tickets, primo weed, or good old-fashioned cash. The more objective Soundscan data revealed how certain genres of country routinely outsold moldy arena rock. The prime example of this was country music, as indicated by Garth Brooks's chart-topping record in 1991. The major labels' working models of popularity, audience size and location, and market stability had to be thrown out the door. Most of the small stores that independent distributors served weren't reporting to Soundscan, which required expensive point-of-sale computer systems, but enough did that some indie releases registered sales there.

In 1993 Urge Overkill's "Sister Havana" video, taken from their debut major-label release, went into rotation at MTV and Smashing Pumpkins' *Siamese Dream* album debuted in the *Billboard* Top Ten. Both bands made no apologies for their ample musical nods to '70s arena rock signifiers and a desire for stardom. A Neil Diamond cover appearing in *Pulp Fiction*, and synched to a sequence of Uma Thurman writhing around, powered Urge's rise. The track had been released on a final EP on Touch & Go. Both groups paid no mind to and were motivated by the gnashing of teeth and rending of garments amongst some elements of the underground. An August 1993 issue of *Billboard* called Chicago "Cutting Edge's New Capital," complete with a map for treasure seekers. As Patrick Monaghan observes, the "audience waxes and wanes, with the biggest late '80s/early '90s factors clearly being MTV and Nirvana, but there has always been outsider music, even when the mainstream co-opts a bit of the left of center. On the upside, loads of artists were able to make a living that previously would not have. I'm thinking of the Jesus Lizard, Veruca Salt, Smashing Pumpkins, Handsome Family, Urge Overkill, Liz Phair, Pulsars, etc. locally."

Every week Joel sorted through a mountain of seven-inch single submissions in his office. Bands were rushing to release records, and we liked to say, only half-jokingly, that the single had become the new demo or demonstration recording: a means to gather attention for a band as opposed to a self-supporting artistic work. The prospect of a brass ring, like signing with one of the bigger independent labels such as Sub Pop or Matador, or being discovered by a major-label scout, seemed to overwhelm any instinct bands had to woodshed and craft identities of their own. The irrational exuberance was such that Phil Hertz finagled a piece of the Geffen action by committing Cargo to sell a thousand seven-inch singles from a band called Cell, pressed on yellow vinyl by Geffen. The ones that didn't end up in the dumpster go for $1.25 on the Discogs marketplace website now. The music writer Bill Meyer remembers, "It seemed like everybody was making a single to the point where I kind of dreaded opening a seven-inch record mailer."

Anyone starting a label would not only have to stand out from the pack, but also keep a white-knuckled grip on costs and inventory and really, really know the promotional and retail environment. Joel and I talked about this. A lot. We knew what not to do. Discussions often concluded with, "If I had a record label . . . "

USE YOUR FREEDOM OF CHOICE

If you walked into your favorite record store where you got your favorite records, you would find a wide selection of music to choose from, if the bins of singles from guitar bands seemed too overwhelming or cookie-cutter. Producer Adrian Sherwood resurfaced in 1995 after a dormant period, with his avant reggae label On U-Sound releasing new albums and with the Pressure Sounds reggae reissue label. The Blood & Fire label was founded in 1993 and issued crucial dub reggae records from the 1970s, most notably the Congos' *Heart of the Congos.* Mysterious copies of German records that were long thought to be out of print started showing up on a label called Germanofon. Titles like *Kraftwerk*, *Kraftwerk 2*, Harmonia's *Deluxe*, *Cluster II*, and *Zuckerzeit* and *Neu 75* seemed to come in and then blow out of the Cargo warehouse shelves. In addition to being intriguing releases from a period of musical history many Americans knew little about, the CDs themselves bore contradictory markings—were they from the Czech Republic or Luxembourg? Later on, bootlegs of the bootlegs showed up. There's a movie with a character named "Nick the Greek" in there somewhere. The *Krautrocksampler: One Head's Guide to the Great Kosmische Musik—1968 Onwards* book by English musician Julian Cope was released in 1995 and served as further illumination for those interested in that overlooked period of rock music. We couldn't keep those on the shelves, either. A widening of access and taste was developing within the indie rock core audience. In the United Kingdom, as David Pearce of Flying Saucer Attack, then a clerk at Revolver Records in Bristol, affirms, "Krautrock was pretty well known. Fairly plentiful secondhand copies of Can, Neu, Amon Duul 2 LPs had been intriguing young impressionable types for quite a few years, e.g., myself, in the mid '80s onwards."

Tomas Palermo was a college radio DJ and record store clerk in Los Angeles; he remembers, "Customers at the shops were all very eclectic. They bought across the whole spectrum of bands and labels, from DC punk to British indie pop, musique concrete, experimental and ambient sounds. By the early '90s LA was solidly a rave city, so house, techno, downtempo, and early jungle were selling big too, not to mention the Golden Era '90s hip-hop. It was an insane time for music."

Josh Madell of the New York record store Other Music, which opened in 1995, notes, "We were known for the 'weird' categories that we used to divide up the store selection, and 'Krautrock' was a hugely popular section. Before the CD era, other than Kraftwerk's later releases, it was mostly just really hard to hear in America."

In Chicago the audience had nearly immediate access to recordings from around the world in or close to their neighborhood, a huge variety of performing groups to see, clubs to go dancing in, and access to free weekly publications that were covering the latest happenings. The *Chicago Tribune* music critic Greg Kot summarizes the advantages of the city for musicians: "Inexpensive apartments in neglected but still livable neighborhoods, plenty of places to play, a beehive of indie labels and booking agencies, tons of record stores, an attentive local media—all made Chicago an attractive place for creative people to live and make music without playing by the big music-industry rules that dominated places like Nashville and Los Angeles." Musician Brent Gutzeit takes a more sentimental view when he says, "The Chicago music scene back in the '90s was magical."

3 that that is . . . is (not)

1991–1992

The poster at Jim's Grill told a small part of the tale. It showed Smashing Pumpkins posed at the back of their van, equipment stacked up, with "ON TOUR NOW" emblazoned at the bottom. A white rectangle extends across the bottom of the poster, a standard design element that allowed local promoters to fill in show details. The quartet was doing their roadwork, "getting in the van," to paraphrase the book by Black Flag's Henry Rollins. Smashing Pumpkins played the same venues as ostensibly "cooler" bands did. They played for free at the tiny Blackout Records store. Their mix of '70s arena rock gestures and bubblegum pop was no more or less legit than that peddled at the time by other bands. Why then was animosity directed toward the band? It grew as the Pumpkins' trajectory upward became more and more apparent.

Was it because Billy Corgan was reputed to be "difficult"? He didn't bother to hide his ambitions, or his artistic control over the band and what he later called an "attack posture." Smashing Pumpkins were quickly taken on as management clients by Joe Shanahan, owner of the Cabaret Metro club—the venue every band wanted to play. Choice bookings at the club followed. One example was opening for English punk rock legends the Buzzcocks in November 1989, a highly coveted gig. When I was working at Touch & Go, the Minneapolis trio Arcwelder opened for a Smashing Pumpkins show at Metro and were eager to display and mock a list of requests from Corgan posted on the door of the band rooms backstage that began with an entreaty for silence in the dressing rooms before Smashing Pumpkins played. It was a demanding and controlling list, but Arcwelder did accept Corgan's invitation to open the show. Their house, their rules. Was the source of the hostility that Smashing Pumpkins avoided the gatekeepers? In fact, they jumped the gate altogether, scoring a Sub Pop single and then signing with the quasi-indie Caroline Records and positioning themselves to move up to major label status. There was no lip service offered to any independent ethos, no mea culpas for arena ambitions.

Say what you want about the music or Corgan as a person, Smashing Pumpkins presented their fans with carefully considered branding and packaging that obviously reflected Corgan's interests and aesthetics. The debut album was well titled, as *Gish* after the 1920s movie star Lillian Gish, which evidenced Corgan's interest in silent film. Expressionism, chiaroscuro, melancholia, and large-scale gestures, all characteristics of the medium, were parts of Smashing Pumpkins' music and performance. As the years passed and the band's success justified more elaborate packaging and presentation, Billy Corgan was able to indulge his tastes. The video for "Tonight, Tonight" in 1996 even included a nod to Georges Melies's 1902 film *A Trip to the Moon*. In 2017 Corgan would create a silent film of his own called *Pillbox* to accompany a solo album.

In 1992 drummer Todd Trainer and guitarist Steve Albini begin playing together in the band that came to be called Shellac. When I announced that I was writing this book, I was immediately asked several times if Albini would be providing a cover blurb. The question was posed partially seriously and partially sarcastically, with the ratio dependent on the questioner. Such is Albini's place on the indie rock totem pole as a musician, producer, and commentator. From the time his group Big Black emerged and Albini wrote for the influential *Forced Exposure* and *Matter* fanzines, the guy has been a prominent, influential, and, at least in earlier times, acerbically unfiltered voice. Written selections like "Three Pandering Sluts and Their Music-Press Stooge" and "The Problem with Music" top his Greatest Hits. Add the prominence Big Black gained, followed by the brief, justifiably controversial life of the regrettably named Rapeman trio and the now long-lived Shellac to the credibility stakes Albini brings to the table. Top it off with his production work for groups like Pixies, Palace Brothers, Slint, and Nirvana, at first in his own home and beginning in 1995 at Electrical Audio studios, and the chips are stacked pretty high. For a lot of people interested in underground rock, Steve Albini ably defended the values of economic and artistic independence, as in the "Pandering Sluts" letter to a music critic: "Out here in the world, we have to pay for our records, and we get taken advantage of by the music industry, using stooges like you to manipulate us. We harbor a notion of music as a thing of value, and methodology as an equal, if not supreme component of an artist's aesthetic."

In late 1993, Albini wrote an article published in Chicago's *Baffler* magazine. The subtitle of "The Problem with Music" essay, "Some of Your Friends Are This Fucked," rang true to many readers.

But the wide-bore rhetorical shotgun Albini took to the issue was problematic. Referring to Liz Phair as one of three pandering sluts was untoward, to say the least, and contributed in a small way to the prurient interest some male fans and writers took toward her. The "no way but the indie way" presented a false choice to many musicians whose bands were not going to get the opportunity to work with Touch & Go or Thrill Jockey or Drag City. Sound engineer and Liz Phair guitarist Casey Rice puts it simply: "It was like 'Satan has come to Chicago.' And you're in league with Satan if you entertain the idea of a major label deal. It could be personal. Being in studio and seeing a lot of the bands that were involved in that stuff, they were kind of closed out of the clique of cool music. People were mean to me because I worked in a studio."

There was, as Lisa Bralts-Kelly accurately puts it, "posturing on all sides." Joel Leoschke and I found the financial figures that Albini broke down in his *Baffler* article to be dead on. We had seen how, even at the indie level where we worked, promotional budgets were excessive and designed more to inflate labels' and bands' self-images than to efficiently promote music. These observations were being integrated into our own plans for a label. Recording and touring budgets were often inflated, as Albini ably demonstrated. Being pretty cynical guys ourselves, we observed that Albini took on major-label recording projects and benefited from the system he criticized. To his credit, Albini did not take "points" or percentage of royalties, a particularly parasitic practice among many producers. Steve Albini stated his fees up front and took on clients from all sources accordingly, while specifying that his services were strictly those of a recording engineer and not those of a "producer," manipulating and guiding bands' musical directions through the recording process.

One prominent target of Albini's ire was Urge Overkill. Given my personal experiences at Touch & Go working with the trio, in 1994 I found Albini's acidic attitude toward the band to be a day late and dollar short. A well-timed "those medallions make you look silly" around 1991 could have saved everyone a lot of grief. Who knows, maybe he tried. By 1994 Urge Overkill were probably beyond shaming and were receiving plenty of positive reinforcement for their velvet-jacketed schtick. They received plenty of press and MTV play, and toured across the country.

There were some bands working on the fringes of the scene who were less interested in the guitar-centric template that dominated Chicago. Sometime in 1991 I witnessed an in-store performance by a five-piece band called Shrimp Boat at the new Tower

Records megastore in Chicago. The quartet explored non-rock time signatures and jazzy song structures, and played multiple instruments with a light touch that was idiosyncratic without wallowing in self-indulgent artiness. The band was honed via a residency at Phyllis's Musical Inn in Wicker Park, playing mostly to School of the Art Institute of Chicago students. Brad Wood joined the band in 1989, after recording the *Speckly* album at Idful Studio: "I was tired of uber-pro musicianship. Shrimp Boat was a band of musicians who couldn't play (yet) and who did not give a damn. Expression was their main goal. We played some epic, long sets that defied what a night of 'rock' music was supposed to be. I enjoyed playing ten-minute-long versions of our songs. If the audience was dancing and sweating, we would keep playing and let Ian (Schneller) and Sam (Prekop) unwind a bit on guitars."

At the Kansas City Art Institute in Missouri, four seniors in a quartet called the Coctails were pondering their next move. Mark Greenberg remembers, "We decided to self-release an LP of the songs we had made together. It seemed weird to put out a record and walk away, so we agreed to move together to Chicago to see what we could do. Archer Prewitt had played Shrimp Boat tapes for us, and we were all excited that a band like that could exist in Chicago." Patrick Monaghan, who was managing the Wax Trax! store at the time, visited a friend in Kansas City who took him to a show: "One of the bands played slightly jazzy garage music in beat-up thrift store tuxedos. I was confused and charmed. They were not cool, but they sure were fun and different than anything I'd run across. And they were fearless in tackling instruments that only one of them had really yet mastered. They were moving to Chicago, and (a friend) Anne had given them my number at Wax Trax! to carry their record. They used the Wax Trax! turntable to play it for Sue and Julia of Lounge Ax. When their LP came out, I gave them the front window."

David Grubbs moved to Chicago in 1991 to attend graduate school at the University of Chicago. He had a band called Bastro that worked the noisy, razor-edged side of the street where Touch & Go bands were often found. He had started a band called Gastr del Sol. His bandmates John McEntire and Bundy Brown were playing with a new outfit in town called Tortoise. As David puts it, "The fact that I was returning to school and John and Bundy were committing more time to Tortoise made it a propitious time to reimagine the group. It seemed kind of comic to us: Gastr del Sol's lineup on our first record, *The Serpentine Similar*, was the same as the final lineup of Bastro, but the m.o. had shifted: a greater use of space, the introduction of acoustic instruments, and a very different relation to singing and lyric-writing."

Gastr del Sol would be joined by Jim O'Rourke, a native Chicagoan whose experience with tape editing, the form of avant-garde collage music called musique concrète, and connections to the world of improvisation would propel the band into wider waters and make Gastr "a group that had no fixed membership."

Grimble Grumble began as a duo playing at workmen's bars in the evocatively named far southside Chicago neighborhood Slag Valley, once the site of steel mills. Named after a gnome in an early Pink Floyd song, the band wore their '60s psychedelia influences on their sleeves. The group began as the duo of Christine Garcia and Reuben Rios playing in workingmen's bars, then eventually moved to Hyde Park, got involved at the University of Chicago radio station WHPK, and took on two more members. Drummer Michael Bullington had been in a band called Pritchard and remembers that he joined Grimble Grumble via a "very '90s Chicago" way: "some WHPK DJs moved to Wicker Park from Hyde Park and happened to live near us. The Pritchard guitar player would practice very loudly in our apartment, and they heard him and thought, 'That must be the guitar player from Urge Overkill,' rang our doorbell, and asked if we'd want to play."

Grimble Grumble, complete with a fog machine for live shows, was a band intent on playing long, exploratory songs featuring cloudlike guitar textures in the tradition of English bands like Spacemen 3, My Bloody Valentine, and the band they got their name from, Pink Floyd. As the drummer, Bullington, says, "I'd only started playing drums a few years prior . . . so I was like, 'If you're willing to work with me through my learning curve, I'll be your drummer.' Luckily, they were willing, and it came pretty quickly. In some ways, the drums would lead the band through dynamics and a lot of the songs were open-ended, so if I kept playing, everyone else had to."

The group befriended a Dearborn, Michigan, duo Windy & Carl after opening for them at a college rock showcase at the Metro. The groups toured together. Grimble Grumble also found sympathetic listeners across the international underground. By 1996 they were releasing singles on English labels like Enraptured and Ochre Records, appearing on split singles, and putting out a ten-inch EP on the Dearborn-based Burnt Hair label. Eventually their self-released debut CD was combined with other tracks by a German label. Despite operating at a geographic disadvantage from their Hyde Park base, removed from the northside clubs and record stores, Grimble Grumble were able to record at the University of Chicago and reached listeners across the Atlantic.

THE PROLIFERATION OF JUST INCREDIBLE MUSIC AROUND THAT TIME REALLY HELPED

Tim Adams started Ajax Records in 1989, releasing singles by post-punk and noisy bands like Antiseen and Modern Vending and an LP by the inexplicable, hard-to-categorize Chicago rock trio Repulse Kava. He quickly expanded his business by taking singles from other labels into his efficient mail-order operation, including future indie rock household names like Nirvana, Pavement, and Sebadoh. The Ajax mail-order catalog grew, and his customers came to depend not only on Tim's reliable service, but also his powers of selection and a well-written, personality-infused newsletter. Ajax became associated with the poorly named, inconsistently applied genre called "lo-fi." Bands and individuals were recording themselves at home on tape decks, taking independence to its natural conclusion. If the 1960s and records like *Sgt. Pepper's* and *Dark Side of the Moon* had established the critical notion of "studio as instrument," musicians in the late '80s had established four-track tape decks as instruments, manipulating the limitations of the technology to incorporate tape hiss and claustrophobia as voices, of a kind. Ajax was also an early advocate for rock music from Australia and New Zealand, especially those bands from New Zealand that had been alienated from the poppier and more prominent Flying Nun label. Many of these artists recorded cassettes for a label called Xpressway and ended up releasing music stateside via Ajax or Drag City Records in Chicago. Later on, kranky would connect with the Dunedin quartet Dadamah, who appeared on an Ajax seven-inch compilation single and released two singles and an LP between 1991 and 1992. The attention that Ajax mail order and releases drew was one more way Chicago came to be seen as a center for musical happenings and cross-pollination beyond the aggressive "Touch & Go sound." As Andrew Beaujon of the Washington, DC, band Eggs says, "All that Touch & Go stuff kind of scared me, they all seemed like such big beef-munching, imposing people and we were these spindly vegetarians from the D.C. suburbs who loved bossa nova. I used to order records from Tim and gradually Chicago seemed less intimidating."

Mail-order services were crucial in distributing music. *Forced Exposure* was a fanzine edited by Jimmy Johnson and Byron Coley started in 1982. Beginning with an interest in hardcore punk, the magazine transitioned to covering a wide range of music reflecting the tastes and connections of its editors, who were both inveterate record collectors and dealers. Slowly but surely a mail-order operation arose alongside a record label. By 1993 the fanzine had come to an end and a record distributor opened. You could find anything from reissues of Peruvian psychedelic bands to free jazz in the catalog that Johnson built. It was another example of the points of access and widening taste range of some independent music fans. A musician named Keith Fullerton Whitman would come to work at the distributor, penning brief record reviews under the name "Hrvatksi," eventually becoming sales manager there. He describes his introduction to the Forced Exposure wholesale operation like this: "I'd been an avid reader of FE and was surprised to hear that the 'mail-order catalogue' section of the magazine was enough of a concern to justify a city-block-sized warehouse. When I arrived, it unlocked the idea of what distributors really were; these insanely large operations funneling records in and out in volume for a relatively small percentage of the retail take. He had definitely found his niche, and I think the proliferation of just incredible music around that time really helped."

Whitman made his own complex, beat-centric music, and his experiments with computer-processed guitar eventually came to my and Joel's attention.

1991 was the year that the final Spacemen 3 album, *Recurring*, was released. The Derby, England, band gathered a significant audience playing a repetitive, trance-inducing psychedelia that referred to obscure '60s precursors like Red Krayola and 13th Story Elevators and '70s electro-minimalists like Silver Apples and Suicide. By the time the band broke up, the two main drivers, Pete "Sonic Boom" Kember and Jason Pierce, were working on their own solo projects. Throw in some dodgy management, and a multitude of record labels stateside and in Europe releasing albums, and at Cargo Chicago it seemed that a new Spacemen 3 record (Live in Germany 1989! Jason's mix of the final album! Sonic Boom's mix of the final album!, etc., etc.) came out every week. But they sold nonetheless. The band's influence only seemed to grow. Despite the band's obvious nods to their predecessors, the Spacemen 3 formula had an impact on indie rock and dance music. Kember and Pierce layered simple chord progressions of guitar and organ to produce cross-hatched overtones matched by simple, forward-moving rhythms. Techno producers in particular would adopt this tactic to extend and enhance the impact of electronic melodies and rhythms. Kember and Pierce both used the band to detail/brag on their respective drug experiences, naming an album *Taking Drugs to Make Music to Take Drugs To*, which didn't hurt their appeal to elements of the indie rock and dance audiences. As the music writer Ned Raggett puts it, listening to Spacemen 3 "was probably my first sense that 'psychedelia' as such wasn't this thing that was reverently referred to in *Rolling Stone* articles or the like." That's as good a summary as any of what truly was a gateway band.

Kember began to work more with analog synthesizer in his Spectrum and Experimental Audio Research guises after Spacemen 3 broke up. He collaborated with a couple of kranky bands live and in the studio, and provided crucial support by booking bands to support his live appearances in North America and his English home base.

The Coctails had released two albums and a seven-inch single on their own Hi-Ball label before crossing the Cook County line in 1991. The group had an advanced audiovisual aesthetic formed by their mutual art school background and interest in '60s cool jazz, Jewish klezmer music, cartoon scores like the compositions of Raymond Scott, lounge music, and the genre of music that had come to be known as "exotica"—the "tropical ersatz . . . non-native" (as the "Hipwax" website calls it) appropriation of musical elements from Oceana, Latin America, and Africa transformed into cocktail-bar friendly mood music. Mark Greenberg says that the Coctails "moved to Chicago with our first full-length record and a bunch of songs ready to go. Along with Archer's art on the flyers and popcorn bags and hand-made merchandise, it helped us pull in people pretty quickly. We were young and full of art school creativity and youthful energy and the ability to sleep very little, so we got a lot of things done. We constantly worked and wrote and recorded and toured. And with our training as art students, I think we had a good idea how to visualize things we wanted to do and be able to get there as a team pretty quickly."

The quartet released a single of children's music, holiday records, and, as Joe Tangari noted in the taste-making website *Pitchfork*, "when facelessness and a supposed lack of affect ruled the underground, and anonymous post-rock collectives lumbered their way to shining reviews, they made their faces into Beatlesque icons, wore their personalities on their sleeves, embraced comic book art and toys as promotional devices, and exuded humor, unfettered creativity, and high spirits." Patrick Monaghan started the Carrot Top Records label expressly to work with the Coctails: ". . . nobody had a stronger sense of their own aesthetic than the Coctails. Their design was somehow both broadly conceived but so tight that the aesthetic could be carried over to all kinds of different objects and uses and still be unmistakably the Coctails. They were exceedingly exacting about their presentation and design and really fun to work with."

By 1992 the band had made an appearance on *The Week in Rock* on MTV showing their self-made dolls and screen-printed newsletter, and found their self-released album on the *Rockpool* magazine Top 100 chart. Patrick Monaghan confirms, "The band were vinyl fetishists running their own tiny label, and they badly needed a CD to sell, so I offered to figure out how to do it myself. I'd already worked at two distributors and in retail, so the label side was a curiosity, and I had $5,000 sitting in the bank. I offered it to Cargo first, and they passed on it, so I picked it up and ran with it." The Coctails became the Lounge Ax house band of sorts, and their releases would anchor the Carrot Top Records label catalog.

Joel Leoschke and I were observing these developments. We had ambitions of starting a record label and plenty of ideas about what we didn't want to do. Chicago was a-bubble with bands and labels, but we didn't see where our potential label would fit in. The impetus arrived from outside.

In Richmond, Virginia, keyboardist Carter Brown and guitarist Mark Nelson started playing together as Labradford.

4

accelerating on a smoother road

1992–1993

> Read Labradford's bio, which gives a good summary of reference points—F/i, ambient Eno, Spiritualized, Dead C, Thomas Koner, Cluster, etc.—which need only a little fleshing out with the Durutti Column, Zoviet France and Felt, for an idea of the greatness that is Labradford.
>
> —*Nils Bernstein*

One afternoon Joel motioned me into his office and showed me a seven-inch single. The cover had a maroon and black cartoon picture of robotic arms pouring liquid into a test tube. He cued it up on the turntable and played the first release from Labradford.

The music I heard was nothing like the indie rock that flowed into and out of the Cargo warehouse, even the "lo-fi" recordings being made by isolated musicians with four-track tape decks. The accepted definition of indie rock was confined to singer-songwriter or the traditional guitar-bass-drums "band." It was unusual to see a band without a drummer. And the differences beyond that between Labradford and their indie rock peers rapidly became apparent to us.

Labradford had a keyboardist. Carter Brown played a bank of synthesizers with names like Memorymoog, Polymoog, Korg Polysix, Roland Vocoder Plus, and Moog Taurus II bass pedals. You might know these names if you closely examined the liner notes to '70s progressive rock albums, especially the Yes records that Carter enjoyed. Mark Nelson played six- and twelve-string acoustic guitars, electric guitar, and manipulated tape loops.

The music on the single was expansive, grainy, and decidedly cinematic. Joel and I immediately started talking about the 1970s German albums that were coming into vogue, but also the obscure proto-industrial collective Zoviet France and the moody post-punk band Felt. Labradford were not playing pastel-tinctured, new age pablum. Their first show was loud enough that a lightbulb fell out of the ceiling on stage. There was nothing like it coming into the Cargo buyers' room. We agreed that what Labradford were doing, though not without precedent, was way outside the parameters of the indie rock we encountered each workday. If we were going to start a label, we wanted to differentiate ourselves immediately from a scene focused on releasing wave after wave of tiresome, sound-alike seven-inch singles. Our label had to release music that transcended the moment. Otherwise, it would be lost in the sauce.

Those many discussions about having a record label, at that moment, began to transform into a plan for an actual record label. For a long time, Joel had envisioned founding "Curmudgeon Records." But the name was too long to fit on the spine of a record and lacked a certain zing. "Cranky" had been suggested. In the tradition of intentionally misspelled American brand names like "Rite Aid" and "Kleenex," we swapped out the "c" for a "k." Out of sheer contrariness we insisted on lowercase letters and ditched the word "records." There was also a Teutonic hint to "kranky" that meshed well with our prevailing interest in '70s German music. I registered the business name.

Our coworker at Cargo, Patrick Monaghan, had recently started his own label. He was kind enough to share a contract template with us. His contract and way of doing business were heavily informed by the labels and distros that we all respected as well-run, ethical operations that we would be wise to take lessons from: "I always looked up to Corey Rusk at Touch & Go, Gary Held at Communion/Revolver, and Ruth Schwartz at Mordam, and said that if they were doing something, I didn't necessarily need to do the same thing, but I sure as hell needed to understand their reasoning for their choices."

The labels Joel and I respected like Touch & Go worked with artists on a handshake basis and did not sign contracts. We liked their respective 50–50 split of royalties with bands, but also realized that we would be asking people we didn't know to cast their lot with a brand-new label. Something had to be written down for mutual reference, as Patrick Monaghan had confirmed. A simple contract would spell out the label's obligations to the band and define some terms. How long does a recording need to be to be called an album? How exactly are royalties calculated, and when are artists paid? What does either party need to do to get out of the contract? We decided to limit the term of our contract to two albums, with an option for either party to renew on a handshake basis. Dischord and Touch & Go operated that way. This approach was conceived as an alternative to the multi-album major-label contracts that extended to hundreds of pages; put ownership of master recordings "throughout the universe," including any recording formats yet to be invented, into the clutches of multinational corporations; and contained hidden codicils that allowed the royalty-free sale of thousands of CDs via "record clubs." In contrast, trust between individuals was the golden ticket in underground music. What had started as an arrangement between friends had grown. Tons of records and CDs moved across continents based on personal relationships and reputation. Success bred confidence between parties. A contract stipulating an option for a second album would allow kranky to build on the investment put into the debut and for the artist to develop material assured that a second album would be released. The proof of this approach is found in the number of groups that have stuck with the label for years: Labradford, Pan•American, loscil, Windy & Carl, and Stars of the Lid all released multiple recordings on kranky long after their initial two-album contract terms expired.

Much of what came to guide label decision making was outlined in what Joel and I called "the kranky kommandments":

1. "Thou shalt pay royalties on time." Fulfilling our obligations to the artists was the first priority for us. There was no guarantee that kranky albums would make a profit, but Joel and I were committed to accounting to the bands on a regular basis. Ethically this is the right way to operate a record label, and economically it is the best way to ensure the long-term survival of a record label. Accounting regularly to bands meant there was no fooling anyone, including ourselves, about how much money was in the coffers and where it came from. On an operational level, we had seen how indie labels lost their best-selling bands when royalty payments were few and far between.
2. "Thou shalt not make an exclusive distribution deal." The financial health and distribution channels of the label would not be dependent on the integrity or business savvy of a single distributor. Spreading distribution across several companies would lessen risk. Nor would kranky accept offers from distributors to manufacture CDs or LPs on our behalf.
3. "Thou shalt not make decisions based on commercial rather than artistic concerns." You would think this

would be the obvious priority for any truly independent label. Joel and I accepted that our tastes were way, way outside those of mainstream music audiences and possibly most indie rock fans. Guessing at the direction of public tastes was a fool's game as we saw it. We knew what we liked, and for better or worse, that's what kranky would release. Hence the label slogan "what we want, when you need it."

4. "Thou shalt not put song lyrics on album artwork." We both strongly felt that lyrics should be left to the imagination of the listener.
5. "Thou shalt not put pictures of bands on album artwork." Something else that should be left to the listener's imagination. Putting yourself on the front cover of your record is dumb unless your band is the Ramones or the Ornette Coleman Quartet.
6. "Thou shalt not start affiliated labels." This was motivated in main by Touch & Go, which had the Quarterstick imprint for some bands and Touch & Go for others, as well as the other companies that had sub-labels devoted to reissues. If we liked a particular recording, we'd put the kranky logo on it. Joel and I were focused on building the kranky brand, which could and would reissue recordings while building a catalog and narrative. A recording was either good enough to put on the label or it wasn't.
7. "Thou shalt not make limited editions" was an important part of our intentions. Small editions elaborately packaged and sold at high prices were not something we were interested in producing. As much as we enjoyed interesting packaging and would come to use semi-transparent papers, screen prints, letterpress covers, and the like, keeping the music accessible and affordable to customers was important to us.

8. "Thou shalt not release tribute albums." We were interested in original music, not in rehashing the old, or patting ourselves on the back for our tasteful record collections. To us, the growing fad of indie rock bands appearing on compilations of covers indicated artistic dry rot, not a tip of the hat or clever bit of irony.
9. "kranky artists shalt not talk about mr. kranky specifically, only kranky as an entity." We encouraged artists to keep us out of it when asked. Joel and I wanted attention focused as much as possible on the artists and their recordings and not on ourselves—or the composite entity "mr. kranky" that we adopted to speak on behalf of the label. As the promotion guy, this restriction frustrated me from time to time. People were interested in talking with us. I had to turn down the occasional interview. I accepted this necessary limitation as the price of keeping the focus on the musicians and their work and not on the guys at the record label.
10. "Thou shalt not release seven-inch singles." Joel and I saw the deluge of singles on the market and did not want to add to it. From a financial point of view, the costs of mastering and pressing singles were close to those of a twelve-inch single or LP with a much smaller list price. This narrow profit margin discouraged us from investing in the format. We placed our kranky bet on the long-playing album format.

Our next priority was branding. I gave a "Doctored for Sound/Super Stereo" sound effects record I had sitting around to my old Touch & Go colleague and graphic artist Matthew Taylor. He took the Audio Fidelity logo from the record, with its tilted, rounded rectangle and stylized soundwave, and elongated it, inserting "kranky." The logo was black and white, easy to replicate and resize, and has stood the test of time. Being the kind of guys we were, Joel and I, with assistance from the wits at Cargo, quickly came up with slogans like "Honk if you hate people, too," "You're with stupid," "Let a frown be your umbrella," and "What we want, when you need it" that were suitable for bumper stickers, T-shirts, and advertisements. They expressed a confidence in the label and artists, and the assertion that kranky was not necessarily for everyone. As critic Bill Meyer observes, our peers at Drag City expressed something similar with their "it's a Drag City thing, you wouldn't understand" tees. Meyer summarizes: "This is what it is. There was no apology. When you were projecting personality, you were projecting music that was different."

Our colleague at Cargo, Lisa Bralts-Kelly, passed along a "Honk" sticker to Billy Corgan, who put it on his so-called "Bat Strat" guitar and did the label a solid by advertising kranky on Smashing Pumpkins tours until the sticker wore off. Our label's "almost recreational negativity," as Peter Margasak put it later in a *Chicago Reader* article, signaled that kranky was in no way some namby-pamby, wind chimes and good vibes New Age label.

The process of reaching out to Labradford began shortly after we set up the business. Joel spoke with Andrew Beaujon to make sure there were no plans to release a Labradford record on his Retro 8 label. Mark Nelson recalls, "At some point Andrew called and told me someone from Cargo was interested in what we were doing—I think I assumed this would mean the possibility of being on one of Cargo's labels—it was really exciting. I didn't even have an answering machine at the time so spent a couple harrowing days waiting by the phone until Joel called." Beaujon had moved to Washington, DC, and started a new band called Eggs with Rob Christiansen, who also happened to be studying audio engineering at American University, where he had access to late-night studio time. As Nelson puts it, Labradford was "intrigued by free recording time. We were going to do another seven-inch, and we had a couple songs done. We'd gone up for a weekend and had two days in the studio. We did one more weekend of sessions at American and that's *Prazision.* I had a Mazda B2000 pickup, so we loaded our shit in the back and drove to Arlington. Recording itself was easy—we just set up and played. I did a few vocal overdubs. We were evenly split between what we thought of as pop songs, stuff I'd written that had vocals and some chord structure, and the more open-ended semi-improvised stuff which was more what we sounded like live."

Carter Brown says, "I don't know if we ever talked about wanting to make a double album. It was always, 'Okay we need something else. Okay, just start doing something, just make this noise start.' A lot was done on the fly. We had a handful of songs when we went up there, and the rest was completely improvised in the studio."

Those late-night sessions became *Prazision*, the debut kranky double-LP release. As the Instagram user *need_more_records* said of *Prazision* years later, "This changed everything, don't think there's an easy way to describe how important this release was."

The album had a distinctive lime-green and white artwork with a caliper in black and white. The cover was an offset print, folded over to cover two twelve-inch records and fit in a plastic sleeve. Joel and I got a rubber stamp made and used it on each side of the plain green labels, and wrote the side number of each record in the space provided with sharpies. Joel cleared out some space on the floor of his apartment, and we spent a few nights assembling albums. The first thousand LPs were hand-packaged in this manner and printed on marbled green and white vinyl. We bought a batch of singles from Retro 8 and threw those in the first batch of albums. Joel and I had no idea how long or even if the label would continue after our first few releases, so we made *Prazision* look as nice as possible. As we got the label organized and while *Prazision* had been in the recording and manufacturing process in 1992 and 1993, we had been busy reaching out to other bands and making arrangements to release follow-up albums on kranky. Joel and I understood the basic dynamic of record distribution: labels only get paid when distributors wanted the next release.

We included a note in the LPs that started out, "You don't know how lucky you are!" The note explained the presence of the seven-inch and detailed upcoming kranky releases from Jessamine, Spiny Anteaters, and Dadamah. This was the public debut of "mr. kranky," the composite persona who has symbolically represented the label ever since, and eventually became identified with Joel.

COMMUNICATING/RECEIVING THROUGH THE SAME TINY TRANSMITTER

The release of *Prazision* in late November 1993 was a spear in the ground. The new record label was positioning itself as offering something new for adventurous listeners of indie rock. Labradford was a band taking elements from bands on the indie rock tree like Codeine, Galaxie 500, and Slowdive and using them to extend a branch of their own. In Bristol, England, David Pearce was working on his own band Flying Saucer Attack while he worked at a record store. He recalls how the Cargo London office was pushing records: "They got excited by the first Fuxa and Windy & Carl singles and then very excited by the first Labradford LP. Those things were something a bit different from lo-fi. We were stocking kranky with vigour I can assure you. So, Stereolab, Fuxa and Windy & Carl, Labradford and kranky, I guess we'd (Flying Saucer Attack) done a single or two by then through Cargo UK unsurprisingly. These things seemed to have started off their own bat pretty separately to each other. Certainly, in our case with no idea if anyone would be particularly interested. And it turned out people were interested."

We also had some instinctual aesthetics beyond these that became defined over time, especially as we interacted and worked with more musicians. A sense of timelessness was important to us. Joel and I were looking for forward-facing bands who could make music that could not be immediately pigeonholed as coming from a particular place or time. Nor did we want music that, as we liked to say, "pushed the wacky meter into the red." The bands kranky worked with were not too absorbed with kitsch. We wanted bands that provided an accessible point of entry to listeners. Deliberately difficult music and overly academic efforts, or as we liked to call it, "homework music," was not for us.

This isn't to say that kranky recordings wouldn't touch distortion or have sharp edges, as later albums by Charalambides and Keith Fullerton Whitman evidence. Emotionally, much of the music we issued inspired or was inspired by disorientation, regret, isolation, or melancholy that was out of step with the raucous, beer-drinking indie rock guitar jams of the time. The early and mid '90s were a boom time above and below ground in America, or appeared to be on paper. Joel and I couldn't identify. Our innate contrariness drew us to musicians who were expressing unease and looking to mess with the prevailing formula. Labradford slowing things down was, as we saw it, as revolutionary as Minor Threat speeding things up had been a decade earlier. Operationally, we saw the label as being in the tradition established by Touch & Go and Dischord. Aesthetically, we identified with British post-punk labels 4AD and Factory, who had enraptured us as teenagers with their visual and sonic look and feel.

We deliberately cloaked kranky in a veneer of mystery. The few ads we ran featured graphics I cut and pasted from thrift-store books on space travel, hi-fi stereo equipment, economic theory, or the Cold War. Captions like "analog technology makes space travel possible" caught my eye. We avoided using band photos in ads or sales sheets. We didn't play up the fact that we were based in Chicago and often referred to the label locale as "planet kranky" in communications. The goal was to make any given kranky release appear to be a transmission from an unknown source. It worked for at least one person, as the filmmaker Braden King confirms: "kranky seemed like this mysterious planet to me. I couldn't understand exactly what it was or where all of this music was coming from. It seemed fully formed and intentional. That was as true of the label itself as it was of the bands. There was an intentional, unified aesthetic. It was almost intimidating."

Mat Sweet, later to release music on kranky under the name Boduf Songs, had been a fan of hardcore punk and doom metal. He remembers discovering kranky music, and that "there was an appeal in the way that the dark themes I'd been obsessed with in loud guitar music were being channeled through quieter, more surreptitious methods." David Bryant says, "Before that first godspeed tour, there was this beautiful halo of mystery surrounding kranky for me. I felt a heavy connection to some of those records, as though a bunch of us, for a tiny moment, were communicating/receiving through the same tiny transmitter."

Joel and I both had to enthusiastically back a project for kranky to undertake it, and the place where our tastes overlapped in a Venn diagram of musical interests was a sweet spot that lasted for a long time. We knew it when we heard it. There was a thrill connected with discovering a new band that we both enjoyed. One of the most enjoyable things about working at a record label, the one that I really, really miss, is the secret planning. The knowledge of putting hidden processes in motion was a big kick for me that compensated for long hours and poor pay. Unleashing something on an unsuspecting public is a lot of fun. Thus, "you don't know how lucky you are."

Keeping our label plans a complete secret wasn't possible. Everyone involved in the production of *Prazision* knew what was going on, and our Cargo coworkers needed to prepare for the release. Joel is a more reticent person than I am, and even I was reluctant to talk without a physical release in my hand. The people I did tell about kranky were supportive. More than a few friends at labels and in bands conveyed their approval, tempered with warnings about the steep climb kranky faced. When we got some advance copies of the album, my answer to "What have you been doing lately?" was to say "This" and slip a Labradford CD across a bar or onto a desk and suggest that the recipient's life was about to change.

I took very few chances at the beginning, doling out promo CDs carefully. With the early kranky releases in hand, I started promoting the bands to press. It was a time when there were dozens of national monthly magazines dedicated to music. Looking back from 2018, Aaron Gilbreath wrote how "*Spin*, *Blender*, *Magnet*, *FILTER*, *The Big Takeover*, *Under the Radar*, *Alternative Press*, and *Rolling Stone* covered rock and pop. Alt-weeklies like *Chicago Reader*, *Washington City Paper*, and *Minneapolis City Pages* were bastions of sharp, influential criticism."

Some of these publications wouldn't give the time of day to kranky releases. We were competing for coverage against major labels that would back their biggest-selling artists with large advertising budgets. And I was promoting music that was almost defiantly hard to pin down. There were no guitar heroics, no verbose singer-songwriter lyrics to analyze ad infinitum. The subject matter was not the soiled and bloody underside of American culture that Touch & Go bands often referenced. The bands were not connected to any identifiable youth subculture;

there was no special clothing associated with being a kranky fan. Without being too simplistic, I think it's fair to assert that the hazy smears of Labradford and the releases that followed expressed a warm, enveloping feminine sensibility that stood apart from the grunge sausage party. The kranky bands had no personal stories of sin and redemption, nor were they academics assiduously exploring the outer limits of music theory. The cult of the lone musical genius did not apply. It was not always an easy sell.

We got a foot in the door with publications like *The Wire* and *NME* in England and *Alternative Press* stateside. I had some established relationships with writers, editors, and fanzines from my time at Touch & Go and directed promos to those I figured would appreciate what kranky was up to. There was a galaxy of fanzines to consider, and our location at Cargo helped us make connections and evaluate where to send out promos. Joel knew which fanzines had a regular publishing schedule and sold well. It could often take six months for a review or interview to show up in a self-financed and produced fanzine, so those that did get kranky promos were carefully vetted. Scott Rutherford had a fanzine called *Speed Kills* and got what Labradford was up to right away. Gail O'Hara from *Chick Factor* was one of four people to attend the first Labradford NYC show.

We were taking bigger chances with record store buyers and relied on the advice of our Cargo coworkers in Chicago and the expertise of the Cargo London office, who received a supply of Labradford CDs for UK stores. Joel and I were surprised that it took several years for the first accusation of "New Age" to be leveled at a kranky album. We had steeled ourselves for it when *Prazision* came out.

My job was to direct free CDs to the right people and keep the promo budget as low as possible. The San Francisco–based dance music magazine *XLR8R* had writers and editors like Vivian Host, Tomas Palermo, and Philip Sherburne who were interested in what kranky artists were doing and believed their readers would be interested as well. There were freelance writers who could get reviews and stories printed every now and then in major metropolitan daily newspapers. Match those with more enthusiastic and knowledgeable writers at fanzines and alt-weeklies, college radio airplay, coverage in the publications *CMJ New Music Report* and *Rockpool* that existed to inform college radio, and promotional service to the right record store buyers, and you had something that looked like a proper marketing campaign if you squinted.

Bill Meyer was a Chicago-based writer who wrote for underground magazines like *Option*, *Puncture*, and the *Chicago Reader*. He remembers, "When that first Labradford record came around, it's like, 'How do I deal with this?' Could anyone make sense of that record if it had come out in 1988? I don't know, it was important that it happened right when it did, like the wedge driving something open."

Another person who got a CD in the mail from me was Phil McMullen at the English magazine *Ptolemaic Terrascope*. Reflecting on *Prazision*, he says, "As soon as I heard it, I knew that it belonged in the *Ptolemaic Terrascope*. Don't ask me how I knew. I would probably say it had something to do with the amount of thoughtfulness that had gone into every element of the release in question, from the passion the musicians experienced when recording, down to the care that's gone into the cover art. When everything works together like that an extra element seems to come into play. Whatever it is, the Labradford album had it in spades."

Some LPs arrived at Cargo from England, packaged in heavy cardboard sleeved with the old-style glued-on, wrapped around paper on cardboard artwork record nerds call "tip on." The words "rural psychedelia" appeared on the cover. It was self-released by a group called Flying Saucer Attack. There were tracks entitled "Popol Vuh 1" and "Popol Vuh 2" after the '70s

German group, and a cover of "The Drowners" by the contemporary English band Suede. The LP had followed two self-released singles. Electric and acoustic guitars were layered to the point of distortion, vocals were sung simply (or whispered), and percussion was simple at best. It was a singular recording, from Bristolians named David Pearce and Rachel Brook (now Rachel Coe) who recorded at home with various collaborators. As Phil McMullen puts it, "You can just tell that the artist has thrown everything into that release because they had something that they desperately needed to express." Jessica Bailiff recalls, "I heard the first Flying Saucer Attack album sometime in 1994, I think. I was obsessed, I bought every single, album, EP, etc. as they came out after that. I never heard music the same way again. FSA's attitude and manner of existence in the music industry was inspiring." For kranky that first Flying Saucer Attack LP was a transmission from a kindred spirit. As David Pearce confirms, Flying Saucer Attack and the bands on kranky were "operations that set up in isolation initially. Kind of serendipitously, because of 'something in the air.'"

Eventually, kranky would work with some of the musicians associated with the Bristol scene FSA came out of, and with David Pearce himself in a recording project with Jessica Bailiff called clearhorizon. Our pal Bill Kellum at VHF Records in Washington, DC, released the album on CD and LP in early 1994. The two Dans were paying attention, too. In October 1994, Chicago's Drag City label had released a second Flying Saucer Attack record called *Distance*. As Pearce puts it, "We hooked up with them because they were the people who were kind enough to ask us. VHF, and a bit later Domino and Drag City, were the ones that outright up front said 'Let's do something', so first with VHF, then Domino/DC, we did. I could understand that, and mostly understand them."

A kranky-UK connection was established very early in the life of the label. A variety of supporters, from John Peel on the

BBC to *Ptolemaic Terrascope* to Peter Kember to our colleagues at Cargo Records in London, were able advocates for the label. In the fall of 1994, a little under a year from the release of *Prazision*, Labradford were playing their first English shows and opening for UK bands on the East Coast and Midwest. In September 1994, Labradford played a show in Manhattan with two English bands, Seefeel and Main, that inspired Jon Wiederhorn to coin the descriptive phrase "gothic cathedrals of sound" in a review for the English music weekly *Melody Maker*. The term has been repeated to the point of cliché.

Beginning in 1967, for generations of music listeners in the United Kingdom and beyond, John Peel's BBC radio program was the point of first contact with the most adventurous music available. On April 10, 1993, Peel played "Preserve the Sound Outside" by Labradford. John Peel sent a supportive postcard to kranky early in the label's development, which was a major affirmation for us. Labradford, godspeed you! black emperor, and Low would all make the live, in-studio appearances known as Peel Sessions between 1996 and 2003. Peel Sessions were one example of how the UK market could be reached with relative ease compared to that of the United States. In Canada, the Canadian Broadcasting Company program *Brave New Waves* similarly broadcast underground music to a dedicated audience of late-night listeners. Patti Schmidt, the show's host from 1995 onward, was very supportive of kranky releases. She tipped me off to a nine-person band in Montreal performing in underground venues to experimental films called godspeed you black emperor! The band moved that exclamation point in 2002, modifying their name to godspeed you! black emperor, to the consternation of writers, copy editors, and other anal retentives everywhere.

Sometime in 1993 Joel and I went out to see a band from Columbus, Ohio, called Monster Truck 5. Their initial single had impressed us. The indie rock biosphere at the time contained a large number of bands recharging garage rock models from the early '60s, and Monster Truck 5 were not too far from that scene, or subscene. One critical catchphrase you could apply to Monster Truck 5 is that the band "deconstructed" rock music. What we saw during that memorable experience was an exploded view of rock music, put back together again with some gaps left in place between jagged, staticky guitars and phenomenal drumming that was a tumbling car wreck at some points and machine-precise at others. Joel was in touch with the band, but their unstable lineup made working together impractical. That aborted effort was as close as kranky ever came to working with a "rock" band.

PRICED TO MOVE

There were developments in the wider spheres of the music business that would gradually influence the distribution of independent labels. In 1993 the growing electronics chain Best Buy opened nine stores in the Chicago area. Best Buy would get into the music business, selling compact discs at large discounts, often under their cost, as loss leaders to lure shoppers into their massive superstores to buy refrigerators, televisions, and the like. By the end of the 1990s this tactic played havoc with independent record stores and chains alike, which could not afford to match Best Buy's prices on the best-selling CDs that were record stores' bread and butter. As *Fortune* magazine reported in August 1997, "From 1993 to 1994, Best Buy's home-entertainment software revenues more than doubled, from $352 million to $729 million. While a portion of that figure was contributed by computer software and videocassettes, the lion's share came from CDs, and those dollars came directly from the record stores' bottom lines." I knew indie record store buyers who would go to the closest Best Buy stores on Tuesday mornings to buy new major-label releases at prices that were cheaper than they could get from their distributors.

By 1997 a group of small regional record store chains like Peaches, Peppermint, Camelot Music, and the larger, national Wherehouse Music group filed for bankruptcy. It was a body blow to record stores and to the distributors and major record labels that lost money, and precursor to the even greater culling that would happen when digital downloading became common with the founding of peer-to-peer music sharing sites online. In 1994 the Clinton administration transferred control over the technological backbone of the Internet, previously operated by the federally run NSFNET, to corporate firms. Broadband Internet began spreading across the country via the existing cable television infrastructure.

A MIND MAP

These were small blips on the radar at kranky, Cargo, and for most people involved in underground music. At Cargo we were positioned in the center of the country and within reach of much of the United States. As Lisa Bralts-Kelly describes it, "I can still picture record store dividers on the shelf. I had a mind map, geographically linking record stores and venues." This mental placemaking allowed those of us selling records at Cargo to "experience scenes by seeing what was taking hold." In my case, that mental map of record stores and venues across the country was overlaid with college radio stations, alternative weekly newspapers, and fanzines. I had the opportunity to connect with music fanatics across the United States, and via Cargo's export shipments to offices in Montreal and London as well. A few posters, a press kit, and a promo CD in a box could make a difference. More importantly, I could make informed decisions about where to expend promotional efforts because Cargo salespeople and the record store buyers I spoke with would tell me what stores were selling kranky CDs and LPs. When bands started to tour, this set of references became doubly helpful.

Distinctive new record labels were established in Chicago. Skin Graft Records, a "comic book company that puts out records," was an extension of Mark Fischer and Rob Syers's self-published comics. The duo moved to Chicago and quickly hooked up with local noisemakers like the Flying Luttenbachers. Their comic/seven-inch-single combos were unmistakable, and the label eventually got distribution via Touch & Go. I even got to contribute artwork to a single by Jim O'Rourke's Brise Glace band. Among other bands, Skin Graft released the first recordings from a quartet called U.S. Maple, who would stress the structure of guitar rock to near breaking point across five albums. In 1994 Bloodshot Records began releasing a mutation of country music informed by reverence for the forms past and energized by the punk rock impulse. Their first album was a collection called *For a Life of Sin: A Compilation of Insurgent Chicago Country*. The cover artwork was a painting by Jon Langford of the Mekons. A quartet called Trenchmouth had emerged from the punk rock scene, infusing reggae rhythms, jazzy touches, and the declarative poetry of singer Damon Locks into the templates created by Washington, DC, bands on the Dischord label. The band connected with a St. Paul, Minnesota, punk label called Skene! Records and toured the punk rock circuit. David Bryant of godspeed you! black emperor, then singing in a band called Bliss, recalls playing with Trenchmouth in Chicago: "We toured a bunch in the states in the early '90s and put out a split seven-inch with Trenchmouth and at some point played a show with them in Chicago. I remember all of us visiting Damon in his apartment and him playing Art Ensemble of Chicago records."

SOUNDS IN MOTION

The crisscrossing of musical influences from a wider selection of recordings to listen to was also a product of what Jim DeRogatis calls "the economics of the esoteric." Between 1988 and 1992, analog synthesizers like the ones Carter Brown of Labradford collected were relatively inexpensive after the advent of digital sampling keyboards motivated many musicians to cast aside their bulkier analog kits. Some musicians were combing the used racks at music stores and digging through thrift shops for equipment. Carter Brown describes how he accumulated his collection of synthesizers: "There was a magazine called *The Trading Post*. That's where I got my Memorymoog. I started with a Korg PolySix. Then, a friend of a friend had three keyboards, and I got one. One was the vocoder. I had a Polymoog that I found in Maryland. I had a pair of Moog Taurus bass pedals that I sold to Doug, the bass player for Tortoise, for $100. Now I could easily get $3,000 or $4,000 just for that vocoder. But the one that I just had to have was the Oberheim Matrix. A sound man at 9:30 Club where I worked had a friend. He couldn't get any money for it, but he knew who Labradford was, and ended up selling it to me. I had lusted after that keyboard for years."

There were other musicians equally obsessed with analog synthesizers. If the English band Stereolab didn't exist, it might be necessary to invent them to advance the narrative of this book. Not only did the "Groop," as they called themselves, create an effervescent mix of '60s French pop, Krautrock, synthesizers, stereo testing albums, the "exotica" albums of Martin Denny and Arthur Lyman, easy listening, and Velvet Underground pulse, but they released albums on Drag City Records and had recordings out on Elektra/Warner Music beginning in 1993 with "Transient Random-Noise Bursts with Announcements." In August 1993, Carter Brown recalls, "I don't remember where I got this information. But it was something to the effect that they couldn't bring their Moog with them. Those songs needed those bloops and bleeps! At the time I had (an inoperative) Moog, and a Moog Opus 3. And I decided to give it to them."

Brown drove the keyboards from Richmond to New York City and delivered them in person to the band. Thus began a relationship between Stereolab, their management, and Labradford. Stereolab played shows with Labradford, most notably at Metro in Chicago in September 1994, and their Duophonic label released a ten-inch single by Labradford in 1997. Stereolab recorded their 1997 album *Dots and Loops* in Chicago with John McEntire of Tortoise and the Sea and Cake and a host of Chicago musicians.

The Coctails had also been recording with a group of Chicago musicians, including Ken Vandermark on bass clarinet, Hal Russel on saxophones, and Dave Crawford on trumpet and flugelhorn. This was in addition to the core quartet playing alto saxophone, tenor saxophone, clarinet, lap steel guitar (John Upchurch), baritone saxophone, guitar, bass (Barry Phipps), piano, alto saxophone, vibraphone, bass, drums (Mark Greenberg), trumpet, guitar, bass, and more drums (Archer Prewitt). The result was an album called *Long Sound*. Mark Greenberg describes the process of corralling the band's multiple influences and directions: "We always had many, many musical interests and loved playing together. It all seemed game. By the time we were making our third full-length record, we decided to try and pull together songs we were making that seemed to hold together better as a group instrumentally and sonically."

The record merges the two seemingly disparate worlds of jazz and the Coctails' previous albums into varied, tingling instrumentals somewhere between the Cool Jazz of the 1950s and the taut rock music of Slint and Codeine. As Patrick Monaghan rightly notes, "From an artistic standpoint, it was clearly a quantum leap in ambition on their part, inside and out." The group's follow-up, *Peel*, was focused on the interplay of guitars, where, as Ari Wiznitzer notes on the *AllMusic* website, the "band's constant swapping of instrumental and vocal duties gives the record a varied, complex feel while saving it from monotony . . . the album's instrumentals serve as fine palate cleansers between pop songs. A consistent listen from top to bottom, *Peel* brims with polished talent, making it among the most vital recordings of Chicago's early-'90s underground scene."

In 1992 the Chicago company Midway released an arcade video game called Mortal Kombat. The soundtrack of the game was composed by Dan Forden, who also played bass from time to time in the idiosyncratic Chicago progressive rock band Cheer Accident. The music on the popular game, the home version, and subsequent volumes in the Mortal Kombat franchise, as well as Forden's presence as a literal talking head in the games, arguably means that his music and voice were heard by many more people in total than those of any of the musicians and bands mentioned in this book. In those years when video games were played in arcades, players paid to hear that music and voice a quarter at a time.

5 analog technology makes space travel possible 1994

Bricks of sanity topple at your feet.
—*Jon Wiederhorn*

Smashing Pumpkins' third album, *Mellon Collie and the Infinite Sadness*, was a double LP released in October 1995. The band had toured for thirteen straight months after *Siamese Dream* came out in 1993, and then began recording with Alan Moulder and Flood (aka Mark Ellis). The latter had worked with New Order, Depeche Mode, Nick Cave & the Bad Seeds, and other electronic and post-punk artists. Moulder had engineered recordings by the Jesus and Mary Chain, My Bloody Valentine, and Ride, English bands focused on immersive guitar tracks often called "shoegaze." Flood would go on to work with U2 and Nine Inch Nails that year. Aside from a career working with groups Billy Corgan obviously emulated, Flood was able to expand and gloss the band's moody music to stadium-level stature and heft and, with Moulder's aid, combine layer upon layer of guitar tracks into high-impact riffs.

The album debuted at number one in the *Billboard* charts. The single "Zero" inspired a T-shirt that you still see around, and that in many ways represents, if you will, the band's brand. Craig Marks wrote in the July 1996 issue of *Spin*, "The T-shirt could be seen peering out from magazine covers, from CD booklets, and from behind the mic nightly. You, too, could be a Zero. And if you couldn't score tickets to the show, not to worry: A recent trip to my local Urban Outfitters clothier turned up a well-stocked rack of the silver and black tees."

I've always found the silver, bolded sans-serif ZERO on a black tee design to be a fitting counterpoint to Sub Pop's LOSER T-shirt. Self-deprecation sold in the stadiums and the dive bars alike. We were having none of that at kranky. Branding-wise, the label would move forward with a confidence bordering on arrogance. When the time came to make our own T-shirts, we chose slogans like "You're with Stupid" or "Let a frown be your umbrella," and made bumper stickers that said, "Honk if you hate people, too." Oftentimes our coworkers at Cargo suggested some snappy one-liners that were too good to pass up, "What we want, when you need it" being one such example, courtesy of Dag Juhlin. We never got around to making "My other car belongs to my parents, too" bumper stickers, though.

THEY WANTED TO BE INVOLVED SOMEHOW

Water tends to find its own level, and the cold-shoulders experience that Smashing Pumpkins may have gotten from "real" indie rockers was passed along to other major-label moneymakers. Sheryl Crow recently recalled that time in an interview with the *Guardian*: "I came up with Smashing Pumpkins, Beck, Hole, REM . . . But I was totally shunned. I always felt like I was in no man's land. I'd go to the Grammys, but I was never 'in' with the popular kids, do you know what I mean?"

After years of touring and legal wrangling with his record label, Trent Reznor released the sophomore album from Nine Inch Nails, *The Downward Spiral*. Like Billy Corgan, Reznor was inspired by English electronic artists such as New Order and Depeche Mode. Alan Moulder was a recording engineer in the sessions. And like Smashing Pumpkins, NIN pumped up the teenage angst for stadium viewing and listening. The album went to number 2 on the *Billboard* Top 200 chart. At the end of the decade, Reznor would use his leverage with his major label to release music from cutting-edge electronic artists like Autechre, Plug, and Aphex Twin.

One Chicago musician received a windfall from the alt rock boom, or rather the pop-punk boom that began in 1994. Unbeknownst to Rick Sims of Touch & Go's Didjits, a Los Angeles pop-punk band called the Offspring covered Sims's "Killboy Powerhead" on their fourth album, *Smash*. The album was suitably titled, rapidly hitting gold and then platinum sales levels to become the best-selling indie record of all time for Epitaph Records. Music writer Tim Stegall recalls, "I was on the phone with my friend at Epitaph when the RIAA auditors certified that *Smash* had gone platinum. I hung up and called Rick. I told his answering machine that he was about to become a very rich man." Songwriting royalties netted Sims a house, car, retirement account, and presumably continued income, as *Smash* has sold over eleven million copies.

The tune you were most likely to hear in Chicago in the hipster districts in the summer of 1994 was "Seether" by the quartet Veruca Salt. They recorded the song with Brad Wood and released it on the Chicago indie label Minty Fresh. It was frustratingly catchy, ably channeling the loud/soft dynamic that Pixies had perfected and taught to Nirvana, centered on Louise Post and Nina Gordon's vocals. Singles left the Cargo warehouse as quickly as they came in. Minty Fresh owner Jim Powers was an experienced hand who had signed Cowboy Junkies to RCA

Records, where they had a moment of MTV-driven prominence. Minty Fresh had released an early single by Liz Phair. In short, Veruca Salt had a label ready to take advantage of the moment a very good single gave them. Did I mention how irritatingly memorable that song is? By September 1994, a debut album called *American Thighs* had been recorded at Idful with Brad Wood producing and Casey Rice engineering. Minty Fresh released an LP and CD, which was quickly licensed to the major-label DGC/Geffen Records. The album was on the *Billboard* Top Album sales chart for twenty weeks, peaking at number 69 and certified Gold. Seemingly, there was nowhere to go but up.

The major-label talent scouts were now out in force sniffing around Chicago. At a March 1994 show a trio called Loud Lucy "wowed a jostling crowd that included reps from Geffen, Sony, RCA, several publishing companies, and smaller labels as well, most notably Maverick, a vanity label owned by a certain someone named Madonna." The Chicago independent label March Records released a Loud Lucy seven-inch single that year, and by 1995 a debut long-player called *Breathe* recorded by John McEntire at Idful was released by DGC/Geffen. Groups with names like Local H, Smoking Popes, Triple Fast Action, and Fig Dish all got scouted, and all put out recordings on major labels between 1995 and 1997. A similar mini-signing spree was happening to the south in Champaign, where Menthol, Hardvark, and Hum all put their names on the dotted line. The Chicago bands mostly played some variation of "power pop," using loud-ish guitars tied to catchy songs reminiscent of '70s predecessors Cheap Trick, Big Star, and the Knack, or more tuneful punk rock like Green Day. As Casey Rice notes, this cohort of bands was "closed out of the clique of 'cool' music in Chicago. Why bother to wait to get into that club, we're just gonna do this instead. They had the kind of music that the major labels were interested in." Except for the distinctly heavier duo Local

H, who had an Alternative Charts radio hit with "Bound for the Floor," none of them made any kind of commercial impact.

This cadre of guitar bands were all following in the footsteps of Material Issue, a Chicago trio headed by guitarist/singer/songwriter Jim Ellison. After releasing a series of singles on small labels, Material Issue signed with Mercury Records/Polygram and released *International Pop Overthrow* in 1991. The album artwork featured lettering by Urge Overkill's Nathan Kaatrud. Like Urge Overkill, Ellison was outspoken about his ambitions for stardom and relentless in its pursuit. He called me once when I worked at Touch & Go to ask if I could add his band to an Urge Overkill tour, saying, "Because they rock, and we rock." What could I say in response to that? I didn't book tours. I was the promo guy for Urge Overkill's label. There wasn't much I could do or wanted to do to help Ellison. The debut Material Issue album had the goods to back Ellison's agenda, with the propulsive guitar pop of "Valerie Loves Me" and "Renee Remains the Same" being especially memorable. The album sat on the *Billboard* Album Charts for nine weeks, peaking at number 86 on May 4, 1991. The 1992 follow-up, *Destination Universe*, was anchored by the peppy "What Girls Want" but did not chart. Material Issue were too early to the party, "far too carb-heavy and Anglophilic for the meaty scuzz of the era," as *Time Out Chicago* put it looking back in 2014.

David Trumfio co-owned a recording studio, and eventually his band Pulsars signed to a major-label deal. He describes the allure of the Chicago scene for major-label talent scouts like this: "We were making music for each other and the indie network bubbling up worldwide. That's what got the majors' attention. The fact Liz Phair was a major breakout from a very DIY/indie approach really put the scene on the map. They saw that we were all doing it either way and they wanted to be involved somehow. It sounds cheesy but there was an energy and excitement they saw that frankly was happening with or without them, which made them even more attracted to it."

Bill Meyer puts it this way: "Companies realized that not everybody's going to be the next Fleetwood Mac, not every record is going to be the next *Rumours* like in the late '70s." Some major labels were willing to put relatively small bets on working with indie labels and bands. Greg Kot, then covering music for the *Chicago Tribune*, remembers that most musicians in the city were "more bemused than excited. A few were eager to cash in, but most saw through the notion that this was somehow sustainable." At kranky, we were more concerned with larger independent labels poaching bands from us and profiting from the investments our label had put into new, unknown bands. Joel and I did not want to see kranky used as the farm team for a bigger label. Beggar's Banquet, what one could accurately call a "major indie," did this with kranky band Bowery Electric. Later on, Warp Records courted godspeed you! black emperor during kranky's relationship with the band.

Trenchmouth's label had gotten themselves a manufacturing and distribution deal with EastWest Records America, an imprint connected to Elektra, a subsidiary of Warner Brothers. On an indie level, Trenchmouth were able to tour for as many as six months out of the year and sell around five thousand copies of each album. The major-label connection on *Trenchmouth vs. the Light of the Sun* did nothing to improve those numbers, and the label's distribution deal evaporated by the time Trenchmouth's final album, *The Broadcasting System*, was released in 1996. Singer Damon Locks and bassist Wayne Montana formed a band called the Eternals. Drummer Fred Armisen went on to a comedy career on *Saturday Night Live* and as the co-creator of the show *Portlandia*. In the latter, he skewers the indie rock milieu he rose through with Carrie Brownstein of the band Sleater-Kinney.

Major labels had not done a whole lot for most of the Chicago bands that had signed the dotted lines for labels hooked into the lower tier of manufacturing and distribution arrangements offered via Warner's Alternative Distribution Alliance beginning in 1993. Bands that worked slight variations on the indie rock template had trouble differentiating themselves in a saturated post-Nirvana marketplace.

Critical praise and sales did flow toward one band that worked with an independent label and had a unique take on how guitars and drums could interact. Consisting of experienced players from Bastro, Poster Children, Eleventh Dream Day, and Tar Babies, Tortoise epitomized both the potential for artistic growth among some indie rock musicians and the potential for sales growth that existed in Chicago. They also drew, and continue to inspire, hyperbole like few other bands. John Bush ladles it on in a biography on the *AllMusic* website, claiming that Tortoise "revolutionized American indie rock in the mid-'90s" and that they "practically stood alone in American indie rock by actually focusing on instrumental prowess and group interaction." This review is not untypical.

Begun by bassist Douglas McCombs and drummer John Herndon with the intention of creating a production and performance rhythm section a la reggae's Sly Dunbar and Robbie Shakespeare or the in-house band at r&b label Stax Records in the '60s anchored by bassist Dennis Duck Dunn and drummer Al Jackson Jr., Tortoise quickly grew in membership and released two seven-inch singles in 1993 and 1994. The second, "The Lonesome Sound," initiated a relationship with Thrill Jockey Records that continues to this day. The artistic and commercial development of Tortoise would make the band a focal point of the Chicago scene as well. Douglas McCombs describes the birth and growth of Tortoise like this: "By '92–'93 Herndon and I had a few sketches that we thought we could do something with. Brad Wood generously offered to record us. I would do two or three bass parts on each song and John would do multiple drum parts. We wanted it to be more than a studio project, so we asked John McEntire and Bundy Brown to be involved. By the time we played our first show we knew that we wanted a two-drumkit, two-bass line-up."

McCombs's experiences in Eleventh Dream Day working with label head Bettina Richards made Thrill Jockey a natural home for Tortoise. The label had a licensing arrangement with the German City Slang label, which placed Tortoise releases in the collective hands of an experienced and connected distributor in Europe's largest market beginning with the first, self-titled album.

Tomas Palermo's colleague in the Los Angeles band Slug, Steve Ratter, says, "As far as the shift in Indie Rock, I do distinctly remember the saying going around between us Slug members upon hearing Tortoise et al.: that 'Quiet is the new loud . . .'"

Herndon, Bundy Brown, and Casey Rice also joined a DJ collective called Deadly Dragon Sound System that played a weekly residency at the Empty Bottle. Deadly Dragon was founded by Rik Shaw, aka Richard Smith, who became a member of the band Rome. The enthralling mix of reggae, hip-hop, dancehall, and jungle made the night a must for indie rock party people. The immersion in the beat-centered jungle and drum-and-bass music also had a big influence on Herndon and Brown and their input into Tortoise music, and on Rice, who mixed Tortoise live shows and would release his own music under the Designer moniker. Tortoise embraced the opportunity to have their music remixed by cutting-edge UK electronic music makers, and John Herndon would release hip-hop and dub-influenced music under the name A Grape Dope.

YOU CAN'T TELL THE PLAYERS WITHOUT A SCORECARD

Tortoise were at the center of an interconnected group of Chicago musicians, many of whom recorded for the Thrill Jockey label. The links between musicians and groups came to resemble the intricacies of a Chicago Transit Authority train map. John McEntire had joined Sam Prekop and Eric Claridge from Shrimp Boat with Archer Prewitt from the Coctails to form the Sea and Cake. The quartet was named after McEntire's mishearing of a Gastr del Sol song title, "The C in Cake." The 1994 self-titled debut album was a fetching blend of interlocking grids of guitar, Brazilian bossa nova pop stylings, Prekop's low-key vocals, and the tight pull of McEntire's drumming. The group went on to release five albums between 1995 and 2003 with the requisite touring around each.

Jeff Parker was a guitarist with jazz training and experience who had played with Chicago jazz mainstay Ted Sirota and in Ernest Dawkins's New Horizons Ensemble. By 1998 he augmented and then replaced Slint graduate David Pajo in Tortoise in addition to playing and recording on Rob Mazurek's Chicago Underground projects and his own groups. Dan Bitney, John Herndon, Matt Lux, and Jeff Parker played with cornetist Mazurek in Isotope 217, a band that mixed jazz, funk, and electronics beginning with the 1997 album *The Unstable Molecule.* That title ably describes the combining and recombining of style and band lineups that was happening in the city. You really did need a scorecard to keep track of all the band lineups.

John Herndon drummed for Five Style, or alternately 5ive Style or 5 Style, a four-piece instrumental funk band anchored by bassist LeRoy Bach. Bach's Champaign, Illinois, band Uptighty was intensely popular, and when Bach moved north to Chicago with the founders of the T-shirt printing company Propaganda their communal live/workspace became a beehive of activity. Five Style released two albums and three seven-inch singles on Sub Pop between Herndon's Tortoise duties. The group played a technically focused update on the chicken-scratch funk pioneered by the '70s New Orleans trio the Meters. The trio were practically the intersection point of the Chicago scene. Bach tended bar at Wicker Park's penultimate hangout spot the

Rainbo Club and joined Wilco in 1997. Bach also booked recording and playing time with Joan of Arc, Will Oldham, Rob Mazurek, Liz Phair, Beth Orton, Andrew Bird, and Iron and Wine. Five Style's keyboardist Jeremy Jacobsen performed and recorded as the one-man band the Lonesome Organist, releasing three albums on Thrill Jockey and touring North America, the United Kingdom, Europe, and Japan.

Rob Mazurek grew up in the Chicago area, where witnessing the avant-garde jazz legend Sun Ra and his Arkestra at the 1981 Chicago Jazz Festival as a sixteen-year-old set him on a course of playing cornet. He took advantage of the city's jazz teaching infrastructure, studying at the Bloom School of Jazz and with teachers from Roosevelt University, DePaul University, the University of Chicago, and others. In 1994 he formed the Chicago Underground Collective as a loosely organized grouping of musicians ranging in size from duo to orchestra. He sat in on Tortoise sessions, as well as recordings by Stereolab, Jim O'Rourke, Sam Prekop, the Aluminum Group, and Gastr del Sol. Mazurek describes how Jeff Parker influenced his music, conversations with jazz greats, and the fertile music grounds in Chicago: "Jeff was responsible for reintroducing me to the world of the avant-garde and total free improvisation. I would go to the Jazz Showcase all the time and beg Joe Segal to let me in to hear all the jazz greats coming through Chicago all the time. Art Farmer really turned my head around in the early '90s. He wanted to listen to what I was doing, so I gave him my first three records. He told me it was not good enough just to try and sound like the masters."

Musicians based in Chicago could play in a variety of venues, from the basement of a coffee shop to the one-thousand-capacity Metro. The two bars that attracted the most local and touring bands were Lounge Ax and the Empty Bottle. There was a little push and pull between the two. It was an inevitable rivalry that got chippy between the club owners at times but was largely beneficial to concertgoers. As Jay Ryan confirmed, "Getting to the Bottle or the Lounge Ax meant knowing you weren't going to get screwed." Patrick Monaghan adds a crucial detail to the appeal of the women-owned Lounge Ax: "They probably did have a higher percentage of women attending shows there because toxic masculinity was definitely not tolerated." Mark Greenberg worked at the club. He remembers the time: "Seeing seven to ten bands a week really, really widened my experience and inspiration. Looking back at the calendar of shows it seemed I wanted to be there twenty-five out of thirty days. It was also right at the right moment in my life when new inspirations and experiences were desired and welcomed and able to be at the center of my life."

If you frequented the bar, there was no telling who might show up. It was hard to miss Luc Longley of the Chicago Bulls. Former teen heartthrob Donny Osmond appeared at a Jesus Lizard show while he was in town performing in *Joseph and His Amazing Technicolor Dreamcoat*. Any given crowd would have musicians present from any number of bands.

Keith Fullerton Whitman describes the view from Boston: "From afar it all seemed incredible; the Lounge Ax, the Empty Bottle, kranky, Thrill Jockey, Drag City, Atavistic. Everything coming out of Chicago just seemed so refined and aware of what was happening in the world."

As the nascent kranky label developed, we cast our eyes and ears outside Chicago. Joel and I believed that our counterparts at Touch & Go, Drag City, and Thrill Jockey were better placed to work with the best local bands. The boomtown atmosphere in the city was such that many new bands were not interested in taking time to craft their own sound. Smaller labels were popping up to grab bands seemingly as soon as they played out. We were well situated at Cargo to find bands from many other points of origin, and we took advantage of it. In April 1993, Joel went on vacation in New Zealand and connected with Peter Stapleton and Kim Pieters of the quartet Dadamah. We were both enamored with Dadamah's records, which hit a sweet spot between the droning guitars of the Velvet Underground and the synth-addled discord of the American "avant garage" band Pere Ubu. Drummer Peter Stapleton noted, "We were together for around two years; I think over 1991–92. We only played four live shows, although for a time we would practice every week." Dadamah's vinyl releases were pressed in small editions by an American label called Majora. The band had broken up by the time Joel arrived, with "half the band moved to Dunedin, five hours from Christchurch." Stapleton and Pieters had a new band going called Flies Inside the Sun, joined by guitarists Danny Butt and Brian Crook.

Joel persuaded the former members of Dadamah to let kranky compile the hard-to-find LP *This Is Not a Dream*, two seven-inch singles, and a compilation track onto one compact disc. We wanted more listeners to have access to the music, and the CD became catalogue number KRANK-002. Stapleton said that he and Pieters agreed: "We felt that the limited-edition vinyl thing was a bit elitist and wanted our music to be more widely available to anyone who was interested." As James Lien noted in *CMJ New Music Report*, "The idea of a band being unlike any other is by now a concept so shopworn it's almost meaningless, but in Dadamah's case it was really kind of true." The Forced Exposure catalog called the quartet "one of the most overwhelmingly great exponents of layer-shifting drone-on master-rock."

A single, beautifully wrapped in silver paper, with a cover of electro-punks Suicide's "Cheree" on a label named after the electro-rock pioneers Silver Apples, arrived at Cargo from a Seattle band called Jessamine. As I wrote later in a press release, Jessamine were "swimming against a flannel tide." "In the beginning we were just some weird kids playing music nobody really got. We did stand out. We didn't fit in to the grunge or riot grrrl scenes or even the psychedelic rock that had a little scene here," singer/bassist Dawn Smithson recalls. Describing her bandmates, she says, "When I joined the band, Rex was really into Opal, T. Rex, Blue Cheer and that kind of thing. Andy was really into analog synths, so that added another dimension. And I came from a place of '80s wave and prog rock, so it was a real mix we had going for us." A second single followed with two originals, "Cellophane" and "(I'm not Afraid of) Electricity." Joel got in touch, and Jessamine signed a contract. The band used an advance from kranky to purchase recording equipment.

In December 2014, David Segal acknowledged the twentieth anniversary of the release of Jessamine's self-titled album by kranky in Seattle's weekly alternative newspaper *The Stranger*: "In 1994, Jessamine were creating a dreamy, exploratory strain of rock that found fascinating ways to reinterpret the tropes established by totemic experimenters Pink Floyd, Can, and Miles Davis' groups from 1970–1975." He went on to call *Jessamine* "one of the greatest records to come out of this city." Sub Pop Records took note, releasing a seven-inch by Jessamine that year. It was packaged with four double-sided inserts held together by a bolt in a nice comment on the lures and frustrations of record collecting and limited-edition releases. In 1999 Jessamine would release a single called "Houdini" via the Barsuk label, which the graphic designer Henry Owens calls "Hands down one of the most insane packages I've ever seen. Cardboard with glued on paper (4/c with 2 spot varnishes and two foil stamps!) and the whole thing is locked in with a real FUCKING LOCK!" At kranky we printed the CD booklets and LPs for Jessamine on semi-transparent paper, with a layered design. Promotional posters were also screen-printed on translucent paper.

Jessamine was the second kranky release sequentially, despite having the catalog number KRANK-003. The Dadamah CD was in the production process and came out in May 1995 as KRANK-002. Such are the vagaries of a business dependent on multiple individuals and organizations contributing parts to a production process. Jessamine took on touring, working from their base in Seattle and moving up and down the West Coast.

Simultaneously in New York City, Martha Schwendener and Lawrence Chandler started rehearsing and playing as Bowery Electric. They had met while volunteering at La Monte Young and Marian Zazeela's Dream House in New York City, an art installation measuring the passage of time by continuous outputs of sound and light frequencies put together by the two artists with a deep background in the avant-garde and interest in immersive drone music. Martha played bass and sang, and Lawrence played guitar and sang. Various drummers joined them as Bowery Electric started playing around the East Coast, beginning at the birthplace of New York City punk rock, CBGBs. By the fall of that year they had released a double seven-inch single called "Drop" on their own label, Hi-Fidelity. A copy came to Cargo in the mail, Joel ordered a bunch to distribute, and we asked the band if we could hear more. As would happen with many working relationships the label had with bands, we acted quickly when we heard something we liked. As Chandler recalls, "Joel rang us after receiving the record at Cargo. We were listening to Flying Saucer Attack when Martha answered the phone." We were immediately attracted to the band's mix of insistent rhythms and atmosphere, with Lawrence's guitar tracks containing hints of Manhattan haze and grit, and the duo's moody, hushed vocals. And as was the case with Labradford and Jessamine, Bowery Electric impressed us with their self-reliance. We were not interested in directing band's careers. The flipside of our hands-off approach to music-making at kranky was the burden placed on the bands to direct their own affairs, from album art to recording to booking shows. A contract offer was extended and accepted, and Bowery Electric recorded their debut self-titled album for kranky.

Bowery Electric also heard from Peter Kember of Spacemen 3 almost immediately after releasing their double seven-inch.

Kember had a new project called E.A.R. (or Experimental Audio Research). Lawrence Chandler describes how Kember supported the band and got involved musically with them: "Out of the blue Pete rang us to tell us he liked 'Drop' and was with the *Melody Maker* writer who was reviewing it. After *Bowery Electric* was released, we toured the U.S. and Canada twice, the second time co-headlining with Pete and E.A.R. He was incredibly supportive. He released "Out of Phase" on the *New Atlantis* compilation on Space Age Recordings and invited me to record and perform with E.A.R."

Martha Schwendener remembers playing shows with E.A.R.: "Sonic (Pete Kember) was inventive, but practical. He'd show up with these hacked toy instruments and just be making music all the time. At the same time, he'd show up with these young kids. He'd put together a band and bring them over and it was just a nice mix of experiment and performance."

Bowery Electric had the track "Out of Phase" included on a Virgin Records compilation called *Monsters, Robots and Bug Men—A User's Guide to the Rock Hinterland.* As was the case with appearances by Labradford and Stars of the Lid on Virgin compilations, their inclusion got the word out on the band via Virgin's promotion and distribution networks. From the beginning the group had played around their home base in New York and soon undertook more extensive touring. Bowery Electric were powerful in a live setting. Schwendener details the live setup: "I played through an Ampeg eight-by-ten amp and Lawrence played through two Marshall stacks—it was really noisy to begin with. I used signal processing with the bass and didn't really play walking bass lines. Lawrence would put a layer of guitar on that was more atmospheric. It was physical music. I also went to a lot of clubs, so I liked that visceral feel of sound systems in clubs and dance music."

The band did have difficulty with drummers, though. Wayne Magruder, who had ably served during touring after the first album, stepped away from a tour appearance in Detroit to play a showcase show in New York for another band he was in, leaving Lawrence and Martha to play as a duo at a big show in St. Andrew's Hall. In time, the duo would make themselves less dependent on humans behind a drum kit.

Working at Cargo provided us with a vantage point where Joel and I could discover new bands easily. It was a big advantage. But there was one big constraint. Part of our understanding with management was that Cargo Chicago and the offices in Montreal and London had exclusive rights to distribute kranky releases. Phil Hertz made it clear to us that keeping our jobs at Cargo Chicago depended on aligning the label with Cargo Distribution. The kranky kommandment "Thou shalt not make an exclusive distribution deal" had been broken before the label's first record came out. Joel was especially chafed that his long hours and years of service to Cargo didn't count for much. As he said to Hertz in our meeting, "Throw me a bone." No bone appeared.

One ill effect of the limitation this arrangement created centered on pricing. Other, larger distributors would buy kranky titles from Cargo, add their own markup, and make kranky releases more expensive to stores. We would have preferred to charge one price to all our distributors over this two-tier system. Even so, we understood the partnership, coercive as it was, could be beneficial. Cargo salesperson Lisa Bralts-Kelly says, "You put yourselves in the place of the record store buyer," and kranky was able to "anticipate the needs of people all the way down the chain to the consumer." An advance copy of a CD or posters could go in an order to a store, and a buyer could have a copy to listen to before record release day. When the Cargo salesperson made a call or the new releases fax came in, that buyer would be familiar with the new kranky release and more inclined to order it—and play it in the store to raise the interest of shoppers. The Cargo sales offices in Montreal and London had incentive to promote their exclusive kranky releases to their client stores and distributors in Europe. It wasn't a completely disadvantageous arrangement, but it had been imposed on us. We weren't sure how successful kranky could be, but should things go well, we were motivated to leave Cargo as soon as we could.

The singles kept arriving at the Cargo warehouse, and we hooked up with a quartet from Ottawa, Canada, called the Spiny Anteaters. Their "Soundcheck" seven-inch reminded us of the obscure English grimy pop bands Meat Whiplash and Slaughter Joe, with a singalong indie rock song structure subverted by layers of distorted guitars. Spiny Anteaters' *All Is Well* album was catalog number KRANK-004, released in the fall of 1994. A second album, *Current*, followed in 1996. The label catalog was growing.

FACILITATORS OF TIMBRE AND TEXTURE

The music writer Ann Powers has stated, "I think that the most useful way to think about genre is as a set of categories, imposed externally, that musicians make use of, build community around, deify, or discard." Someone was bound to coin a phrase to try to capture what a widespread group of musicians were up to. Beginning in 1994, two Englishmen took on the task of defining what musicians, including kranky artists and Chicagoans like Tortoise, were putting together.

Attention was being directed in England toward kranky releases. As Peter Kember describes him, Kevin Martin was ". . . a journalist with a small j, and a musician with a large M . . . and a mover and shaker in the cooler shadows of the London music scene." In 1994 Martin compiled *Ambient Four: Isolationism* for Virgin Records and included a Labradford track alongside a host of predominantly British artists, including Peter Kember's E.A.R. project. It was a good fit, as Mark Nelson notes when he recalls how he and Carter Brown started the band: "We shared a few favorites—Spacemen 3 probably would have been an area of commonality. Carter brought a background in church music (organ) playing—so those gospel chords fit really well into a noisy abstract sound world. He was also well into more abstract composition." In the *Ambient Four* liner notes, Martin posited, "The proliferation of sanitized chill-out zones in the clubs of 1994 stands as both a testament to and indictment of Ambient's current resurrection. The explorations of Ash Ra Tempel, Terry Riley, Cluster et al., are now being eagerly recycled by Silicon age hippies on the quest for eternal highs . . . Dropping inwards instead of reaching out, this compilation's furtive music sounds as paranoiac as it does panoramic and is in direct contrast to its mellow relative."

Isolationism never caught on as a genre per se, although one could argue that it was influential in the formation of the currently used genre tag "dark ambient," which can be applied to artists on the compilation like Lull, Zoviet France, Total, and Final who came from the noisy industrial and metal scenes. Labradford's presence on the *Isolationism* album was an indication of how a discerning observer like Kevin Martin saw them as operating outside any notions of rock music. It was also a boost for Labradford, as Virgin could spend much more money promoting *Isolationism* than kranky could afford to spend on *Prazision*.

Simon Reynolds defined the term "post-rock" in *The Wire* magazine in May 1994 as "[the use of] rock instrumentation for non-rock purposes, using guitars as facilitators of timbres and textures rather than riffs and power chords." Just as Martin used *Isolationism* as a response to the perceived inadequacies of ambient music, Reynolds held "post-rock" up as the reaction to stale grunge and indie rock scenes. In a 1995 follow-up article in *The Wire* on American post-rock, he used Labradford as an example: "Grunge literally means 'grime,' 'muck,' 'dirt.' So, it's appropriate that so many of those in revolt against grunge's earthy passion have turned to science fiction and outer space in order to free up their imagination. For instance, all the tracks on Labradford's *A Stable Reference* are loosely inspired by the space race. Mark Nelson talks nostalgically of the space race as 'a monument to the human spirit, a desire to see something fantastical' before adding, poignantly, 'I was one of those kids who thought we'd all be taking trips to the Moon by now.'"

Post-rock won out in the battle of the genres. This was aided by Reynolds's status as a full-time writer, able to define and expand his argument in multiple articles across several publications. *The Wire* had become a must-read for would-be and actual music sophisticates on both sides of the Atlantic. Reynolds cast a wide net, including in the genre bands like Tortoise that were rhythmically centered alongside Jon Spencer Blues Explosion, who most listeners would have likely categorized as indie or garage rock, and Labradford and Stars of the Lid, who didn't have drummers at all. As the scholar James Hodgkinson noted, "Music categorized as post-rock is extremely hard to define because it attempts to escape mere classification by genre and because it does not represent any subculture." Reynolds made a point to differentiate English bands, which he argued had inherited "Dub's . . . impact on British left-field rock," and adopted what he called "hip-hop's sampladelia." He thought that "UK bands could respond to hip-hop as yet another exotic imported 'street sound,' white American bohemians feel that it is black cultural property, to be given props, but not to be trespassed upon . . . UK post-rock outfits, influenced by various admixtures of dub, hip-hop and techno, tend to be studio-centric sound laboratories for whom live performance is an irrelevance; whereas American post-rockers remain deeply committed to the band format and playing live."

The interest in live performance by American bands was also an inheritance from the avant-garde of the 1950s and 1960s.

The Theatre of Eternal Music, the mid-'60s group centered on La Monte Young, Tony Conrad, John Cale, and Marian Zazeela, was one major example. Theirs was an ethos linked to the performance-art Fluxus movement via poet-percussionist Angus MacLise. Cale would go on to join the Velvet Underground, and Tony Conrad reemerged in the 1990s with reissued and new recordings working with Chicago musicians Jim O'Rourke and David Grubbs. MacLise's recordings were also reissued in the '90s. Other musicians who participated in the Theatre of Eternal Music, called the Dream Syndicate by Conrad and Cale, were Jon Hassell and Terry Riley, who were also major influences on the American bands Simon Reynolds came to associate with post-rock.

American bands were cautious to avoid what we now call cultural appropriation, especially when it came to hip-hop. They were also cognizant of the musical risks in crudely grafting hip-hop onto rock. The Red Hot Chili Peppers could not count many fans among underground musicians. White musicians in the American underground scene listened to hip-hop and admired it, but were wary of overtly integrating it into their music.

One place in Chicago where indie rock musicians and audiences were able to express their love of and influence by music of the African diaspora was at the weekly Deadly Dragon Sound System DJ night at the Empty Bottle. Rick Smith had begun playing reggae records on the bar's turntables, when Casey Rice suggested, "Why don't we play reggae through the PA? It would sound so much better. And then people started coming and then people started coming, coming. And we just kept doing it. And because we all were kind of interested in music that wasn't rock and roll, we just started playing all those records there because it was fun."

Chicago was, and is, one of America's most segregated cities. Those of us involved in the independent rock underground did not deliberately look beyond where circumstances landed us. Patrick Monaghan observes, "I've often wondered why indie rock and punk were so largely skewed to whites, and I still don't have an answer for that. I know that when they filmed *High Fidelity* at Lounge Ax, Lisa Bonet made them go out and round up some black extras to bring in, because the extras they had were so white, which mirrored their normal audiences." Most venues, audiences, and musicians were white and located on the largely white northside of the city.

As Rice describes, the Deadly Dragon night "attracted a much different crowd, and I would say a far more racially integrated one. And queer. It didn't have as much of the white-boys-their-arms-crossed kind of vibe, it was more about dancing and fun and you could talk, it wasn't like a performance by a band, so you didn't have to be reverential and stand there." Smith, Rice, Bundy Brown, and John Herndon all held down turntable duties spinning a mélange of reggae classics, dancehall, hip-hop, and the energized new music from the United Kingdom called jungle. As Tortoise occupied more of Herndon, Brown, and Rice's time beginning in 1998, Smith took on solo DJing under the Deadly Dragon name in venues across Chicago.

The American emphasis on live performance Reynolds mentioned was also an inheritance from punk and indie rock and a reflection of the artistic strength of many bands that could not afford to spend the time and money to learn how to "use the studio as an instrument," but who could afford spaces to practice. In a continent-spanning country that lacked a national radio service and a few powerful music papers like the United Kingdom had, touring was something of a necessary evil. Musicians were compelled to take time off from jobs, or give them up altogether, for touring and take on the costs of transportation. For bands like those on kranky, whose music did not naturally accompany beer drinking in smoky bars, long tours across the middle of the country were not the best use of time. Trips to the East Coast, where cities, colleges, record stores, and alternative venues were concentrated, and where the alternative newspapers were inclined to publicize left-field music, were a better idea, mixed in with occasional West Coast excursions. Even then, bands like Labradford found that "it was difficult to play live for a host of reasons—so frustration with that led us to kind of give up on it." Brian McBride from Stars of the Lid confirms the difficulties of performing extended compositions for indie rock audiences when he remembers the duo's first US tour: "Many people didn't know how to receive our little sound baths. Nashville was kind of a disaster with a couple of bottles thrown our way."

Working with a good booking agent who could organize tours and secure good shows was invaluable, but the number of bands far surpassed the openings good booking agencies had for clients. English bands could go out for a couple of weekends in their smaller country, score some radio airplay on the BBC, and get coverage in the weekly papers. They might even hop the channel and play European dates. The hill was steeper in the United States. As kranky artist Jessica Bailiff notes, "It really says something that I could cover the cost of one or two plane tickets to Europe, vehicle rental, fuel, missed day job wages, paying one or two other people to play in my band, and more, for a European tour. But I had trouble even getting shows here, and when I did, I could never cover the cost of travel, let alone all else."

Logging in extended studio time was expensive, so groups tended to get what they could on tape quickly. The best way to do that was to simply record at home or in a practice space. This took away the time pressures and expense of working in a studio setting. Adam Wiltzie from Stars of the Lid notes, "We never had any money to record in studios. We've always had these old archaic four-track reel-to-reel cassette recorders that we recorded all of our stuff on 'cause that's all we could afford, and we made the best out of our predicament." Home recording gear mitigated this problem for some groups, as with Bowery

Electric's adoption of samplers, Roy Montgomery's recording on a portable four-track tape deck, and Windy & Carl's home studio. Jessamine used an advance from kranky to purchase equipment for their own studio, where they could record practices for further reference or to use on albums. The complicated calculus of aligning day jobs, touring, and recording seemed to work out differently in the United States than in the United Kingdom, and not always to the advantage of American musicians.

Simon Reynolds did not invent the term "post-rock" out of whole cloth. James Wolcott deployed it in describing Todd Rundgren's work in the July 1975 issue of *Creem* magazine. I don't believe that Reynolds intended for a group of articles and reviews that examined a wide group of musicians to become an ironclad genre. I always took Reynolds's articles as the beginning of a conversation. But that conversation between writers never really materialized. Or rather, it was directed toward a low common denominator. Most other music writers liberally applied the term as if "post-rock" had been defined for posterity and everyone knew and agreed with that definition. The scholar James Hodgkinson observed, "Without the discourses of post-rock, the phenomenon could not truly be said to exist. . . . The discourses that surrounded it in fact constructed it." As Reynolds observes, "Post-rock was not conceived as a genre so much as a 'possibility space'—that would allow for a very diverse, open-ended range of sounds and approaches. You go beyond the strictures of a conventional rock band and there are all kinds of different outcomes. Post-rock ended up being something much more defined and quite unlike what I'd imagined, or indeed what I had been inspired by (groups using loops, sampling, swirls of texture, either groove-oriented or edging into ambience). By the 2000s, post-rock had become much more like instrumental rock with a sense of drama and epic crescendos."

In any event, as Ann Powers noted, musicians habitually dismiss the categories and genres that are applied to them. In my experience, that certainly was the case with the musicians I worked with at kranky. Reactions to the post-rock genre being applied to their music could range from amusement to exasperation. Mark Nelson aptly describes Labradford and Tortoise as "temperamentally sharing something" in common, which is a more useful way of describing what linked those two bands than a musical genre. Lawrence Chandler from Bowery Electric looks back on how he and Martha Schwendener saw post-rock: "We were both in graduate school at the time studying with some of the major proponents of all things 'post'—'post-colonialism,' 'post-feminism,' etc. So 'post-' this or that was a bit obvious in that moment. Without knowing about Simon Reynolds's use of the term, writing tongue-in-cheek I described our music as 'post-rock' in the press release for the *Drop* EP."

Douglas McCombs from Tortoise looks at the tag from another perspective: "I'd prefer 'post-rock' to 'jazz fusion.' The term seems to mean something different to every journalist. The one implication I used to disagree with and resent was that 'post-rock' was initiated by musicians who believed that 'rock 'n roll' was dead or a dead end. The music that I want to play is thought-provoking and rebellious. 'Rock 'n roll' still has a role to play, I don't care what you call it."

Having your art thrown into a category alongside other bands you may or may not feel an affinity with is definitely irksome to musicians. I had some experience with this at Touch & Go Records, where a wide variety of groups were often described as adhering to a "Touch & Go" or "Chicago" sound. As *Fact* magazine later put it, "The first rule of post-rock is that you definitely don't call it post-rock." I never used it in conversation without applying a protective layer of sarcasm. Reynolds's articles laid out elements that subsequent writers picked up and ran with, gradually forgetting the original premises until the present moment, in which the genre is used to describe mostly bands that sprinkle in longer tempos and the odd non-rock texture into instrumental guitar-centric rock music.

Simon Reynolds's writing was focused on Tortoise's use of the studio as a compositional tool, which was aided when drummer John McEntire established his Soma recording studio in 1993. The band's live shows were remarkable. The members of the band often switched up instruments on stage, which was a novelty of sorts in an indie rock scene where most bands assumed static instrumental roles. Another big factor in Tortoise's live show was Casey Rice's live mixing on the sound board, a role she held beginning with the group's first shows, and that allowed for the use of supplemental sound sources and effects that made Tortoise shows unique. The band acknowledged her contribution in the credits on album artwork, giving "special thanks to Casey Rice 'The Designer' for live sound."

INTRIGUING LITTLE THREADS

One group of people tied together a range of new recordings into one worldview in what became a scene as opposed to a genre, or perhaps, as Ned Raggett offered, "a through line." Phil McMullen started editing the *Ptolemaic Terrascope* in 1989 from his home base in western England aiding artist Cyke Bancroft and publisher Nick Saloman, and became an early, ardent supporter of kranky releases in its pages. The masthead defined it as "an illustrated occasional." That antiquated term describes an approach both reminiscent of an idealized rural English past and flexible enough to take on inspiration as it arrived. The *Terrascope* staff covered music new and old in an idiosyncratic mix of folk, rock, psychedelic, and experimental music. David Pearce recalls that once while he was working in a record store, "A customer lent me all the issues. I kept mentioning in the shop bands like Trees and who were they and what had happened to them, and eventually there were enough of these bands that the *Terrascope* had tracked down and interviewed that this chap lent me the whole *Terrascope* set up to then. So, I found out loads of stuff."

Raggett describes McMullen's editorial approach as a "reasonably broad embrace of psychedelic legacies—from full-on noise squall to fragile solo weirdness." As the producer and guitarist Jack Endino put it, "The accent is on what must unfortunately be called 'psych' for lack of a better term, but they are as likely to interview Tom Rapp or Silver Apples or other overlooked sixties/seventies cult icons as they are to cover modern stuff." There were many fanzines on both sides of the Atlantic, but the *Terrascope* stood out as one of a few that expanded beyond regular publication to host a yearly festival that provided a physical space for musical collaboration and networking.

Initially started to aid the magazine financially, the Terrastock festival was held seven times between 1997 and 2008, first in Providence, Rhode Island, and then in San Francisco, London, Boston, Seattle, and Louisville, with return stops in Providence and Boston. Terrastock featured artists that kranky worked with like Roy Montgomery, Charalambides, and Windy & Carl, who played the first fest after Bowery Electric dropped off the bill, and then went on to play all seven fests. Each featured a wide variety of groups from reformed electronic rock pioneers Silver Apples to Woodstock veterans Country Joe and the Fish. Did the *Terrascope* and Terrastock represent an actual movement or genre? Not quite. But as Endino confirms, readers were always likely to find something interesting there. Editor Phil McMullen describes the *Terrascope* founders' interests as "broadly speaking classic psychedelia, contemporary underground rock and traditional folk," and notes that "somehow it all seemed to belong—there were often intriguing little threads which tied them all together." McMullen confirms, "A lot of people who previously knew one another only through correspondence or by reputation met one another for the first time and lifelong friendships were formed." The Terrastock festivals became "a true gathering of the tribes, one that united a hitherto obscure community that looked beyond consumerism and strived to connect with something deeper and more spiritual." Windy Weber of Windy & Carl remembers, "The call never came until nearly the last minute after Bowery Electric bowed out. The *Ptolemaic Terrascope* had been one of our favorite magazines, and we were absolutely thrilled to have been part of Terrastock no matter how we got there."

Michael Bullington describes the musical experiences and connections that Grimble Grumble made at the 1998 festival: "I remember getting our gear off stage quickly because I really wanted to see Kendra Smith, who was playing in the other room right after us. Jello Biafra [of the punk band Dead Kennedys] stopped by our merch area to tell us he really was into our set. And we got mentioned as a highlight in an article in the *New York Times*. We met Hans Martin Gross, who runs a German label, and he offered to release our ten-inch and LP in Germany."

The magazine directed its attention to bands on independent labels, which was fitting as the founder Nick Saloman released albums from his band Bevis Frond on his own Woronzow label. McMullen says, "Independent labels were our life-blood: labels like kranky and VHF and Drunken Fish could be relied on to not only advertise every issue, but also provide us with interesting new releases and interview opportunities." The *Terrascope* in turn inspired journals like *Broken Face*, *Deep Water*, and *Worlds of Possibility*. *Ptolemaic Terrascope*, as Joel and I had noticed from working at Cargo, always sold out of its print run, too. It became one of a few publications that kranky regularly advertised in. In return, Phil McMullen notes, "kranky was a hugely important label to all we were striving to achieve."

A GRAND CHAPTER IN TOUCH & GO'S HISTORY

The most important music business development in Chicago in the 1990s was the growth of the distribution operation at Touch & Go Records. As Adam Reach, a Touch & Go production manager, recalls, "Atavistic, Drag City, Emperor Jones, Merge, Skin Graft, Thrill Jockey, and Trance Syndicate all had manufacturing and distribution deals with Touch & Go Distribution."

The distribution company split profits with each label catalog-wide after costs were recouped. Touch & Go Distribution took 30 percent, while each label received 70 percent. The arrangement gave Touch & Go Distribution operating funds for manufacturing, sales, and warehouse staff. Splitting profits across a label's entire catalog after costs were covered meant that, in most cases, less-selling releases did not end up in a financial hole.

And as Reach elaborates, savvy labels "channeled those releases they deemed suitable/ready via the distribution deal, while manufacturing and selling smaller releases on their own. Many times, it was more advantageous for a label to make smaller releases (i.e., seven-inches, or any obscure, esoteric, or smaller—at the time—artists/albums) on their own. This allowed the labels to grow, to refine their 'brand' if you will, since they were able to combine the 70 percent from releases put through TGD with the 100 percent profit they were able to make on their own."

This arrangement carried some risk for labels, which could expect to get paid only after recordings "recouped" manufacturing costs and on a catalog-wide basis, not release-by-release. It worked to the benefit of Chicago labels like Drag City beginning in 1993 and Thrill Jockey starting in 1994. Their experienced owner/operators judiciously managed their release schedules, inside and outside of the Touch & Go system. Not every label in the system operated in that way. In the case of Atavistic Records, the deal prompted the creation of the Unheard Music Series in collaboration with John Corbett, and sixty (!!??) releases in six years, plus a sublabel called Truckstop run by filmmaker Braden King, Michael Krassner, and Joe Ferguson and numerous releases on Atavistic itself. From the outside, that did not appear to be sustainable.

All the labels involved benefited from the volume manufacturing discounts Touch & Go Distribution received. The price per unit of compact discs decreased as the size of duplication orders increased, which in turn increased the profit margin on each CD sold. This worked to the benefit of kranky when we received Touch & Go pricing from the CD plant in Quebec that we all used. When albums from Tortoise or Will Oldham took off, Touch & Go had the resources to meet demand and the staff to solicit and ship sales. Touch & Go also sent releases to other distributors, like Cargo, which optimized coverage for all involved. By the turn of the century, label and distribution operations employed two dozen people. Leslie Ransom was head of domestic sales and describes an operation where "Initially, the labels were smaller than Touch & Go and they got a leg up with someone who had the ear of retail and distributors to get them into more stores and with greater support. The distributed labels at Touch & Go were also growing, and their releases were often bigger than the Touch & Go label releases."

The Truckstop crew had moved to Chicago from Los Angeles, where King had gone to the University of Southern California for film school. His senior film project featured music by a band with himself and Krassner called the Boxhead Ensemble. They opened Truckstop Audio Recording Company in a loft not too far from the former Chess Records offices. Braden King looks back on those days: "I've always felt how beneficial it was that there was no real overarching entertainment industry to aspire to like there was in LA or New York. There was nothing to gain by posing or image-making; everyone was just trying to do good work. That was the currency that mattered.

I remember an open, collaborative, helpful community of people, especially surrounding the Rainbo Club. Everybody seemed game for anything."

Truckstop Records was formed in collaboration with Kurt Kellison and released early Bobby Conn recordings as well as work by Simon Joyner, Songs: Ohia, and Chicago bands the Lofty Pillars, Pinetop Seven, and the Goblins. Michael Krassner describes the loft space as ". . . our headquarters. We lived there and built a recording studio that is still in operation to this day. Chicago seemed like the center of the universe back then, at least from my perspective. So much inspiring music from just about every genre. So many great labels, each with a razor focus. That really was a PhD-level education for me on all levels." Braden King left Chicago to take a "very impulsive trip" to the westernmost tip of the United States, the village of Dutch Harbor on Amaknak Island in Unalaska, Alaska, to film the fishing fleet based there.

Invisible Records, operated by Martin Atkins, had used Touch & Go distribution to build an operation powered by Pigface, a touring powerhouse and recording entity made up of many Wax Trax! veterans. The label served an audience hungry for the beat-heavy, impactful "industrial" music that Wax Trax! pioneered. Wax Trax! itself had lost momentum by the mid '90s, hampered by overexpansion and then purchased by TVT Records. Patrick Monaghan, who managed the store, explains how prosperity and a profligate release schedule had combined to ill effect for the label and store: "The unexpectedly meteoric success of Front 242 had caused a huge cash crunch at the Wax Trax! label, and Jim Nash had started pulling cash out of the store to cover his pressing plant shell game. Shortly after I left and moved to Cargo Chicago . . . the store closed and moved to a smaller space in the label building, and then the whole Wax Trax! mini empire collapsed."

Mark Spybey released music on the Invisible label under the name Dead Voices on Air and recalls, "Invisible was in a south-side loft warehouse, a great space in what was at the time a bit of a dodgy area. Every time I was there, bands would be staying whilst recording. Conversations became fully fledged ideas, no matter how impossible they seemed. Most of my ideas were vigorously embraced, my music was heavily promoted, and I was well supported."

The music scene created around the Invisible nexus may not have been to the tastes of many indie rock scenesters, but there was no denying the sheer productivity going on there. Once again, available space and good distribution combined in Chicago to great effect.

COMPARISON IS THE THIEF OF JOY.
—TEDDY ROOSEVELT

Liz Phair's second album, *Whip-Smart*, was released in September 1994. Recorded in part at Idful in Chicago and at Compass Point Studios in the Bahamas, it featured the same group of Chicago musicians that had backed Phair on *Exile in Guyville*. Atlantic Records and Matador Records had signed an agreement allowing Atlantic to manufacture, distribute, and promote select Matador titles, with *Whip-Smart* as the first entry in the new partnership. The songs "Chopsticks," "Shane," "Go West," "Whip-Smart," and parts of "Jealousy" had all originally appeared on Phair's Girly Sound cassettes. The track "Supernova" spent fourteen weeks on the *Billboard* Hot 100 chart, peaked at number 78, and was nominated for a Grammy for Best Female Rock Vocal Performance. Phair made the cover of *Rolling Stone* and made frequent television appearances. *Whip-Smart* peaked at 27 on the *Billboard* Album Chart in early October, shortly after its release. The critical reactions were more or less positive, even if the sophomore release could never really equal the impact of Phair's debut. As *Rolling Stone* put it, the album was "a little less than just right." Phair was getting songs placed in movie soundtracks as well, and "Don't Have Time" from the *Higher Learning* official soundtrack was nominated for a Grammy in 2005. All in all, *Whip-Smart* was a reasonably successful follow-up to *Exile in Guyville*, and Phair's career was in the ascendant.

BALANCED ON ITS OWN FLAME

After recording *Prazision*, Carter Brown and Mark Nelson decided to expand Labradford to a trio. As Nelson describes it, "I think we were ready to move on from the noisy/less structured side and wanted to develop arrangements. This was going against the grain a bit given the time and place, and I was probably more vocal about wanting to structure our sound a bit more. We were interested in a bass player to anchor the thing and force ourselves into more structure."

Bobby Donne from the Richmond trio Breadwinner joined the band. He says, "It was perfect timing for me. I liked the challenge of figuring out how to fit in with what they had established." The group rehearsed and began forming the material that would appear on their second album. Nelson says, "We tried it and it worked pretty much right away." Or, as Brown says, adding Bobby Donne to the band was "the best decision we ever made." The album was recorded once again with Rob Christiansen at American University, entitled *A Stable Reference*, and released in May 1995. Jon Dale described the album as "Songs—of a sort—that forever spiral inward, fractal and hypnotic, unsettled by a micro-active bed of noise percolating at the edges of audition. It's gorgeous stuff, but edgy with it, and miles beyond the gormless drone/ambience peddled by most in this field."

Carter Brown notes that Labradford "were thinking about repetition and subtle changes and repeated notes," and Donne's contributions on bass and baritone guitars and his later use of a sampler widened the spectrum of sounds Labradford used to cycle through extended musical figures.

Bobby Donne's addition to the Labradford lineup also resulted in the opportunity to record a single for Merge Records, the North Carolina label run by members of indie rock favorites Superchunk. Merge had released music from Breadwinner, and as Mark Nelson observes, "Connections between the two scenes [Richmond, Virginia, and Chapel Hill, North Carolina] were very strong." The "Julius / Columna De La Independencia" single came out in 1994 and exposed fans who followed the guitar-centric indie rock bands on Merge to Labradford's unique sound. More singles would follow, including one on Stereolab's Duophonic Super 45s label called "Scenic Recovery / Underwood 5ive," with the B side featuring drums played by Scott Minor. At kranky, we saw these extracurricular releases by Labradford, Bowery Electric, Jessamine, and other bands on the label as a great way for bands to get exposure to audiences, radio, and press that kranky could not reach. And it provided the audience with music that bridged the gaps between full lengths, keeping a band in the public eye. Mark Nelson looks at them from a creator's perspective and says, "I guess singles/EPs were a way for us to try new things. I don't think any of them were very successful—but they pointed the way forward or revealed dead ends."

The New Zealand label Flying Nun Records had gained an international profile releasing music "grounded in smart, melodic guitar pop, shot through with a dose of mystery and magic that people began to call the Dunedin Sound" by bands like the Chills, the Clean, the Verlaines, and others. The first Flying Nun release had been a seven-inch single by Pin Group, Roy Montgomery's first band. Joel and I were both fans, as were many in the American underground scene. The Flying Nun influence on American indie rock has been astutely described as a "subtle shift in aesthetics that happened slowly over a number of years, coming to the fore in the mid '90s when revered bands such as Pavement and Guided by Voices started admitting the influence of Flying Nun bands on their music." The Australian recording and publishing corporation Festival Records, a wholly owned subsidiary of Rupert Murdoch's News Corporation, bought a 50 percent stake in Flying Nun Records in 1990 via their Mushroom Records imprint. It was yet another example of how larger corporate entities were placing a few chips on indie rock. Flying Nun's founder, Roger Shepherd, moved to London in 1994 to open a Flying Nun UK office. We were surprised when Shepherd contacted kranky to propose licensing Labradford records for distribution in the United Kingdom and Europe. The opportunity to have Labradford albums manufactured and distributed there appealed to us, and with the band's permission, *Prazision* and *A Stable Reference* ultimately were licensed to Flying Nun and sold from offices in London and Germany. The Flying Nun partnership was the first opportunity for kranky to have a direct European manufacturing and distribution arrangement, and we hoped that it would not be the last.

6 slow thrills
1995

> Once so electrifying, US underground rock is emitting precious few bolts and flashes these days.
>
> —*Simon Reynolds*

The Chicago label Pravda Records released *Super Fantastic Mega Smash Hits!* in 1995, a CD compilation of bands covering '70s mainstream/schlock hits including Smashing Pumpkins' version of "Jackie Blue," originally recorded by the Ozark Mountain Daredevils. The cover artwork was a picture-perfect homage to the TV-sold hit LPs of the soft-rock years. Graphic designer Sheila Sachs remembers that she and label owner Ken Goodman "scoured thrift stores for old K-Tel records. I based my design off of those—taking parts and ideas and melding them into that first record. Then we did it three more times—*20 More Explosive Fantastic Rockin' Mega Smash Hit Explosions!*, *STAR POWER!*, and a greatest hits version: *Super Fantastic Mega Smash HITS!*" An obsession with covering top-40 music and classic rock from childhood had become one identifying characteristic of the indie rock bands of the '90s. You could call it irony, or an attempt to reckon with influences, or a passive-aggressive effort to stake a place on the cultural map, but oodles of record labels and bands were involved with cover albums. There were so many releases in this vein that Joel and I proclaimed one kranky kommandment to be "thou shalt not make tribute albums." The English label Imaginary Records specialized in these "tributes," with albums compiling covers of the Velvet Underground in three volumes (!!??), Bob Dylan across two volumes, Syd Barrett, the Kinks, Jimi Hendrix, the Byrds, the Rolling Stones, Captain Beefheart, and the years 1966 and 1967. There was even a band called the Mock Turtles dedicated to covering songs for these records. Sonic Youth released covers of songs by the New York Dolls, the Carpenters, Aerosmith, and Alice Cooper. Did the phenomenon indicate a hardening of the creative arteries among a wide range of indie rock bands? It certainly was "influence signaling" that indicated a codependent relationship between indie rock and corporate monoculture.

Urge Overkill was unabashed in parading their references, and when director Quentin Tarantino picked their cover of Neil Diamond's "Girl, You'll Be a Woman Soon" from their final release on Touch & Go for the soundtrack to his film *Pulp Fiction*, the band's fortunes took a turn upward with the film's general release in the United States in the fall of 1994. Elysa Gardner wrote in the *Los Angeles Times*, "Urge Overkill's approach certainly seems to be flying these days. The group's 1993 Geffen Records debut, *Saturation*, firmly established the Chicago group as a favorite of critics and the college-rock crowd . . . Then Urge gained widespread attention when its darkly passionate version of the Neil Diamond chestnut 'Girl, You'll Be a Woman Soon' was featured memorably in last year's hit film *Pulp Fiction*—in the scene in which Uma Thurman's character has an unfortunate run-in with some high-powered heroin."

This October 1995 interview, part of the press campaign for the second Urge Overkill Geffen release, *Exit the Dragon*, ironically points to the band's impending demise. On the occasion of a 2011 reunion, the *Milwaukee Sentinel-Journal* observed,

"Unfortunately . . . *Exit The Dragon* wasn't a big deal upon its release in 1995, and that's when minor cracks among the band members widened into yawning rifts. [Blackie] Onassis had become a heroin addict, while [Nate] Kato and [Eddie "King"] Roeser had soured on collaboration." A 2015 *Mojo* article revealed that Nate Kato even had a heroin-related near-death experience of his own that mirrored the one depicted in *Pulp Fiction*: in 1996 Kato was offered a "line" at a party. "I rationalised, 'Well, it would never be that big if it was heroin . . .'" Cue a life-saving adrenalin shot—sans John Travolta—and Kato found himself waking up in hospital face to face with Urge bandmate Roeser . . . "Me and Nash weren't on speaking terms anymore, but I got the call to come to the hospital," Roeser says. "There he was. The nurse told me, 'This guy, he almost died.' Nash almost went out in the most inopportune way . . ." As Roeser later told the *Sydney Morning Herald*, "We didn't really officially break up; we kind of silently disbanded." In the end, the swinging Rat Pack image Urge Overkill adopted and lived out derailed and then deflated the band.

In March 1995 an album came out from a Chicago band newly signed to a major label. Jeff Tweedy formed Wilco after the collapse of Uncle Tupelo, an influential country rock band whose final album, *Anodyne*, had sold 150,000 copies on the Sire label. Wilco's *A.M.* was released on Reprise Records, the Warner Brothers label founded by Frank Sinatra in 1960 and famous for a roster that included Jimi Hendrix, Joni Mitchell, the Beach Boys, Gordon Lightfoot, and others who dominated FM radio play in the late 1960s and beyond. *A.M.* peaked on the *Billboard* Heatseekers Chart at number 2 in April 1995. The album continued in the roughed-up country rock vein of Tweedy's earlier band. The addition of Jay Bennett from Champaign's Titanic Love Affair on lead guitar and keyboards prompted Wilco to widen their sound to include psychedelia, '60s rhythm 'n blues horn arrangements, and orchestral flourishes. In 1996 a double-CD set called *Being There* followed and "broke them out of the alt-country ghetto," as Mark Deming puts it. The double CD peaked at number 73 in the *Billboard* Top 200 in November 1995. It was not the stratus clouds that Smashing Pumpkins albums customarily reached, but with Urge Overkill going through a stealth breakup and the extended absences of Liz Phair and Smashing Pumpkins, Wilco gained a consistent profile in and outside of Chicago. Their mix of classic-rock swagger, country twang, and Tweedy's lyrics appealed to many, and the band toured constantly.

Red Red Meat were another Chicago band that used blues and rock structures as a point of departure. Anchored by Idful founder Brian Deck and Tim Rutili, they self-released some recordings on their own label Perishable, toured opening for Smashing Pumpkins, and were picked up by Sub Pop, where they released three albums between 1993 and 1996, each "peering through the codeine haze of skewed Chicago art school glasses," as one critic puts it. In an example of how the major labels could get involved in the underground rock scene in strange, inexplicable ways, or perhaps of how effective a hoax can be when music writers copy news releases verbatim, A&M Records was purported to have commissioned a collaborative effort between Red Red Meat and the Brooklyn band Rex called Loftus. The two groups toured together, sometimes sitting in on each other's sets. The Loftus album, recorded by Bundy Brown in a truck stop where Red Red Meat practiced, was intended for a sublabel called Treat & Release, which evaporated before opening. That was the story, at least. Perishable released the self-titled Loftus album, which sold enough to finance a relaunch of label operations. After the demise of Red Red Meat, Rutili pushed past the few remaining genre guidelines that confined the band in the succeeding group Califone.

There were nods to the past at work in the underground that referenced far more obscure and mundane points on the musical timeline. Stereolab ruled this particular roost, with album and song titles referencing the Bachelor Pad; there was also M.O.R. or "middle of the road," a term used in describing '70s mainstream rock music; the Ronco label that produced compilation records advertised on TV in the '70s; the avant filmmaker Stan Brakeage; the Mellotron synthesizer; the postwar European avant-garde collective COBRA; and more. The interest in lesser-known musicians of the late '60s and early '70s had the beneficial effect of encouraging some to step back into the admittedly small spotlight that had shone on their pioneering work.

Jessamine had named their label after the Silver Apples, who in turn reemerged in 1994 and recorded an EP with kranky artists Windy & Carl. After the group Cul de Sac covered John Fahey's "Portland Cement Factory at Monolith, California" on their 1991 *Ecim* album, the pioneer of finger-style steel string guitar had a revived career. Cul de Sac's Glenn Jones, a longtime advocate for Fahey, was able to record *The Epiphany of Glenn Jones* with Fahey and his band in 1997. Likewise, the 1970s German group Faust reconfigured and resurfaced. The filmmaker and musician Tony Conrad began to reissue albums, including his 1973 effort with Faust called *Outside the Dream Syndicate*, and collaborated with David Grubbs and Jim O'Rourke. The latter played crucial roles in the production of the Fahey, Faust, and Conrad records. All these activities and more were made possible by real appreciation and material support on the part of fans and musicians.

An Atlanta label, Table of the Elements Records, was especially instrumental in releasing music from AMM, Tony Conrad and Faust, John Cale, Rhys Chatham, and others whose '60s and '70s experimental music had seeped into the '90s underground. Their releases were exquisitely packaged and released in limited, and expensive, editions. The label had an organizational gimmick too, giving each release a catalog number matching an entry on the Periodic Table of the Elements and naming their music festivals after elements like manganese. Steve Dollar described the 1994 festival in Atlanta as "a kind of avant-garde debutante ball for Table of the Elements . . . a Lollapalooza for fringe-dwellers." The Table of the Elements Yttrium Festival in Chicago at the Empty Bottle in November 1996 featured John Fahey, Gastr del Sol, Jim O'Rourke, and others, and was an acknowledgment of the central position the city held in the underground scene and marketplace.

In July 1995 the Lounge Ax hosted the second OOPS (!) iNDOORS Festival over two nights. Skin Graft Records organized the event, featuring Chicago bands Cheer Accident, Brise Glace, U.S. Maple, Shellac, Mount Shasta, Jim O'Rourke, and You Fantastic alongside the Japanese groups Space Streakings and Melt-Banana. It was a glorious, bubbling stew of progressive rock, noise, theater, self-indulgence, and the label's comics-powered dynamic that stood in contrast to both the monotony of indie rock and the po-faced seriousness of the "experimental" scene.

WHAT WE WANT, WHEN YOU NEED IT

At kranky, we were working with the New Zealand musicians who had once been in Dadamah. Kim Pieters and Peter Stapleton had formed a quartet called Flies Inside the Sun. The new quartet was decidedly more improvisational; as Pieters puts it, "Dadamah was a little more ordered. There were songs which could be played again, but differently each time." Their first album, *An Audience of Others (Including Herself)*, was, as Pieters confirms, recorded by "setting up the mics and pressing the record button." Dadamah's compositional approach "was gone by *An Audience of Others* . . . (It was) improv from then on, especially if I was involved in any recordings." As Stapleton described the quartet, "Unlike Dadamah, Flies played out fairly regularly, mostly in Dunedin, but also in Christchurch. You never knew quite what might happen, and I remember some of those shows being very intense!"

The album is possibly the most "out," and in my opinion grossly overlooked, record kranky ever released, with Pieter's vocals especially compelling on the centerpiece track "Sleepwalk." Stapleton described the recording process by noting, "Songs were very loosely structured. They'd be built around some sort of motif (often from Kim's vocal), but apart from that they were largely improvised. Each time we got together we'd record on a four-track portastudio tape deck and then select the pieces we liked." Kim Pieter's subsequent work with Peter Stapleton in other Flies recordings and the successor groups Rain, Sleep, and Doramaar marks her as a distinctive voice in what is often called "free rock," the form of improvisation that starts from the base of bass/drums/guitars instrumentation and moves outward.

After the breakup of Dadamah, guitarist Roy Montgomery moved to Christchurch and formed a duo called Dissolve with Chris Heaphy. In July 1993 they recorded an album called *That That Is . . . Is (Not)* and mixed it in early 1994. Joel Leoschke had met Montgomery on his New Zealand trip, and Montgomery recalls "a coffee conversation in Christchurch with Joel where I mentioned Dissolve and he said send me a tape when you can."

Roy took an extended trip to the United States and Guatemala, and in June 1994 he gave kranky a tape of the Dissolve album while visiting Chicago. His first pass through Chicago involved an extended search with Joel for a Teisco guitar as used by bluesman Hound Dog Taylor and seen on the cover of the 1973 *Hound Dog Taylor and the HouseRockers* album, released by Chicago's independent pioneers at Alligator Records. Montgomery recalls, "Joel took me to guitar shops here and there, but we ended up back in Wicker Park at a pawn shop as a last shot at it and the rest is history. Except that it turns out it was a Kawai not a Teisco (no markings on it and no crazy Japanese guitar almanacs at the time to refer to)." The stark electric guitar interplay of Montgomery and Heaphy operating together as Dissolve was mesmerizing, and we happily released the album in 1995. As Montgomery told *Your Flesh* fanzine, "We wanted to try something that just involved guitars, and which was more soundscape than song-oriented. We tried to keep things simple and most of what you hear is relatively unadorned—first takes, for better or worse." Roy Montgomery's recordings during his sojourn in the Americas resulted in another album for kranky and a slew of releases on other record labels.

The search at kranky extended into the past as well. Joel made an effort to reissue music on kranky from an obscure musician he had discovered. The artist in question was a Californian who went by the title Master Wilburn Burchette. As Joel explains, "I have an older, genuine hippie friend who was moving in the early '90s and he asked me if I wanted to store his records for a bit with the idea that I would also be able to listen to them. When going through them I found a copy of the *Guitar Grimoire* album, and when I heard it the first time of course I did a 'WTF?'" With the aid of his brother Kenneth, Burchette had self-released record albums and a printed psychic meditation course available via mail order from 1971 to 1977. *Guitar Grimoire*, released in 1972, was packaged in Burnette's ornate, hand-drawn artwork and presented as a set of musical incantations. The spindly, reverberant electric guitar creates a decidedly spooky, occult atmosphere. We both found it riveting.

The Burchette Brothers advertised the LPs in specialty magazines ranging from *Gnostica News* to *High Times*. Then the Master abandoned music, destroyed all his work, and went into seclusion. Joel made several efforts via mail to persuade Burchette to let kranky reissue *Grimoire* and his other records. His entreaties met with a blanket refusal. The Master would take no phone calls. Things were moving along at kranky, and so Joel took no for an answer. Twenty years later, the Chicago-based reissue label Numero Group "tracked Burchette down and kept calling him until he agreed to talk and bless the reissues."

In the winter of 1995, a booking agent named Tom Windish moved to Chicago from upstate New York. Working under the name Bug Booking, he had a trio named Low on his roster, as well as Peter Kember's Spectrum band, Hum from Champaign, and a few other indie rock bands. Windish also played music himself. He managed to unintentionally work the rivalry between Bruce Finkelman, the owner of the Empty Bottle, and Sue Miller and Julia Adams, who owned Lounge Ax, into living quarters for himself. As Windish tells the story, "I was broke. I moved to New York City. Then I was completely broke. I had booked a bunch of shows at the Bottle, and I was playing shows. Bruce Finkelman said, 'I want to thank you and fly you out. I want you to play and you can stay above the club.' While I was there people said you should move here, it's really, really, cheap. Either I mentioned it to Bruce, or he mentioned it to me, and next thing I know he says, 'You can live above the Empty Bottle. I'll charge you $150 a month.' I was having dinner with Sue and Julia, who I had never met before. I mentioned super nonchalantly that I was thinking about moving to Chicago, and that Bruce has offered for me to live at $150. Julia blurted out, 'Fuck that you can live above Lounge Ax for $100 a month, utilities included.' I drove out in my 1971 AMC Hornet. Of course, it gets snowed in like a week later."

Windish quickly established himself in town, eventually joining a larger agency run by Dave Viecelli, who had been my predecessor as promo guy at Touch & Go.

THE LONG ARM OF COINCIDENCE MAKES MY RADIO CONNECTIONS

Jessamine had put the recording equipment they purchased with their advance from the first, self-titled, album to good use. Powered by a tightness gained through extensive live performance and the settled presence of Michael Faeth in the drummer's seat, the quartet recorded their second album *The Long Arm of Coincidence* in December 1995. There were some serious delays with a printer who could not/would not complete his work in the agreed-upon time and has since been accurately described as "insanely flaky," but when the letter-pressed chipboard covers for the CD and double LP finally arrived, they were magnificent. The band had taken their free-form approach to playing together and expanded and stretched their song structures. Critic Dave Segal wrote, "If there is any one band that's really doing something interesting with the rhythmic and experimental concepts behind '70s bands Can and Neu! it is Jessamine." He added, "*The Long Arm* . . . will sometimes sound like it's dissolving completely, becoming lost in a bubbling cauldron of guitars-leaned-on-amps and gurgling Moog noises, with only the drums holding it together."

As a band with a keyboard player working a seam of music at odds with the prevailing guitar-centric music Seattle had become known for, Jessamine faced more than a few challenges. Bands were moving to Seattle hoping to make it big in the grunge business, taking up space on bills and vying for attention. Jessamine found kindred spirits in Engine Kid and Silkworm, two bands with distinctive takes on guitar rock varying from the Seattle blueprint. The city, like Chicago, had many hole-in-the-wall joints where Jessamine could play live and hone their dynamic as a live band. Dawn Smithson remembers, "We played a lot of little places. I remember the Storeroom was particularly gritty and had a lot of bikers and metalheads and they were kind of looking at us sidelong, but we had enough rock and heavy sound when we played live that I think we won them over that first night."

Joel Mark, a booking agent and member of the Chicago band Nectarine, listened to Jessamine's album on the advice of his client Greg Anderson from Engine Kid. As Mark recalls, Anderson always steered him toward "bands with ultimate focus." He added that Jessamine was "trying to be part of a lineage of other groups that weren't as heralded as they should have been. That's what drew me to Jessamine was when I heard the first record and thought, 'I don't really know what this is but it's incredible.' They were picking up where other people have left off and felt like that's what you guys were doing at the label also." Dawn Smithson says that Jessamine "did eventually form a little group of 'misfit bands' with Silkworm and Engine Kid because bookers didn't know where to put us so they would just put all together. We eventually started playing a lot of good (more appropriate) shows. We didn't really fit in in Seattle, so we had to get popular enough to be allowed to open for out-of-town bands that actually were in a similar or close enough genre." Some of the visiting bands that Jessamine opened for in Seattle included Labradford, Stereolab, and Stars of the Lid. On September 17, 1994, Jessamine, Engine Kid, and Silkworm played a memorable show in Chicago at the Empty Bottle with Flaming Lips, a former indie band rapidly rising with a major label behind them.

Jessamine toured nationally with Nectarine. Joel Mark remembers that Rex Ritter sent him tapes of Neu! and Can "as preparation for the tour." Rather than discuss the logistics of stage setups or money details, Ritter wanted the members of

Nectarine to know where Jessamine were coming from musically and how the two bands could each present their music to best effect. An extensive tour with the Philadelphia psych band Bardo Pond followed, which Dawn Smithson calls "a major boost" for the band, and numerous releases for other labels. Darren Mock connected with the band at a San Francisco show and offered Jessamine a space in a compilation he was preparing for his Drunken Fish label. *The Harmony of the Spheres* was released in 1996 as a three-LP box set. Each band was given a side to contribute an original recording. Jessamine and Roy Montgomery participated alongside Flying Saucer Attack, avant blues guitarist Loren Mazzacane Connors, Houston free-form psych weirdos Charalambides, and Bardo Pond. It holds up nicely as a testimonial to the threads of psychedelia that were weaving through the underground in the early to mid-'90s.

Extensive practice and touring had led Jessamine to consideration of how the band was making music. Dawn Smithson describes the artistic development of Jessamine in this way: "Hours and hours of listening to prog rock really developed my sense of dynamics and drama. Rex turned us on to Talk Talk's *Laughing Stock* and we were all gobsmacked. A little later it was Can, and then '70s Miles Davis. I bought Andy's Big Muff from him and paired it with a volume pedal and a Boss Feedbacker pedal and got WAAAY more heavy. Rex and Andy also increased their pedal lineup to achieve more evil sounds. We had all started listening to Sabbath again. Michael Faeth was very precise and got great at going with the flow, so that was kind of a strange juxtaposition, but it worked."

As Rex Ritter describes it, to avoid a hierarchic dynamic, Jessamine decided, "Everyone could play whatever they wanted." Dawn Smithson recalls things a bit differently: "Rex definitely had ideas about how the drums should sound and gave suggestions to Andy regularly. Although with Andy, they would geek out on sounds and plot the purchase of rad equipment. Vocals were where I didn't feel like I could express myself. Rex had very specific ideas about how he wanted the vocals to sound."

The Long Arm of Coincidence was a product of a more open compositional approach, even if the members' recollections of the degrees of that freedom differ. As the *Portland Mercury* described the album much later, they "connected the sparking wires of Krautrock, modern classical, and the shadowy regions of psychedelia without getting burned." Smithson, who was romantically involved with Ritter at the time, puts the album in personal and artistic context: "I had started to stick up for myself and Rex and I had just broken up. I was asserting myself and he was trying to be more open to other people's ideas—you can hear it in our back-and-forth. We were deep into stoner-land and just thought the journeys we went on were incredible and that everyone would find them fantastic too! And maybe they did, because we sold as many of that album as we did the other two."

Jessamine recorded *The Long Arm* between October 1995 and February 1996 on an eight-track tape machine in their basement studio, between constant live performances that included five straight weeks of touring in 1996 alongside the Philadelphia heavy psych band Bardo Pond. "I think that five-week tour we did before we moved to Portland in '96 was so long that it now seems like all tours we went on were part of that one tour," Smithson says. From my perspective doing promotion back then, Jessamine had the highest press and radio profile of all the kranky bands. They had adapted to touring and performance and were better received as a live band than their label peers were. Even with the widening of the audience's musical interests, live performance was still the main way artists drew attention to themselves.

In late 1996, the quartet moved from Seattle to Portland, Oregon, where space for recording equipment meant that a sixteen-track studio could come together. They started their own record label called Histrionic and released a compilation of Jessamine singles called *Another Fictionalized History* in 1997. They also began work on their third studio album.

LEARNING FORGETFULNESS

In the summer of 1995, a package arrived in the kranky P.O. box. Inside was an old leopard-skin eyeglass case containing three cassette tapes. It came from a trio based in Redmond, Washington, called Magnog. Each of them was under twenty years old. Magnog had formed in 1994 when Jeff Reilly and Dana Shinn met Phil Drake after the collapse of their band Space Helmet. Reilly states that the band name "came from a misunderstanding of the word 'Magog.' Dana and Phil were watching an old sci-fi film called *Gog*. And no, it has no biblical connections." The trio recorded all their practices with a Tascam four-track tape deck because, as Reilly put it, "We thought of them as not practices but acts of creation. The goal was not to record a song, but rather to capture a moment in time and space." Magnog "decided to send our demos to kranky due to the fact we had seen a Jessamine show and ended up loving them. We figured any label that would dig them might like what we were doing. The sending of multiple tapes in the bizarre case was something we thought might grab the attention of the label."

It did grab our attention. The music on the cassettes would have been a surprise if it had been made by musicians in their early thirties. The fact that a bunch of teenagers could make music that thundered and flowed as it did was mind-blowing. Magnog touched on predecessors like Spacemen 3, early Pink Floyd, and some of the music that influenced them like the Indian-influenced side of jazz saxophonist John Coltrane. They also had some rhythmic stretch and flexibility that many "space rock" bands of the mid-'90s lacked. Shinn and Reilly, on drums and bass guitar, respectively, had played together for several years before Magnog began and "had an amazing chemistry, almost psychic. We could turn on a dime without even looking at each other for changes," as Reilly describes. The addition of Phil Drake on guitar completed the trio. Reilly remembers that Drake "was only seventeen when we started and did not even know how to tune a guitar and yet it all just clicked. I think our chemistry also came from growing up in the rainy Northwest—our music was always a reflection of our environment." All three members of the band contributed synthesizer and guitar to the recordings. After taking a deep dip into the tapes, we got in touch and signed Magnog to kranky. In September 1995, they began recording their debut album with Andy Brown at Jessamine's Private Radio studio in Seattle.

Roy Montgomery's American sojourn in 1994 had taken him through the Guatemalan rainforests in Tikal, where he spent a night atop the ruins of a Mayan temple contemplating the loss of a woman named Joanna. In January 1995 while in New York City, Montgomery recorded his impressions of that night on a Tascam Porta One four-track tape machine, using the Teisco guitar he bought with Joel Leoschke in Chicago, two effects boxes, and a delay pedal. In March he came to Chicago and mixed those recordings to digital tape with Brendan Burke engineering at his Loose Booty Studio. The recordings became a CD called *Temple IV* that kranky released in January 1996. Packaged with a booklet printed on textured brown paper highlighted with woodblock artwork by Jessica Meyer, *Temple IV* is testament to the deep music that a simple set of tools can create. The CD was well received critically, as evidenced by this review in *CMJ New Music Report* by Dawn Sutter: "Roy Montgomery writes on the inner sleeve of *Temple IV* that it was inspired by a trip to the Northern Guatemalan rain forest where he endured physical discomforts and attempted to come to terms with the death of a love. Though it's nice to have a concrete description, those words are unnecessary. . . . The lush songs on *Temple IV* are brimming with an aching sadness, violent anger and exhausting relief."

During his mixing sessions with Brendan Burke, Montgomery compiled his New York recordings into another album called *Scenes from the South Island* and several seven-inch singles. The time spent at 324 East Thirteenth Street, New York City, between December 1994 and February 1995 had been very productive indeed.

HAIL, HAIL THE COMPACT DISC

In New York City at 15 East Fourth Street, between Broadway and Lafayette Street, across the street from a massive Tower Records store, a new record store opened called Other Music. The store took the font for its logo from Spacemen 3 records. Josh Madell, Chris Vanderloo, and Jeff Gibson had worked at a video store called Kim's Underground before they opened their new business. I had sold music to Kim's for Cargo, and Jeff Gibson had been a roommate and coworker at Schoolkids' Records in Ann Arbor, Michigan. Other Music bought a lot of CDs from Cargo as they stocked the store, and I made sure kranky titles made up a large percentage of them. As Josh Madell recalls, it was "the heart of the CD era, a time when tons of amazing but obscure music from the 1960s, '70s, and '80s was being reissued and reintroduced to young fans. For the first time, once rare and expensive music from regional artists all over the world from French Ye-Ye to European psychedelia to African funk was more available. Add to that the diverse young independent artists and labels pushing culture forward in the US, and the vibrant UK-based experimental electronic labels like Warp, and you had a whole new world of sound for fans to engage with."

The popularity of compact discs facilitated the reissue of many free-jazz and improvised recordings on labels like Impulse, ESP, and BYG. Bill Meyer notes, "Record companies went back and found music that was just pressed on vinyl once. It was pretty hard to get these things unless you were in the know. You could get Charlemagne Palestine music again, and it actually reenergized some of the players. And then people could branch out and it got cheaper to make CDs."

In San Francisco, Aquarius Records gave kranky releases lots of love via their pithy reviews taped to CDs and LPs and a much-loved mail-order catalog. "Here at Aquarius, we've coined such neologisms as 'dronology' and 'fuckery,' simply because we hope that such words offer enough connotation even without a lot of context," read one classic entry. Owner Windy Chien had moved the store to the Mission District in 1996 from its earlier Castro Street location. Aquarius prospered at that hipster epicenter and then under the subsequent direction of Andee Connors and Allan Horrocks. At kranky we could appreciate the sarcasm behind the Labradford review that ended with "Labradford may have beaten Andee [in his first solo project after A Minor Forest] to the punch with a blatant appropriation of George Winston / Shadowfax / Windham Hill onto a record for kranky. Beautiful, none the less." Or a review of the 1998 album by Tomorrowland on the label that simply read, "Your parents like Windham Hill, you like kranky." What Joel and I had feared in November 1993 finally had come to pass; the New Age label had been applied to a kranky release.

On July 31, 1995, Stereolab and Tortoise played at the Lounge Ax, alternating as headliners at early and late-evening sets. The two bands had met, as Douglas McCombs tells it, when "Gastr del Sol played a show with Stereolab at their first time in Chicago. We hung out at that show and they became aware that some of Gastr played in another group. Next time they came we played shows with them in the Midwest. Then we stayed at their house when we were in London, they lived at the Tortoise loft when they recorded in Chicago—it went on like that."

This is a textbook example of how underground bands met and made connections. The logistical and communications challenges that bands faced when touring abroad could be smoothed over with the aid of trusted compatriots. The relationship between the two bands would extend across the ocean and over the years.

In January 1995 a Lounge Ax condo-dwelling neighbor was shocked (shocked!) to find that noise was emanating each night from a street filled with bars and filed a complaint against the club. The city liquor commission began citing the club for violations of the byzantine licensing laws that compelled the club to carry what was called a Public Place of Amusement license at the same time that zoning regulations for their location forbade such licenses. Ongoing hassles over these issues and increasing development of the Lincoln Park neighborhood led to a Lounge Ax benefit compilation CD on Touch & Go in 1996 and, ultimately, the closure of the bar in 2000 when a new building owner wanted to run a bar of his own. There were a lot of great shows before that point arrived, but for anyone aware of the intricacies and biases of city government it seemed that the writing was on the wall for Lounge Ax.

Farther south in Wicker Park, saxophonist Ken Vandermark and music critic/radio host John Corbett were presenting free-jazz and improvising musicians at the Empty Bottle. Out-of-town musicians played regularly, and Vandermark's various bands held a midweek residency. Listeners had the opportunity to catch a set or two from a predictable, high-quality lineup at a familiar venue, and musicians had a regular gig to meet and play together. With the night's performance split roughly into two forty-five-minute sets, I particularly enjoyed stopping by at nine-ish on a Wednesday night to sit down in front of the stage for the opening set before heading home by midnight on a work night. Eventually, a series of yearly Jazz Festivals ensued at the Empty Bottle, bringing together Chicago artists and the cream of European and American avant-garde jazz, electronics, and free-rock practitioners. As Bill Meyer noted in the *Chicago Tribune*, "Nowadays it's common to see the same faces in the crowd at jazz, contemporary classical and rock shows."

Located near the critical hipster mass living within a few blocks and on a major thoroughfare on Western Avenue, across from an electrical power facility and with few condos nearby, the Empty Bottle had fewer structural obstacles than the Lounge Ax, which was placed smack dab in a gentrifying neighborhood. The Empty Bottle had a room with a pool table separate from the stage and bar, and suitable for hobnobbing during and between sets. It also had a stage configuration that made sound quality variable. You had to maneuver your way to the sweet spots where bands sounded crisp; otherwise you were likely to hear "a wall of mud with bass and cymbals poking though," as Joel once put it. Lounge Ax was a single, narrow room and much more advantageous for a good sonic experience from any position in the room. Walking into Lounge Ax was a commitment to watching and hearing bands first and foremost, although the back of the bar was available for schmoozing early and late in the evening, if you could grab a barstool. Neither bar had a television set. Aside from some video games, pinball machines, and photo booths, there were few distractions from the music.

The most unlikely story of the year 1995 and the attendant major-label obsession with Chicago bands was that of Chris Holmes and his fistful of bands. Holmes was/is a guy who cannot walk into a room without working it. He had a "space rock" band called Sabalon Glitz that had played droney rock modeled after early Pink Floyd and the English '70s power psych band Hawkwind and released a single and album on a local indie called Trixie Records. Holmes also had a solo electronic/techno project called Ashtar Command. He possessed elaborate verbal blueprints for each grouping, which he was always willing to lay out for anyone willing to listen. Such was the state of flux between each band that a December 1993 Lounge Ax listing for a show read "Sabalon Glitz (we assume)." The endless networking came to fruition when Holmes's persuasive skills converted a representative from Atlantic Records to the cause. The competition between major-label representatives to sign bands from the hot Chicago scene had gotten frenzied, and this created leverage for Holmes, who positioned himself as the genius behind a slew of musical projects. The deal he signed gave him an amazing amount of leeway to release what he wanted through a sublabel called TAG Records. Holmes secured the managerial services of the former Atlantic Records vice president Janet Billig, and as jaw-dropping as the terms of the deal appeared from the outside, there was reason to believe that Chris Holmes could schmooze his way into anything.

(Entered by Charles Andrew Beaujon on Jan. 28, 1993 at 5:19 PM)

Dear Joel,

Hi, my name is Andrew Beaujon, and I'm enclosing a single I just put out by a band called LaBradford in the hopes that you all might be interested in distributing it. They are a two-piece band from Richmond, Virginia who play Moogs and guitars. I hope you might find it acceptable. If you'd like to get in touch with me I live with Mark Robinson. Thanks for your time.

Sincerely,

p.s. I play in a band called eggs, and Hemiola records in the UK just put out what I think is our best single yet. Are you guys carrying that?

The letter from Andrew Beaujon to Cargo Distribution soliciting an order on the first Labradford single, "Everlast" b/w "Preserve the Sound Outside," released on Beaujon's Retro 8 label. Letter from Andrew Beaujon by Andrew Beaujon © Andrew Beaujon. (Courtesy of Andrew Beaujon)

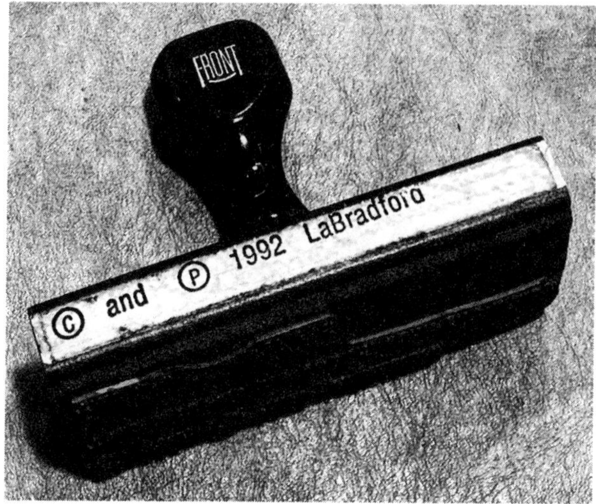

One way for kranky to save money on production costs was to order records printed with standard blank white labels and then use rubber stamps to add release details. This stamp was used on the first Labradford seven-inch.

Nils Bernstein, Caterer, Sub Pop Records, Seattle, WA (206) 441-8441

If you're too busy listening to your Geffen bones and trying to convince yourself that you not only like the Raincoats but have all along, at least read Labradford's bio, which gives a good summary of reference points—F/i, ambient Eno, Spiritualized, Dead C, Thomas Koner, Cluster, etc.—which need only a little fleshing out with the Durutti Column, Zoviet-France and Felt for an idea of the greatness that is Labradford. I'd like to thank Kranky (via Cargo) for developing them for us. Hopefully the

Nils Bernstein, then doing promo for Sub Pop, wrote this for *CMJ New Music Monthly* shortly after *Prazision* was released. His comments sarcastically point out how large indie labels often let smaller labels "develop" unknown artists before swooping in to sign them.

The very first advertisement for Labradford's double LP debut. This layout on graph paper was converted into a photostatic copy for print production. (Courtesy of kranky, ltd.)

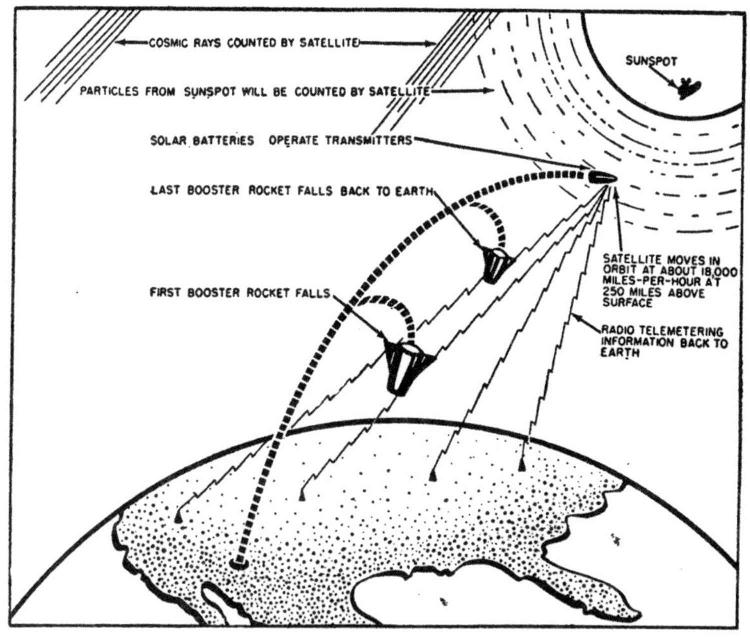

analog technology makes space travel possible

Dadamah This Is Not A Dream CD
Jessamine Jessamine CD/ LP
The Spiny Anteaters All Is Well CD
Labradford Prazision LP CD

Prices
CD $11 ppd USA/ $13 Canada/ $15 Elsewhere
LP $8 ppd USA/ $10 Canada/ $12 Elsewhere
send check or money order to:
kranky P.O. Box 578743 Chicago, IL 60657

This early advertisement is an example of how I sourced visuals for ads from used books—and the allusions to space travel we often used in kranky marketing material.

- YOU GONNA EAT THAT?
- CRYING OUT OF OUR ONE GOOD EYE
- THAT RED STUFF THEY PUT ON PUKE
- WAXING THE BANNISTER SINCE 1993
- A LEANER, 90's HEAD CHEESE
- NO SALT. NO LINT. NO CASSETTES
- HUT, HUT, HIKE!
- "NO, THAT'S JUST AN EXPRESSION. YOU DON'T ACTUALLY BLOW ON IT."
- STARRING JIMMY ROBERTSON AND HIS MAGIC PUPPY JAKE
- LIKE A PANTRY FULL OF SOUP
- FLOSSED, TOSSED AND DOUBLE-CROSSED.

KRANKY

- THE PENIS: MIGHTIER THAN THE SWORD.
- WHAT WE WANT, WHEN YOU NEED IT.
- I'LL GIVE YOU SOMETHING TO CRY ABOUT, MISTER
- KEEP WALKING, TOUGH GUY
- THE CROSSROADS OF ART AND COMMERCE
- LOOK BACK IN ANGER AND COUGH
- HITTING THE SNOOZE BUTTON SO YOU DON'T HAVE TO.
- SHAPELY AND DEFIANT

Our coworker at Cargo, Dag Juhlin, submitted these slogans. One made the cut, and you can still buy "What we want, when you need it" T-shirts. (Courtesy of kranky, ltd.)

Jessamine rehearsing in their basement studio. From left to right: Dawn Smithson on bass guitar, keyboardist Andy Brown, Rex Ritter on guitar, and drummer Michael Faeth. (Courtesy of kranky, ltd.)

Precious and few were the promotional items issued by kranky. These coffee cups expressed the label's mission statement and our view of its function in the music ecosystem.

The Coctails issued an impressive array of consumer products centered on the cartoon version of themselves. As the de facto house band at the Lounge Ax, they even directed patrons to the basement restrooms.

$4
The
CocTAILS
Buttons

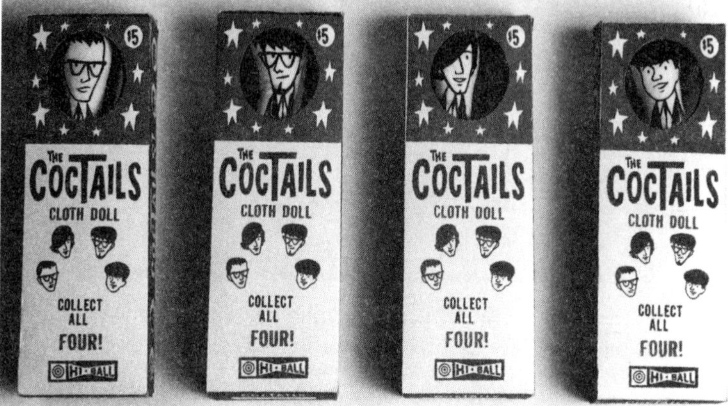
$5
THE
COCTAILS
CLOTH DOLL
COLLECT
ALL
FOUR!
HI-BALL

Cartoonist Chris Ware was beginning his rise to fame when he designed this poster for the Cardigan Festival, a weekend benefit at the Lounge Ax in 1994. Tortoise had just released their debut, self-titled album. Cardigan Festival Poster by Chris Ware © Chris Ware. (Courtesy of Chris Ware)

Melody Maker Sept. 10, 1994

SEEFEEL/LABRADFORD/MAIN
MANHATTAN CENTER, NEW YORK CITY

TONIGHT, we only get to see half of Seefeel in a live mix. Actually, we don't see much of anything, since Darren Seymour and Mark Clifford are trapped behind electronics boards. But there's plenty to feel, as the two manipulate samples from "Quique" into unrecognisable soundwaves. The music starts out sparse and atmospheric, with dreamy keyboard washes and strange effects, but gradually becomes more solid as tribal drums and techno beats are added to the mix. By the end, the band have salvaged a pleasant, if far from mesmerising experience from a near disaster.

While Seefeel attempt to feed your mind, Virginia's Labradford would rather destroy it, or at least damage your hearing a bit. An organic trio who prefer live instrumentation to samples, the group play morose, beat-free ambient rock at intolerable volume levels. Their songs are gothic cathedrals of sound *(!!! – Ed)* constructed with dense, creeping basslines, eerie guitar chimes and minor-key organ lines that drift and swoop like ghosts in a graveyard. Labradford hardly ever use vocals but, when they do, they're the muddled voices of disembodied spirits lost somewhere between limbo and hell. Haunting and hypnotic, the music shudders and rumbles like an earthquake, altering tone and timbre only slightly as bricks of sanity topple at your feet.

Trust Robert (ex-Loop) to take the gliding tones and galactic textures of ambient and contort them into something bleak and sinister. Next to Main, even

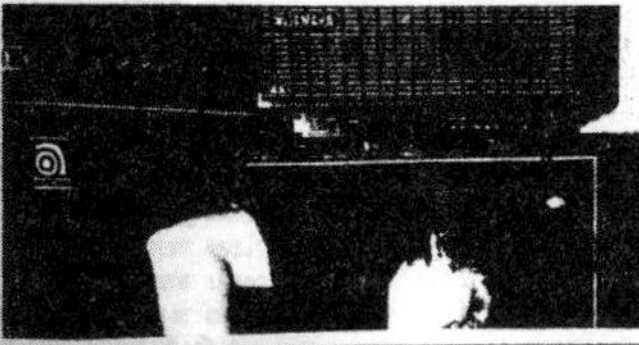

Labradford sound bright and cheery. Like Loop, Main use repetition to freeze time, trapping us in an endless miasma of shimmering reverberations. Then they insert their needle and paralyse us with stabs of feedback, pumping sonic air bubbles into our constricting veins. Their sparse rhythms are driven by dub basslines and an array of crackling and hissing sound effects and

SEEFEEL/LABRADFORD/MAIN
MANHATTAN CENTER, NEW YORK CITY

TONIGHT, we only get to see half of Seefeel in a live mix. Actually, we don't see much of anything, since Darren Seymour and Mark Clifford are trapped behind electronics boards. But there's plenty to feel, as the two manipulate samples from "Quique" into unrecognisable soundwaves. The music starts out sparse and atmospheric, with dreamy keyboard washes and strange effects, but gradually becomes more solid as tribal drums and techno beats are added to the mix. By the end, the band have salvaged a pleasant, if far from mesmerising experience from a near disaster.

While Seefeel attempt to feed your mind, Virginia's Labradford would rather destroy it, or at least damage your hearing a bit. An organic trio who prefer live instrumentation to samples, the group play morose, beat-free ambient rock at intolerable volume levels. Their songs are gothic cathedrals of sound (!!! – Ed) constructed with dense, creeping basslines, eerie guitar chimes and minor-key organ lines that drift and swoop like ghosts in a graveyard. Labradford hardly ever use vocals but, when they do, they're the muddled voices of disembodied spirits lost somewhere between limbo and hell. Haunting and hypnotic, the music shudders and rumbles like an earthquake, altering tone and timbre only slightly as bricks of sanity topple at your feet.

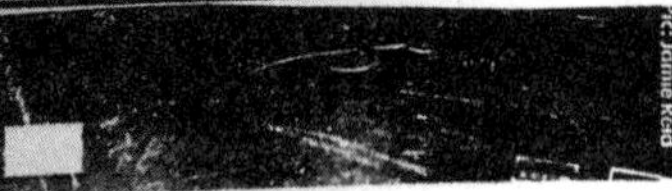

as a hanging judge's gavel slamming down as he sentences a defendant to the electric chair.

Main are a band to die for.

JON WIEDERHORN

This 1994 live review from the English weekly *Melody Maker* may mark the first appearance of "cathedrals of sound," a descriptive phrase that has been repeated to death, with and without sarcasm, since then to describe long-form or ambient music.

August 10, 1997

Dear kranky—

How are you?

We are godspeed you black emperor!

enclosed is our new record...

We had a show lined up in Chicago

mid-september but it fell through...

We're passing thru your town

September 12+13 but have no

show lined up...

hoping wishing hoping

You might like this record

and help our sorry asses out...

hope all is well w/you...

love,

godspeed you

black emperor! x

DAVE

[illegible] our adress is in the [illegible]...

The letter that godspeed you! black emperor wrote to kranky asking for help booking a show in Chicago in August 1997. A tape of *F#A#∞* was included in the package. August 10, 1997, letter to kranky from godspeed you! black emperor © godspeed you! black emperor. (Courtesy of godspeed you! black emperor)

LOW ON THE ROAD AS USUAL

MARCH

FRI	8	NORTHFIELD, MN	THE CAVE
THURS	14	MADISON, WI.	THE CHAMBER
FRI	15	AUSTIN, TX	721 CONGRESS
MON	18	DETROIT, MI	ZOOTZ COFFEEHOUSE
TUES	19	N. CUMBERLAND, PA	THE WIRE
WED	20	CAMBRIDGE, MA	T.T. THE BEAR'S
THURS	21	PHILADELPHIA, PA	SILK CITY
FRI	22	NEW YORK, NY	KNITTING FACTORY
SAT	23	WASHINGTON D.C.	BLACK CAT
THURS	28	MOORHEAD, MN	CC MUSIC CAFE
FRI	29	IOWA CITY, IA	GABE'S OASIS
SAT	30	DAVENPORT, IA	SMILE COFFEEHOUSE

APRIL

MON	1	BOULDER, CO	FOX THEATRE
TUES	2	SALT LAKE CITY, UT	CINEMA BAR
WED	3	BOISE, ID	NEUROLUX
THURS	4	PORTLAND, OR	SATYRICON
FRI	5	SEATTLE, WA	PINER SQUARE THEATRE
MON	8	SACRAMENTO, CA	PRESS CLUB
TUES	9	SAN FRANCISCO, CA	BOTTOM OF THE HILL
THURS	11	SANTA MONICA, CA	KCRW (A.M.)
THURS	11	HOLLYWOOD, CA	TROUBADOR (P.M.)
FRI	12	TUCSON, AZ	CAFE LUNALOCA
SAT	13	TEMPE, AZ	STINKWEED'S
TUES	16	NORMAN, OK	THE T BAR
WED	17	DENTON, TX	THE ARGOT
THURS	18	AUSTIN, TX	EMO'S
FRI	19	HOUSTON, TX	URBAN ART BAR
SAT	20	NEW ORLEANS, LA	MERMAID LOUNGE
MON	22	KANSAS CITY, MO	GRAND EMPORIUM
TUES	23	ST. LOUIS, MO	CICERO'S
THURS	25	MINNEAPOLIS, MN	7TH ST ENTRY
FRI	26	CHICAGO, IL	LOUNGE AX
SAT	27	MILWAUKEE, WI	THE GLOBE

MORE DATES COMING FORTHWITH, SO STAY TUNED. THE NEWEST JEWEL IN THE LOW DISCOGRAPHY, THE *TRANSMISSION EP* IS OUT NOW ON VERNON YARD RECORDINGS. FOR A COPY, OR A PHOTO, OR GUEST LISTS, OR INTERVIEWS, CALL US.

AUTOTONIC 2272 DEADRICK, MEMPHIS, TN 38114
901.452.3939 TEL /3928 FAX autotonic@aol.com

By the time kranky started working with Low, the trio from Duluth, Minnesota, was a seasoned road outfit, as this routing from Spring 1997 shows. (Courtesy of Tom Windish)

Foundation & Blast First presents
Labradford Second
Festival of Drifting
Wed 26th May:
Drifting North, Sheffield
> Labradford
> Pole
> Matmos
Thu 27th May:
Union Chapel, London
> Labradford
> Pole
> Matmos
Fri 28th May:
Union Chapel, London
> Durutti Column
> Caspar Brotzman
> Dean Roberts
Sun 30th May:
> Chris n' Cosey
> Oval
> Labradford
1st June:
Royal, Edinburgh
Matmos
Pan American
Union Chapel, Compton Terrace, N1
Tickets £10.00
Drifting North, Club Generation,
Tickets £7.50
Café Royal, House of Dubois, West
Edinburgh
New Labradford LP 'E Luxo So' out Monday 17th May on CD/LP
on Blast First Records

The second Festival of Drifting traveled around the United Kingdom in May 1999. Drew Daniel of Matmos recalled, "A very kind and soft-spoken dude came up to me and said he liked our set and talked to me for a bit and I said, 'Oh thanks I was really nervous because someone told me Autechre were in the crowd' and then he got a funny look on his face because duh it was Sean from Autechre. Also in attendance at the Sheffield gig: Squarepusher and Richard H Kirk from freakin' Cabaret Voltaire." As M.C. Schmidt puts it, "This tour really, really generated a lot of insane events that have turned into legendary stories in our life." (Courtesy of M.C. Schmidt and Matmos)

Residencies at the Empty Bottle were an important factor in building an audience for free jazz and improvised music. Ken Vandermark and John Corbett organized monthly sessions for local groupings as well as festivals at the club. Vandermark 5—This Is Your Music by Dan Grzeca © Dan Grzeca. (Courtesy of Dan Grzeca)

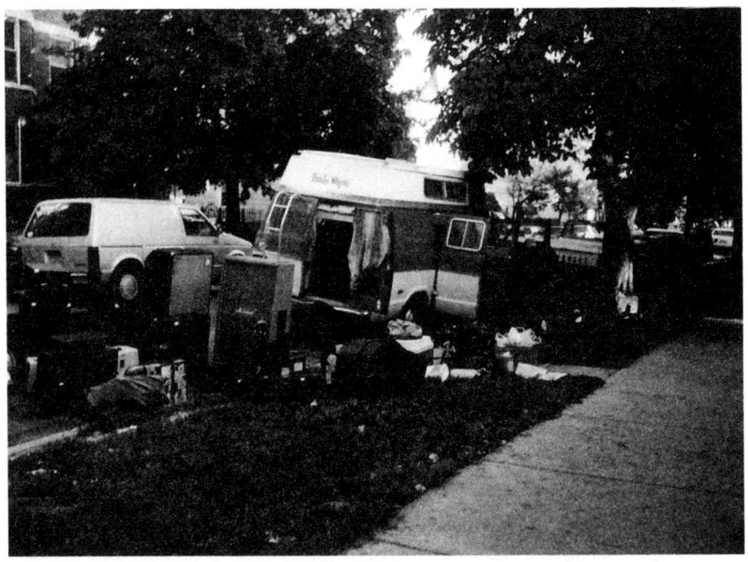
The godspeed you! black emperor touring van lovingly called the Family Wagon, seen here in front of Joel Leoschke's apartment in Chicago. (Photo courtesy of David Bryant)

Stars of the Lid gradually were able to get more and more shows outside the rock club circuit, as shown by this ticket for a concert in a planetarium in Champaign, Illinois. (Courtesy of kranky, ltd.)

7

the taut and the tame

1996

I've lived through a golden age and I didn't realize.

—*Bill Meyer*

The opening track of *Millions Now Living Will Never Die* by Tortoise, "Djed," was and is held up by many as a benchmark of the band's craft. The opener is a collage of recording-session tape splices John McEntire pulled together out of frustration. It's hardly unprecedented in rock music to anyone who has heard the Beatles' "Revolution," much less avant-garde music by the likes of Pierre Henry, John Cage, or pioneering industrial collagists Nurse with Wound. What is distinctive about "Djed" is the rhythm linking the slices of magnetic tape together. The album's closing track, "Along the Banks of Rivers," is decidedly more continuous, especially melodically, with a delicate slide guitar melody floating vaporously above a gentle rhythm. As bassist Douglas McCombs describes the band's approach, "Early on we embraced an anything goes policy. This collaborative policy brings a lot of diverse influence into what we do and in my opinion is our main strength. Most of us had been playing in pretty intense, dense-sounding rock bands, so the use of space and a slightly different palette helped us develop something that we could call our own." Bundy Brown had left Tortoise after their initial album and was replaced by David Pajo, the former guitarist of Slint who lent more cred points to the group along with his measured playing.

There was more to *Millions* than the rhythmic interplay of two drummers and two bassists. The influence of American roots and folk music on the band was apparent in the second Tortoise single, "The Lonesome Sound," which covered a song by the Chicago country duo Freakwater referencing bluegrass legend Bill Monroe's "high, lonesome sound." The band's subtle, melodic sensibility and use of the space between instruments had something in common with Labradford, which was incorporating violin into its third, self-titled album at the same time. The "anything goes" approach was also adopted by Jessamine, who were increasingly drawn toward group improvisation and the electric band sounds jazz trumpeter Miles Davis started exploring on the *Bitches Brew* album. The experience the members of Tortoise brought to the table and a well-considered lineup of songs made the band stand out. Bill Meyer describes the process behind the formation and development of Tortoise like this: "I remember talking with Douglas McCombs early on. His interests were a lot broader than what he was actually playing. For a lot of people who came through, punk rock or some early indie rock thing, they all got to play a thing that was probably a very small subset of what they really liked. There was this point where there were a lot of people [trying to] figure out a way to express all those interests or to bring more of that into the music."

As McCombs puts it, "We were excited about some of the results we were getting in the studio, proud even, but we didn't really expect many people to like it. Maybe a few people who were interested in our pedigree. We knew we were distinctive, for sure."

Many people did like the second Tortoise album. *Millions* was seemingly omnipresent in 1996, with rave reviews in every publication, invariably played in every record store and coffeehouse, and as a preliminary to every rock show in Chicago. The band was equally prominent out of town. At Record Swap in Champaign, Bob Steltman recalls, "We sold Tortoise hand over foot." *Time Out Chicago* would eventually describe the album as "one of the few pieces of music that could have been simultaneously released on [avant techno/electronic label] Warp, [pioneering New Age Label] Windham Hill and [jazz label] Blue Note."

With the resources Touch & Go Distribution provided, Tortoise and their label Thrill Jockey took advantage of the moment. Nitsuh Abebe recalled the mood in Chicago in a 2005 piece for the influential music website *Pitchfork*: "Suddenly the local record stores had long, well-stocked bins labeled 'Tortoise et al.' or 'Post-Rock,' with the discs inside carefully stickered—'produced by John McEntire of Tortoise,' or 'featuring Jim O'Rourke.' Those Urge Overkill records went down in the discount bin; up top, you were more likely to find Gastr del Sol and the Sea and Cake, or Mouse on Mars and Spring Heel Jack. By the time Stereolab released 1997's *Dots and Loops*—an album that had them collaborating with McEntire and Mouse on Mars—the whole thing had . . . shouldered its way pretty close to the center of the indie universe . . . Superchunk, a pretty good indie barometer, would start the decade shouting about bad jobs and end it crooning over the obligatory vibraphone; Yo La Tengo, another good yardstick, would do something pretty similar . . ."

The "revolutionary" effect that Tortoise had on indie rock musically, as John Bush asserts on *AllMusic*, extended mostly via the footprints of the band's members. Tortoise collaborated with many other groups and musicians, and John McEntire was a member of a popular indie rock band, the Sea and Cake. David Pajo recorded under the names Aerial M and Papa M and lent his skills to Stereolab and many other bands. An array of indie rock bands incorporated percussion instruments like glockenspiel or vibraphone into their arsenal, but few could equal, or even attempted to equal, the instrumental skill and compositional savvy of Tortoise's members. None of them had Casey Rice working the soundboard for live shows, as Tortoise did. The addition of the experienced jazz guitarist Jeff Parker into the lineup in 1998 as Pajo's replacement made Tortoise even more difficult to mimic. What ended up happening for most bands was elaboration of instrumentation without substantial structural change on the way they wrote and performed music. Marimba in, Big Muff out.

The fulsome praise directed toward Tortoise often doesn't acknowledge the band's impact in live performance. Casey Rice had been behind the mixing board from the band's beginning, and as time went on her role as sound organizer and enhancer expanded. Rice explains her approach when she says, "I had a tape recorder that I would carry around with me. I had a lapel mic, we're out walking all of the time, and in the pocket the record button is getting switched on and off all the time. Then I would take the recordings, fast-forward them randomly over other bits, so I had these weird kind of Kmart musique concrète cartridges that I would play in between songs. Tortoise didn't talk to the audience, they played different instruments and switched up and there were these weird pauses and gaps to fill. Really big gaps. People don't like that when they're not entertained with something."

No two Tortoise shows were exactly the same. In addition to the improvisation going on between band members and the sound engineer, the group had sonic heft. As Casey Rice describes the reaction of the organizer to the band's first appearance at the All Tomorrow's Parties festival, "I remember Barry coming up to me when Tortoise were playing and saying, 'They just called from six miles down the road and they can hear the bass.' I thought, 'Okay, good.'" David Bryant of godspeed you! black emperor says, "I remember seeing Tortoise in Toronto in 1996. The show was fantastic, but it ended with Casey playing an infrasonic frequency, like an auditory hallucination. The frequency nullified all sound, but you could not perceive it as sound (it was below the audible threshold of the human ear). You could see people talking, but no sound was perceivable, it was the absence of all sound. This is just a guess, I'm not sure this really happened . . . but it was incredible."

My personal favorite band from Chicago on Thrill Jockey was a trio called Rome. Bassist Richard Smith was better known as Rik Shaw of the popular Deadly Dragon Sound System DJ team. Eliot Dicks drummed and Adam Gruel used a Yamaha sampler and tape deck. Rome performed and recorded with an obvious deep interest in the techniques of dub reggae. Space was central to Rome as a compositional and performance tool, with effects and delays filtering rhythms into extended tracks, often with the jagged edge that Tortoise lacked. The self-titled debut album came out in 1996, recorded by John McEntire and, importantly, mixed by Rice. Rice notes that Smith and Gruel came from a scene centered on the Milk of Burgundy venue, which she describes as "trashy, weird art damage" as opposed to "the rock bands like Eleventh Dream Day and Poster Children that Doug (McCombs) and Johnny (Herndon) were in."

MEANWHILE, BACK ON PLANET KRANKY . . .

In the spring of 1996, I left Cargo. Joel had been able to phase out earlier, parlaying a part-time bartender gig into more hours and picking up shifts at Reckless Records. I got a job in the warehouse at Facets Multimedia, a Lincoln Park art cinema and videotape rental and mail-order operation. I found myself in a mirror universe of the music-centric one I had left. My coworkers displayed deep film knowledge and discussed the latest films from Iran and restored silent films. I worked alongside musicians there, including John Forbes from Mount Shasta and Adam Gruel. My car had died earlier that year, so Joel would drop off 120-count boxes of promo CDs, or a box of padded mailing envelopes, in the basement warehouse. At the end of the workday I'd schlep them up the stairs, out the door, and west across Fullerton Avenue to a bus stop at the corner of Damen. Then I'd get up on the bus with my thirty-pound box and ride home, where I'd make the final leg up two stories to my apartment. Joel and I each got early iMac computers and our own printers for ourselves. My "office" was always well supplied with post office mailing tubs, the ubiquitous semi-transparent plastic mail carriers that I would pack with promo packages to go out. They stack up nicely. Technically I was breaking federal law (and still am) by taking them home, but the helpful post office staff were always willing to give me some. I'd take trips down Western Avenue to a nearby Kinko's to run off sheets and stuff them into packages with CDs. Then, back on the bus to carry my tubs to be mailed. I became intimately aware of the best offices to visit, the ones located off a bus line where the lines were short and the clerks were helpful. I would buy mass amounts of stamps at a time to send out promo CDs at the "media mail" rate for books, magazines, and recorded media.

A scandal had ripped across Chicago in the fall of 1994 when a series of discoveries were made of postal workers leaving mail in relay boxes, stashing mail under a viaduct, and hiding bags in their home or under a back porch. In one case, firefighters discovered 2,300 pounds of mail in the closet of a carrier's home. One epicenter of slow and indifferent mail delivery was close to my house, the post office near the corner of Ashland and Lawrence Avenues in the Uptown neighborhood. The evaluation of Chicago's postal service became a regular topic of conversation between me and other label promo folks, fanzine publishers, and interested parties. After one promo mailing, I discovered that a package I had mailed to Vancouver arrived in two days while mail sent across town took weeks. The poster artist Dan Grzeca clued me in to a small post office near his house at the intersection of Wilson and Damen Avenues, and it became my go-to. I put tricks I had learned at Touch & Go into practice, especially how to fill out customs forms and mark envelopes so that the recipients in Toronto or Paris wouldn't be charged customs duties on a promo package. My evenings and weekends were filled with this kind of activity, as kranky had fourteen releases to its credit by 1996.

The third, self-titled Labradford album came out in November. The album starts with the sound of dragging chains and a gas canister on "Phantom Channel Crossing," then picks up squeaking violin from Chris Johnston, who contributed to several other songs on the album, and finishes with a rhythmic pulse that shows the surprises that the trio lineup brought to the studio. Bobby Donne's contributions on bass and sampler indicated he had been fully integrated into the composition and recording processes. The album was recorded in Richmond, Virginia, at a new studio called Sound of Music with owner John Morand engineering. Labradford would go on to record three albums there. A couple of years later, writing for the kranky website, I expressed the frustration Joel and I were feeling with the critical dialogue around music and crazes of the day: "By the time 'post-rock' had coalesced into short-hand for imagination-challenged music writers (let's say around 1996), Labradford were recognized as one of the early entrants in a movement that nobody really wanted to put the energy into defining. At the time of their third album, analog synth fetishists, cocktail nation fritterers and the dabblers in drum and bass and beat science all swirled around like june bugs on a summer night."

From our perspective at kranky, Labradford were simultaneously expanding their sound while retaining the elements that made them distinctly *Labradford*. The subtlety of the music worked both for and against the band, garnering a limited but appreciative following. At a basic nerve-response level, the interaction of bass and drums was still how most audiences connected with music.

Looking back on 1996's *Labradford* album, Jon Whitney wrote, "It was exceptionally focused, both by the balance between the fantastic melodies with subtle effects and the balanced roles of the three members. It comes as no surprise it had such an influence on music worldwide, ringing in a new era of ambient music that isn't boring." Whitney had been a college radio DJ at WMUA in Amherst, Massachusetts, and then at WZBC in Boston, and started a music website in April 1996 called *The Brain* that covered oddball and peripheral music. He also provided hosting service on brainwashed.com to bands including Bowery Electric and Stars of the Lid, and ultimately he designed and hosted the kranky label website.

Labradford was released in the United Kingdom and Europe by Blast First, an arrangement that benefited the band much as it had American predecessors like Big Black, Sonic Youth, and the Butthole Surfers. Blast First, as licensor for UK releases for the above mentioned, played no small role in launching a hype train around noisy American rock in the late '80s, and there was good reason to believe they could do the same for Labradford. As Bobby Donne recalls, label impresario Paul Smith sought out the band as they "were touring the U.K. as an opener for the High Llamas. Paul came to a gig and pretty much asked if he could license our stuff right there." Blast First at the time was manufactured and distributed by Mute, a quasi-indie that had Depeche Mode, Nick Cave, and other high-profile artists on their roster and a network of retail accounts across Britain and Europe. Wider distribution and domestic prices in the United Kingdom helped get Labradford CDs and LPs into stores, and

European touring ensued for the band. Bobby Donne says, "Paul was constantly trying to find ways to branch out our appeal and widen our audience." As Smith recalls, "Finding an audience for Labradford was going to be a bit ticklish—their slow-paced, melodic music obviously didn't suit the indie rock 'n roll circuit, but at that time the contemporary classical world had not yet really embraced 'ambient' music as being understood as 'composed.'" Paul Smith's efforts to raise Labradford's profile and contextualize their music didn't always pay off, but it was more than kranky could afford to do from afar.

What I didn't know at the time was that the compositional impact of Labradford would, arguably, exceed that of Tortoise in the decades to come. The trio's introduction of analog synthesizers, longer-form song structure, and extended tones and textures was picked up by more and more musicians as time passed, to the point where "they could almost be the pioneers of coalescing ambient, drone and rock music," as one reviewer recently summarized Labradford's long-term impact. In 2007 the influential *Hearts of Space* syndicated radio program played a track from Labradford's 1999 album *E luxo so* alongside music from Coldplay, the Grateful Dead, David Bowie, and Radiohead in a program called "When Rock Meets Space," described as "a report on the ongoing diffusion of the space and ambient sound into the world of popular music." Labradford also benefited from the attention of dance music fans. Tomas Palermo, a college radio and club DJ and music writer in San Francisco, observes, "Electronic and dance music listeners picked up on the kranky vein of ambient almost immediately as college radio DJs embraced and played these sounds, and the more savvy dance DJs who knew or played ambient were clued into it. There were many DJs in San Francisco, Seattle, and LA that came from experimental, goth, and industrial dance backgrounds, where ambient music had an influence. By the time I moved up to

San Francisco in the later '90s the kranky sound was definitely key—Stars of the Lid, Pan•American, and Windy & Carl were all being played on the college stations and ambient club nights around the city."

Similar nights happened in small venues in Chicago, such as Mike Javor's /bin series that brought electronic artists like Kid 606 who skirted the boundaries of the dance floor and experimentation to the basement of the Nervous Center coffeehouse. Mark Nelson from Labradford had the opportunity to play an early show in his Pan•American guise. It truly felt like an underground phenomenon and a place where people interested in the interwoven strands of techno, ambient, and avant-garde music were checking out the latest developments sitting on wooden benches under a coffeehouse.

In 1996 a California-based distributor, Darla Records, began a series of twelve-inch single releases called the Bliss Out. The title was inspired by Simon Reynolds's book *Blissed Out* and was designed to spotlight "indie rock and electronic music artists with an acute pop sense to showcase their more ambient side in epic length and form." Windy & Carl contributed the second installment of the series, an EP entitled *Antarctica*. At kranky we thought it was the best thing the duo had produced. After five years of more or less stringing the band along, we agreed to work with them. Windy Weber remembers, "Of course it was frustrating. We wanted to be on the label Labradford was on."

DETROIT: SPACE ROCK CITY

Windy Weber and Carl Hultgren had been issuing seven-inch singles and cassettes beginning in 1993 on their own Blue Flea label and playing shows with a group of like-minded musicians in the Detroit area. Weber recalls, "We all did shows together in ’95, ’96, ’97 and on a regular basis, you could go into downtown Detroit and see groups like Monaural, and Auburn Lull, and us. There were a whole lot of shows all the time and a lot of people involved. It felt like we were really doing something.”

This grouping of Detroit-area bands became identified as Michigan space rock due to the blurring of melodies, extended song structures, and synthesizers many of them used. Windy & Carl’s initial recordings came out as singles on a number of labels, including English labels like Enraptured, Ochre, and Earworm. As Hultgren notes, “Once other labels outside of Michigan (and the USA) started putting out records by us and our friends, there seemed to be a Michigan Space Rock scene being talked about. If someone wanted to put your record out, we would go for it. As long as we ended up with some copies to sell ourselves, it was all fine. It was quicker and cheaper back then to put out a record and we were just happy to have someone willing to put our records out for us.”

Weber adds, “It seemed like getting as much music out into the world as we could was the way to go, especially if other people were paying to press the record and do the shipping, etc. But eventually we realized that we were giving away whole albums of material on a regular basis just to sell a few hundred copies of a seven-inch.”

That shift to longer forms on *Antarctica* pushed all the right buttons at kranky headquarters. The creation of the title track is an example of how home recording aided spontaneity. As Windy Weber tells it: “I had asked Carl about running a keyboard through pedals and if it was the same as running a guitar through pedals. Carl said yes and I went in the basement and hooked up some stuff and pressed a key on the keyboard, and within seconds I heard Carl running down the stairs and through the house and into the basement. He immediately plugged me into the four-track cassette recorder and then turned on his amp and pedals and plugged in. I found a piece of tape and taped down the key I was holding and picked up my bass. We both simply played."

Carl Hultgren says, "Up until that point, everything we did was bouncing back and forth between two separate cassette recorders with on-the-fly live overdubbing. I really do think it happened in one quick take. It was also the first long form piece we've ever done."

Windy & Carl began working on their debut kranky release, *Depths*. In 1996 Windy bought a 1966 Fender Jaguar electric guitar, followed shortly by a Vox Pacemaker amplifier and a Roland RE 201 Space Echo guitar effects unit. Carl justified the purchase to Windy by saying, "It'll sound like Durutti Column," the English post-punk instrumental band Windy idolizes. "The combo was pure heaven to me. I could not stay away. I started playing guitar all the time." So much so that tensions arose as the duo worked on the album, as Windy details: "Carl wrote four pieces that were hazy and gauzy and rather menacing and I wrote three songs. I did not want Carl to play on my tracks and he did not want me on his. We started referring to it as our Spacemen 3 album because we were refusing to work together."

As mastering engineer and musician Rafael Anton Isarri puts it, "Around '97 or so I heard Bowery Electric's *Beat* and Labradford's *A Stable Reference*, which became favorites. Later on, around '99 or so, I heard Windy & Carl for the first time: the *Depths* album. Massive influence on me."

In Philadelphia, Chuck van Zyl had been receiving promotional mailings from me and was formulating his own view of kranky: "Were they an Ambient Music label? or an Ethereal Rock label? or a Collage/Soundscape/Minimal label? ECM records had their own distinct values and vibe. But with kranky, I had never heard of any of their artists, most all of which seemed to have absorbed much of the influential music I knew, so this new music had a strange familiarity, but it possessed a certain contempt for its predecessors."

This describes almost exactly the space that Joel and I wanted kranky releases to inhabit. That space was not, as Joel was wont to say, a "smooth, white, oval room."

Magnog completed their recording sessions with Andy Brown in October 1995, and their self-titled debut came out in May 1996. The critical response was immediate and positive. There is no doubt that some of the reaction was due to the novelty of young men playing free-form psychedelic rock that hearkened back to obscure bands predating their arrival on the planet. Imitative or not, the power of Magnog could not be denied. Simon Hopkins wrote in *The Wire*, "If Magnog are Krautrock aficionados—and as 20 year olds it's perhaps hard to imagine, but then it's hard to imagine 20 year olds making music like this, period—then they have a taste for an earlier, less groove-based take on Krautrock: Manuel Gottsching's Ash Ra Tempel, perhaps, or "Zeit"-period Tangerine Dream . . . Whatever; swathed in echoes and reverbs, with seamlessly melded scorched-earth guitar and synthesizer textures . . . Magnog have a depth way beyond reverential imitation."

Magnog was reviewed positively in *Rolling Stone*, *Guitar Player*, and the *New York Times*. Magnog would play shows in Seattle with Jessamine, the two bands transitioning between sets by adding and subtracting members in an amoebic improvisation. Peter Kember remembers playing shows with Magnog, noting that the trio were "kind of child prodigies of the scene. When I played with them, (guitarist) Phil Drake was only allowed in the venue to play their set. We did a lot of hanging in the parking lot." Looking back on the shows Magnog played after the debut album came out, Jeff Reilly notes, "By the time we were lucky enough to share a stage with Jessamine and Sonic Boom we had matured somewhat and felt fairly confident."

Magnog even got to open for corporate grunge superstars Pearl Jam for a fan club show. Dana Shinn and Jeff Reilly "had played in a band with Eddie Veder's first wife Beth Liebling and Dana's brother Ryan, so we were friends." Reilly notes, "I remember the show as being both incredibly frightening and exhilarating. Magnog was just starting out at the time, so this was very mind-blowing." The trio even played at the Vienna Jazz Festival. "Out of the blue I received a call from a guy claiming to be from the Austrian Arts Council who wanted to book us to play with Experimental Audio Research, Earth, and Godflesh. It turned out we were their second choice to play, as Labradford could not attend (lucky us)." The horizon was wide open for the band.

I CAN'T BELIEVE THIS BAND IS HAPPENING AND YOU DIDN'T TELL ME ABOUT IT

In Chicago, the growth of affordable recording studios was making it possible for more and more bands to access good facilities with sympathetic recording engineers. Mike Hagler and David Trumfio's Kingsize Soundlabs along Western Avenue in Wicker Park had been attracting a diverse clientele since opening in 1993. By the time Greg Kot featured Kingsize in a March 1996 edition of the *Chicago Tribune*, a parade of indie rock artists from the Palace Brothers to Barbara Manning had used the studio. Kot noted how the studio tapped into the pool of Chicago musicians nearby: "Kingsize offers the duo's connections to the fertile Chicago music community; it's not uncommon for them to ring up Poi Dog Pondering multi-instrumentalist Dave Crawford to lay down a fluegelhorn part on a Stuart Moxham record, or have the Jesus Lizard's Duane Denison play guitar on a Sally Timms session." Kingsize was the location of the recording sessions for Chris Holmes's Yum•Yum album *Dan Loves Patti*, and it was Holmes who tipped off his major-label contacts to a part-time, new wave band that David Trumfio and his brother Harry had going called Pulsars. Greg Kot described what had become a familiar process in Chicago: "Every major record label and a handful of indies began courting the duo in Chicago's latest version of a bidding war. When the talent scouts first came calling, based on word-of-mouth from shows the duo was playing around town, the Trumfios didn't even have a demo tape ready . . . Chris Holmes [of Yum•Yum] mentioned us to his A&R guy, and the next thing I know I'm getting a call from the senior vice president of Atlantic Records, who's telling me he loves our tape."

The Brothers Trumfio signed with a new major label owned by Herb Alpert of the Tijuana Brass and A&M Records fame for a reported $2.5 million three-album deal. Joel Mark, who was working as a Chicago talent scout for the MCA label, says, "One day my boss called me and literally yelled at me about the Pulsars. She said, 'I can't believe this band is happening and you didn't tell me about it and I'm in trouble with my boss because we haven't signed anything from Chicago, and that's why I hired you, and why aren't you telling me about this?' They needed something from Chicago because everyone else signed something from Chicago."

A five-song EP, *Submission to the Masters*, came out in late 1996 with Herb Alpert contributing trumpet on a track. The Pulsars' self-titled album was released in 1997. David Trumfio recorded both at Kingsize, wisely investing those advance dollars in his own career as a sound engineer. As the financial advisers always say, "Pay yourself first." As David Trumfio describes it, "Unlike others who may have historically put their advance money up their noses or pissed it away on frivolous stuff we were very careful how we handled our signing. Harry and I spent years in many bands to get to that point. We had no pretensions about what was cool at the time and made guilty pleasure type music we heard in our heads. I spent years developing my career as a producer/engineer and studio owner, so I was doing that either way. The deal just helped solidify it and we spent the advance wisely."

Chris Holmes's reach for the brass ring ended differently. Of his many real and theoretical projects, he chose Yum•Yum, a chamber pop band, to be the first release on his multi-album major-label contract. Recorded at Kingsize with Trumfio and Mike Hagler engineering and a string trio to boot, *Dan Loves Patti* was released by TAG/Atlantic Records. Holmes's version of baroque pop in the tradition of the Left Bank and Electric Light Orchestra landed in the marketplace with a dull thud. The album failed to enter the *Billboard* Top 200 Albums chart upon release in May. Peter Margasak reported in the *Chicago Reader* in August 1996 that Soundscan sales numbers for the album barely topped two thousand.

The second half of 1996 was nothing short of catastrophic for Smashing Pumpkins. A national tour placed the band in Manhattan in July, poised to play two sold-out shows at Madison Square Garden. Early in the morning of July 12, paramedics were called to the band's hotel. Shortly thereafter, touring keyboardist Jonathan Melvoin was pronounced dead and Smashing Pumpkins drummer Jimmy Chamberlain was arrested for possession of heroin. A few days later the band announced that Chamberlain had been fired. The tour resumed with the addition of drummer Matt Walker and keyboardist Jimmy Flemion to the band. Billy Corgan later admitted to *Uncut* magazine that continuing touring was a poor decision. "Did Jimmy being sacked cripple the band?" says Corgan. "Oh, absolutely. I should've quit right then. Instead, I doubled down on a bad situation, and it got worse. The band went into a Cold War vibe. People stopped talking. And with walking away from rock stylistically, I was burning my bridges."

After fourteen months of touring to support *Mellon Collie and the Infinite Sadness*, the Pumpkins trimmed down to a trio and began recording in Chicago in sessions that continued into 1997 at multiple locations with engineering and production provided by Arif Mardin, Nellee Hooper, Brad Wood, Neil Perry, Rick Rubin, and Flood. The latter producer had a deep background working with the '80s electronic acts on the Mute label who obviously influenced Corgan's musical aesthetic. As Lisa Bralts-Kelly observes, "'Adore' could have been a Depeche Mode song." Some tracks ended up on movie soundtracks, while others were rough versions of songs recorded as "demos" to prepare for album sessions. The band was floundering. *Electronic Musician* wrote, "After months of aimless recording, Flood was brought in to sift through the 40-odd songs and assess what needed to be done to make an album out of the mountain of recordings. The final 'Adore' album was a patchwork that drew from these sessions as well as the failed Chicago Brad Wood Sessions, the live CRC sessions and even some home recordings . . ."

The commercial momentum Smashing Pumpkins had built over several albums and years of touring dissipated in the wake of the delays in recording and releasing *Adore*. Corgan had tried mightily to move the Pumpkins' sound beyond the riff-heavy rock he felt had constrained him creatively. As Ian Cohen wrote about a reissued, expanded version of *Adore* in 2014, "It features a highly stylized gothic cover, lacks anything resembling an Almighty Riff, features drum programming . . . and shares a producer with *Exile in Guyville*." *Adore* was released on June 1, 1998, and entered the *Billboard* charts at number 2. It was certified as platinum within five weeks. But it quickly dropped off the charts, falling short of previous albums' sales. Smashing Pumpkins had found their core audience, and that audience would not grow significantly in the years to come. The band had plateaued. But what a plateau it is: 20 million Smashing Pumpkins recordings had been sold in the United States alone as of 2016. Mount Corgan was much higher than the peaks that other Chicago artists scaled after they grasped the ropes handed to them by the major labels.

As the year ended, Liz Phair began work on her third album in a process eerily similar to the one Smashing Pumpkins went through. A series of recording sessions in Chicago and Miami over several years resulted in the sixteen-track *Whitechocolatespaceegg*, released on Matador via a distribution deal with Capitol Records in the summer of 1998. The album peaked on the *Billboard* Top 200 Albums chart at number 35 and dropped off after three weeks. Years later, a distinctly nasty review of Phair's self-titled fourth album on the indie rock barometer website *Pitchfork* expressed what had become the accepted wisdom for many, mostly male, critics: "Things didn't start to go *horribly* awry, of course, until Phair's next album, *Whitechocolatespaceegg*. That record's attempts to radio-ize her sound only dismantled the depth of her music—if not the awkwardness—resulting in an odd batch of songs that perhaps encapsulated Phair's faulty view of what constitutes a radio-friendly album."

Oh, *of course*. That, in a nutshell, is the damned-if-you-do, damned-if-you-don't situation Liz Phair has faced as a recording artist. That same *Pitchfork* review described *Exile* like this: "Phair's gruff voice wrapped awkward non-hooks around flimsy, transparent chord progressions, resulting in (to everyone's surprise) a certifiable indie roadtrip classic."

In other words, she can't really do indie rock right. Somehow Phair had lucked into indie rock notoriety with *Exile in Guyville*. And Phair can't sell out and get radio play the right way. In 2017 Liz Phair showed the *Vulture* website that she knows the score: "I grew up in Winnetka, the preppiest suburb imaginable, and then suddenly I was identified with this downtown Wicker Park scene. Really? I'm going to cleave off an entire part of myself and live in a world that isn't even mine? Exile in Guyville. Exile! Guyville was not my home. I wrote the whole fucking record about having trouble living in Guyville, and then Guyville became my home forever? No."

The metaphysical borders of Guyville stretched beyond Wicker Park. There were few opportunities for women to carve out careers for themselves. Looking around the Chicago scene, one would have found one influential club, Lounge Ax, owned and operated by women and one influential record label, Thrill Jockey, owned by a woman. Susanne McCarthy (now Dawursk) brought her Flower Booking business to Chicago in 1994, growing her roster of clients to include Chicago bands like Joan of Arc and Local H. In 1996, Kathryn Frazier started the Biz 3 publicity firm above the Empty Bottle representing Chicago bands like 5ive Style, The Aluminum Group, Dianogah, and Sally Timms as well as out-of-town acts. For several years the Empty Bottle was managed by Carrie Weston (then Carrie Leech), who began working as owner Bruce Finkelman's office and booking assistant. Sheila Sachs was the art director for the *Chicago Reader* and took on freelance graphic design for a checklist of Chicago record labels: "I started designing for Thrill Jockey with the Sea and Cake *Nassau* record in the mid '90s. Over the years I designed hundreds of records for them. I started designing records for Thrill Jockey, kranky, Bloodshot, Overcoat, March, Carrot Top, 482 Music, Delmark, Cuneiform, Jim Gill Music (children's music) . . ."

DJ Scary Lady Sarah hosted a goth/industrial dance party called Nocturna at Metro beginning in 1988 and supported various bands as they came through town. Terri Bristol and Val Scheinpflug, working as DJ Psycho-Bitch, broke into the house music scene and built big followings playing clubs like Smart Bar, Neo, and the influential juice bar Medusa's. Kate Simko was the hip-hop/dance music director for WNUR and began a career making electronic dance music after graduating. The women who worked at Cargo were confined to sales, promotion, or data entry, with little to no input on decision making. Overall, only a handful of women controlled or owned the businesses they worked at. Detailing these imposed limitations doesn't begin to cover the trauma women in the business and female musicians experienced from sexually manipulative and abusive men at record labels and in bands.

In 2018, Liz Phair toured around a reissue of *Exile in Guyville* and the Girlysound tapes, in a variation on the sad trend centered on the Don't Look Back festivals where indie rock bands turn into tribute bands to themselves and perform their best-known albums in order, track by track. To Phair's credit, she was performing songs many people had never heard, or had only heard of. And she did so with one guitar player backing her in what was as close as possible to a replication of the dynamic of the cassettes and early performances that first drew attention to her.

When the Big 3 of Chicago alt-rock, the Pumpkins, Phair, and Urge, stalled out, a vacuum arose in the city's mainstream music scene. The genre-blending that had been occurring on the underground level came to the forefront. Greg Kot, a keen observer and chronicler of Chicago music for the *Tribune*, recollects, "The scene seemed very stratified in the '80s with house, industrial and noise-rock all in their own silos. But in the '90s the barriers fell away and there was a lot more cross-pollination. I think the non-rock, instrumental/experimental vibe emerged from that."

DEEP AND FORGIVING BUT RIGOROUS

Rob Mazurek, who had started playing straight-ahead be-bop jazz, found his horizons expanding as he collaborated with other musicians. Most notably, he joined Jeff Parker's group Isotope 217 after a weekly series of jam sessions at the Rainbo club.

"There was experimentation going on in various places, but nothing that I experienced as deep and forgiving but rigorous as Chicago at that time," Mazurek says. "I was introduced to the electronic music of Xenakis, Ussachevsky, Kevin Drumm, Dockstader, Autechre, Mouse on Mars, Oval, etc. Jim O'Rourke was great for this, but also John Herndon and Casey Rice. I started to delve into electronics when I joined Isotope 217 and never looked back." Parker and Mazurek were joined in the group by Matt Lux, a bassist whose contributions to multiple bands earned him the sobriquet "the Kevin Bacon of Chicago Music" from Peter Margasak.

Joan of Arc had formed out of the remains of the popular band Cap'n Jazz in 1996. Tim Kinsella was the center of the band, which took in his brother Mike and Jeremy Boyle. Cap'n Jazz was a popular band pointed to as originators of the "emo" genre of tuneful punk. Joan of Arc quickly moved past the limits of that amorphous genre assigned to them by default, especially through the use of fractured electronics and stark acoustic instrumentation. A number of Chicago musicians like Liz Payne, Matt Clark, Ben Vida, and Azita Youssefi cycled through performing and recording incarnations of the group. The group issued a series of inventive and idiosyncratic albums as lineups combined and recombined around Kinsella.

In 1996 an old, unmarked factory bar in the North Branch Industrial Corridor between Lincoln Park and Wicker Park was bought by Tim Tuten, his wife, Katie Tuten, Mike Hinchsliff, and Jim Hinchsliff. They named their bar the Hideout and almost immediately started hosting shows in the back lounge. Although the Hideout came to be identified with the insurgent country scene and Bloodshot labels via residencies from artists like Devil in a Woodpile and Robbie Fulks, its ragged confines also hosted performances by various Ken Vandermark projects, Charalambides, and the inventive guitarist Jack Rose. A yearly Block Party began on the large parking lot near the bar. After the closing of Lounge Ax in 2000, a goodly portion of the indie rock audience began frequenting the Hideout, ideally placed as it was between the locations of Lounge Ax and the old Wax Trax! store and Wicker Park.

In 1988 Chris and Michael Schuba renovated the Lincoln Park tavern that became Schubas and opened the Harmony Grill next door in 1997. The back room in Schubas hosted shows mostly by singer-songwriter and Americana acts, but there was room on the schedule for touring indie bands and the occasional jazz group. The warm, wood-lined lounge suited smaller groups and solo acts, and oftentimes musicians would play residencies there. When the experienced booking agent Matt Rucins moved to Schubas from Columbia, Missouri, in 2000, the club's national profile grew.

LOOPED

Bowery Electric began working on their second album in June 1996. Lawrence Chandler explains the shift the band took in their writing and recording process like this: "I was into music technology and signal processing, and it was a time when samplers were becoming more affordable. The prospect of being able to work outside of a commercial recording studio was very appealing. We started with an Akai S950 and were able to do a fair amount of "pre-production" for *Beat*. Discovering time-stretching was very cool, as was being able to sample ourselves. Working with sampled beats was a big relief after struggling to get drummers to play the beats I wanted to hear."

Martha Schwendener adds, "It's enormously absorbing and fun and conceptual. I love making music that way, especially since I spent very little time practicing or playing. I think Lawrence and I had that in common. He was kind of a signal-processing and tech genius and I could hear how things should 'be' and then direct it, so it was a good match."

The band returned to Studio .45 in Hartford, Connecticut, where *Bowery Electric* was recorded, and worked to knit their homemade samples to in-studio recording. As befitted a band whose main members met while working at Andy Warhol's *Interview* magazine, the cover art featured *Untitled No. 27*, taken from provocateur/photographer Catherine Opie's "Freeways" series. Martha Schwendener says, "I was a baby art historian and art critic back then. She was just a favorite artist and artists aren't hard to contact. We talked to the gallery and they said she was camping, but she'd get back to us later." The album that was released in North America in November 1996, *Beat*, was a major step forward for Bowery Electric and immediately garnered a positive reaction from critics and listeners alike. The English label Beggar's Banquet licensed the album.

Remixing is reinterpreting an existing piece of music by extending, adding to, or subtracting material from the original and/or extensively altering the recorded material through physical or digital manipulation. By the mid-'90s, releasing remixed singles was very nearly standard business practice in the electronic dance music scene; a successor to the tradition of extended disco mixes, the studio-created dub "versions" of reggae songs, and hip-hop singles. More and more musicians like those in Tortoise and Bowery Electric were listening to the techno, drum 'n bass, jungle, and so-called intelligent dance music genre defined by an Internet message board in 1993, and being released on labels like Warp, Rephlex, Mu, and others in the United Kingdom. The Mego label in Vienna was releasing music descended from techno that arched into areas of abstraction or pure ambience. The Finnish duo Pan Sonic had moved from releasing austere, minimalist techno to creating booming shards of electronic buzzes and hums. It was inevitable that contacts would be made and shared. Mark Nelson reminisces, "One of my favorite things about being in Labradford was the interest we got from electronic/experimental artists primarily in Europe who understood what we were doing right away. I wouldn't consider what we did experimental—but they seemed to get the removal from traditional rock without having to consider it or qualify it. But it was very rewarding over those early years to come into the orbit and be sought out by the Mego crew in Vienna, Bruce Gilbert, Russell Haswell in London, Panasonic, Christoph Heeman, Chris and Cosey and beyond."

The late Peter Rehberg, who recorded as Pita and helmed the Vienna-based Mego label, helped Labradford and Pan•American secure slots in the PhonoTAKTIK festival in Vienna in 1999. Mark Nelson recalls, "We stayed about six days, had our own little practice space, hung out at the Rhiz bar and saw shows. It was the best week."

The music writer and DJ Vivian Host explains these affinities by noting, "The mid to late '90s electronic music was seen as cutting-edge and cool and very avant-garde in a lot of cases. That's how it was marketed as well. It wasn't any sort of surprise to me that kranky artists would be listening to that stuff, and I don't even think I made a distinction then. I would almost put Labradford or loscil in the same record store section as Pan Sonic."

Josh Madell of Other Music recalls how electronic music crossed over into the American underground: "for many fans, until the '90s electronic music was considered pop music, and they were not interested. 'Disco sucks' and all that. Then artists like the Aphex Twin started to make waves, and first-wave ambient artists like Eno, or even classically minded minimalists like Terry Riley and Philip Glass, began to creep into the consciousness, and suddenly there were a lot of indie music buyers who were interested in ambient and experimental electronic music. kranky was a big part of defining what the American scene was about, bringing a diverse roster who nonetheless had some sort of a defining sound, and it was an easy fit for many of our customers' tastes."

The writer Philip Sherburne says, "I always saw the two worlds as being pretty porous. I considered Bowery Electric just part of a continuum of adventurous electronic music, one that happened to stretch toward the edges of the dance floor."

Keith Fullerton Whitman observes in retrospect, "For me it was a real bridge-building between several very disparate stylistic and geographic scenes. . . . those Tortoise twelve-inches were years before Reznor used his clout to issue those crucial Squarepusher/Autechre double-discs via Interscope; you kind of had to either be in London or in an especially clued-in dance-music shop to even know about that stuff stateside."

Bowery Electric co-headlined a North American tour following the release of *Beat* in summer 1997 with Main, the project begun by Englishman Robert Hampson after the demise of the heavy psych trio Loop. As Lawrence Chandler recalls, "He was at one of our first shows in London. We ended up doing an improv set with him in the basement of a pub somewhere in East London." Hampson used Main to explore abstract, beat-driven ambience and floating fields of static. His live mixing of Bowery Electric during that tour rattled ribcages across the continent.

A UK tour quickly followed the release of *Beat*, with a Peel Session recorded in July and broadcast in August 1997. The band played shows in Europe to support the album. Gareth Mitchell from AMP says, "I remember seeing Bowery Electric live in London. I really liked the physicality of their sound—very strong, really loud; rhythmic, well-defined pulsing waves; quite unrelenting." The weekly *Melody Maker* described a performance by saying, "For two people to be able to create such a huge, rolling epic sound is surprising; what really hits hard is just how huge it can be, how the inarguable and pulverising beauty of BE's sound simply forces a slacked out crowd into its swell." The duo had connected with several English experimental electronic musicians who took up remixes of material from *Beat*, which were released as twelve-inch singles and then compiled as a double CD called *Vertigo*. Technically a kranky/Beggars Banquet co-release, it was manufactured by the English label. We took a number of the double-CD release for exclusive kranky North American distribution. *Beat* was the final album Bowery Electric released on kranky and the completion of the label's standard two-album agreement. It was obvious to Joel and me that the band would exclusively record for Beggar's, and we wished them well. Two twelve-inch singles, "Freedom Fighter" and "Lushlife," followed on Beggar's Banquet in 1999. The group recorded a third album called *Lushlife* that Beggar's released in February 2000. Martha Schwendener sums up Bowery Electric's Beggar's Banquet experience as "one of those standard things where you think it's a move 'up,' but it's a bad idea. kranky was the best—we still get paid (!!!!)—whereas Beggar's was like, 'Here's what it's like to be on a major (or major Indie).' I wouldn't say that was an entirely positive experience, but it's what people do."

Gathering remixes as twelve-inch singles and then compiling them for release in album form nearly became obligatory for a certain class of artists beginning in the late '90s. Stereolab had *Miss Modular* remixed in 1998 in five versions; Tortoise had the songs "Galapagos 1," "The Taut and The Tame," "Bubble Economy," "Learning Curve," and "Djed" remixed from 1996 to 1998, released a remix single with Chicago house music DJ pioneer Derrick Carter called "Derrick Carter vs. Tortoise," and did an EP of remixes by techno abstractionists Autechre. Thrill Jockey artists Trans Am released a remix EP called *Extremixx* in 2002. "I loved the camaraderie of it all, again, very open-ended and optimistic thinking that someone halfway around the world would even respond to a request to drastically rework something, but that level of trust and the devil-may-care attitude of it all led to some incredible music," Keith Fullerton Whitman remembers. "Those Tortoise singles were just mind-blowing really; I can't imagine the trajectory Bettina Richards would have taken with Thrill Jockey were it not for the doors opened by that series. Similar to what David Grubbs and Jim O'Rourke were bringing into Drag City; that level of trust." In many cases, these were not remixes designed for the dancefloor when artists like Jim O'Rourke, for example, worked on Tortoise's "Reference Resistance Gate." This was the case with an aborted Labradford remix project for the Blast First label, in which pianist Harold Budd, Pan Sonic, the Louisville duo Matmos, German drone auteur Christoph Heeman, and F.M. Enheit from experimental industrialists Einstürzende Neubauten were enlisted by Paul Smith to rework Labradford tracks. Two tracks, the Harold Budd remix of "V" and one of "So" by Matmos, appeared on the promotional CD included in subscribers' copies of *The Wire* in November 1998 and March 2000, respectively. But a compilation album of remixes never saw the light of day. As Mark Nelson recalls, the band saw it as "a Paul Smith marketing idea that we were into for a while and then realized we had no control over." Bobby Donne breaks it down further by saying, "I can only imagine he thought having Pan Sonic and F. M Einheit remix our stuff would do something to bolster our popularity. It was his idea, and he picked the remixers, for the most part. He probably just didn't like the way it came out in the end."

I confess that at kranky we saw the remix craze through jaundiced eyes. Our experiences at Cargo prompted us to view remix singles as a business tactic used to extend the sales life of dance singles. We discounted the significant collaborative remixing activity going on. Bowery Electric had their music remixed by Robert Hampson, who had performed with them and mixed their live sets. This was also the case when soundman Casey Rice remixed Tortoise tracks in his Designer alias. But these combinations were the exception to the rule. Richard D. James (a.k.a. Aphex Twin) later noted that for remixes in those days, "I had met the representative or artist somewhere in central London and got paid in cash." What was oftentimes described as remixing was outright composition, as Simon Reynolds describes: "It was interesting at first but then it got to this daft point where the remixer was submitting what was essentially an all-new piece of music—they were substituting their own track for the track supposedly being remixed. Remixing by the late '90s had become more like re-production, and even then there wasn't much 're-' involved—the name remixers like Richard D. James were just creating new works, with only a tiny element from the original, barely discernible." We never released a remix on kranky until 2005, on a twelve-inch EP by the New York group Out Hud. Vivian Host has a more even-tempered view of remixing than Joel and I did. "To pay for a remix you had to really want one (since you didn't really 'need' that weird drum 'n bass remix). Majors pay for 'dance club' remixes all the time, but I think that's a different animal. Of course, you did get some that seemed trendy, but I think people were excited to hear their music differently. And in the case of drum 'n bass in the mid to late 1990s it was considered pretty avant-garde music from a production standpoint, a band like Tortoise were really inspired by its rhythms and drum patterns. And the opportunity to maybe make that link with artists and fans who were so different culturally."

One Chicagoan had moved from guitar rock straight into making his own beat-focused electronic music. Casey Rice had been introduced to drum 'n bass on an English tour with Liz Phair. A friend turned on the radio, and Rice asked, "'What the hell is this?' He says, 'It's jungle and this is pirate radio.' Sounds interesting to me already: illegal radio station. We went and saw a couple of gigs, and I thought, this is crazy, this is like reggae, but it's really fucked up. I became fascinated by it. At the same time, the bullshit in Chicago was going down. I felt stuck in the middle of it, socially ostracized. Fuck the scene, I thought. It was fully autonomous, with its own labels, radio stations, artists, and live events. It was made by people for themselves because they wanted to hear it. So, it was really a very punk rock and DIY thing that everybody said they were interested in in Chicago."

Rice recorded several EPs under the name Designer, and remixed tracks as well, integrating what blew his mind about jungle/drum 'n bass into his own fractured electronic dance music: "I really needed to do something too because I don't want to just be the recording mixing person for the rest of my life." The multitude of small and often short-lived labels that released Designer singles and Rice's recording work likely kept the music from getting the attention it deserved. Peter Margasak noted in the *Chicago Reader* in late 1996, "While there are traces of electro, dub, and drum 'n bass on these two twelve-inch singles, Rice's trippy production renders most reference points moot." Paul Dickow, who records under the name Strategy, says Designer has been "criminally underrated," and I concur.

BRISTOL WITHOUT A PISTOL

Joel and I had been listening to bands coming out of Bristol, England, with great interest ever since we heard the first Flying Saucer Attack records. A proposed collaboration between Labradford and Flying Saucer Attack never came to pass, victim to both groups' busy schedules. Joel's overtures to the Planet Records label, whose releases by Crescent and Movietone really impressed us, were unanswered. Other Chicagoans were equally interested, and eventually Atavistic released a Crescent album called *Electronic Sound Constructions* and Drag City began licensing Movietone releases in 1997. We were able to make a kranky connection to that productive and tangled group of musicians.

In the spring of 1996, a musician named Richard Walker contacted kranky. In college Richard had been a member of a Bristol band called the Secret Garden, which was made up of David Pearce, David Mercer, Gareth Mitchell, Guy Cooper, Andy Revell, and John Cooper. Many bands and recording projects sprung forth from the band. Pearce formed Flying Saucer Attack, and David Mercer put out music as Light. Gareth Mitchell lays out all the connections and recording identities: "Andrew Revell, Dave Pearce and I formed a band, the Secret Garden, whilst we were at art college. Dave moved to Bristol. A few years later, a few other friends of ours moved to Bristol: Dave Mercer (Light, Amp, Flying Saucer Attack), Andy Revell, and Paul Gulatic (Soundsmith). Richard had also been in the Secret Garden, so there were lots of connections that had formed between us."

In 1992 Walker had started to release singles under the name Amp, joined by Karine Charff. Like others in the United Kingdom, he had picked up on kranky via John Peel: "I was aware of kranky from listening to John Peel, which I used to do every week, and had done since I was a child. Dave Pearce had played me some Labradford, he was very switched on to what was going down in the underground music scene worldwide."

Having keenly followed the Bristol contingent at kranky, we were disappointed that Amp's first full-length album was released on an American label called Petrol. Walker describes how that label "folded for several reasons and gave us some contacts for going forwards, one of which was kranky, adding also that Joel had told them that he wished he could have released the album, so this obviously pricked our ears up . . ." The recordings Richard and Karine sent us became the *astral-moonbeamprojections* double LP/CD released in May 1997. It's a cavernous album, characterized by "a sense of power being held back, a crushing flow of feedback and reverb swelling and filling out the mix," as Ned Raggett noted at the time. Walker had been designing cover artwork for the Creation label, and his artwork for the album added to the mood, with a red and magenta photographic collage redolent of swirling magma and an inner cover resembling a tidal pool in blues. It looks great as a gatefold record cover.

The connection to Amp became doubly productive in the summer of 1996 when Gareth Mitchell, who had briefly collaborated in a live incarnation of the band and contributed to *astralmoonbeamprojections*, sent us music he recorded under the name Philosopher's Stone. Mitchell called the album *Preparation*, and it is unlike any other in the kranky catalog. Mitchell explains, "I really wanted to use a basic home recording set-up as a compositional tool. I adopted several approaches to making that album that I had never previously utilized (in some cases, had deliberately been holding back on using until the time seemed right). I had spent only about six months developing extended technique with the guitar and a musique concrète style approach to composition. Once I decided to work instrumentally and with loops, though, and to make compositional and instrumental decisions based on numerology along with vague ideas of what I could understand of alchemical principles, the floodgates opened."

There is something out of time about the album, as Mitchell's references to alchemical and numerological techniques suggest. It reminds me in parts of the medieval-sounding records the 4AD Records group Dead Can Dance put out in the late '80s, and of the over-the-top cabaret vocal stylings of Scott Walker and others. As Mitchell describes it, "I wanted the singing to be certain and demonstrative rather than, say, whispered and half-hidden, which was quite a trend at the time. I also wanted the vocal parts to remain a novelty, an aspect of the record that might surprise but nevertheless make sense in being encountered there." The final touch that has made *Preparation* such a memorable release was the cover art, a photo of megalithic rock formations awash in sepia tones. Mitchell says, "The photographs were taken by my partner, Shahny Raitz von Frentz, especially for the cover at a place called Wilhelm's Höhe in Kassel, Germany. I was looking for structures that were not immediately recognizable but nevertheless suggestive: images that looked like evidence of a previously unknown civilization which defied immediate categorization."

Jessamine had been playing shows with Peter Kember for some time, and on August 8, 1996, recorded a set at Moe's in Seattle with Kember in his E.A.R. incarnation. Kember played EMS Synthi AKS and Serge Modula synthesizers, a Theremin, and bowed cymbals, while Andy Brown played Micro Moog synthesizer and Farfisa organ, Rex Ritter contributed on guitar, and Michael Faeth drummed. This combination had recorded a cover of the Silver Apples' seminal '60s electronic track "A Pox on You" in 1995. The live session requires patience on the part of the listener as the electronic squiggles slowly cohere around Brown's organ lines, Ritter's guitar, and a subtle drumbeat. Ritter recalls that the initial improvised synthesizer performance, which read out as a sustained square wave, "drove most of the audience out after about three minutes." The session was released as *Living Sound* on Jessamine's Histrionic label and Space Age Recordings in the United Kingdom.

A FREE, OPEN END TO WHAT WE COULD AND WOULD MAKE

The Coctails released their fifth, self-titled album in 1996. The relationship began with Patrick Monaghan's Carrot Top Records, which had brought the Coctails albums into the digital world with the CD compilation of early recordings *The Early Hi-Ball Years*. The group's second release, *Long Sound*, had more jazzy textures courtesy of contributions from Chicago jazz stalwarts Hal Russell, Ken Vandermark, and Dave Crawford. Patrick Monaghan has vivid memories of when the band delivered the recording: "The first CD sold better than we all thought it would and got attention. So, the band and I decided to do a second release together. One afternoon, my doorbell rang, and I opened it to all four Coctails. They'd brought me a tape of their new album to listen to while they watched me. I put the tape on and lied [*sic*] down and by the time the second song started, I was laughing hysterically. I'm not proud of this moment at all, but I was laughing because, as I told them, this was going to be a record without a marketable home. It did force me to look for additional distributors to cover the jazz market. Having Hal Russell's last recordings was a selling point for them, and Vandermark was already starting to be known outside of Chicago. It was just an uphill climb." The climb ensued and band and label established themselves.

The 1996 release *The Coctails* featured band members Mark Greenberg, Archer Prewitt, John Upchurch, and Barry Phipps all singing and playing varying combinations of guitar, bass, drums, clarinet, glockenspiel, marimba, vibraphone, organ, and electric piano. They had become a sophisticated art pop band. There were few vestiges remaining of the band's cartoonish beginnings.

Because of their name, suits, and early graphics, the Coctails were thrown into the "Cocktail Nation" genre getting attention in the mid and late 1990s. A band from North Carolina called Squirrel Nut Zippers had a hit with their re-creation of '30s hot jazz "Hell," and the 1997 film *Swingers* launched the careers of Jon Favreau and Vince Vaughan. *I, Swinger*, the debut from Combustible Edison, who took their band name from a vintage cocktail, had come out on Sub Pop in 1994, and its quirky, effervescent sound prepared the ground for what was to come. The underground had been fascinated for some time by the exotica records of Martin Denny and Les Baxter, centered as they were around bird sounds, Asian percussion, and the gentle pulsations that mixed drinks with umbrellas bring. The Mexican composer Juan García Esquivel had been rediscovered, and the 1994 compilation album *Space Age Bachelor Pad Music* gained a lot of attention for the idiosyncratic mix of Mexican folk music, Latin percussion, and pitched percussion instruments. Stereolab had also referenced a lot of these artists and markers, titling an early album *The Groop Played Space Age Bachelor Pad Music*. Cocktail Nation seemed to be more than a musical genre, though. It was very nearly a lifestyle choice, right down to "the retro-bro look of thrift-store bowling shirts, secondhand wingtips, grandpa's pomade, and, of course, the music," as *A.V. Club* put it. Sartorially and musically, a "slew of backward-glancing outfits like Big Bad Voodoo Daddy, Love Jones, and Cherry Poppin' Daddies peddled a debonair sound tailored toward sipping gin rather than shooting heroin." There were musical nods to the revived ska movement that was popular at the same time. The Coctails were unwillingly swept into the genre, much in the way Labradford were categorized as "post-rock" around the same time. It was a reductive way to categorize an inventive group. Mark Greenberg still chafes at the comparison: "While there was a big push to proficiently recreate seemingly long-lost styles and music with a wink-wink 'we know it's corny' thing, we felt very differently. We were reacting against the slickness and necrophiliac feeling many of these other bands were shooting for. This was an uninteresting plan to us, and it hurt our feelings that we were so easily thrown into that group of bands due to some surface-y and mostly visual details."

Patrick Monaghan, as the label guy, sees the label as "a mixed bag. By the time that really crested, they'd already released all of their studio albums and were well past that schtick.

I saw it as 'no such thing as bad press' and we sold some more of the *Early Hi-Ball Years* CDs."

This was happening at the peak of the Clinton-era "economic boom," when the cigar industry experienced a wild sales boom as movie stars and trendies took to puffing on stogies. It was conspicuous consumption carefully screened behind thrifted clothes and an ironic posture that wasn't too far off from Urge Overkill's libertine rayon fantasies, albeit stripped of distorted guitars and '70s arena rock references. Opposed to the patchy jeans and stringy hair of grunge, the snazzy-looking Cocktail Nation bands also stood apart from what Rafael Anton Isarri perceived as the low-key Chicago post-rock uniform: "Plaid shirts, hoodies and sweater vests—and eyeglasses, I felt like everyone had glasses!"

Carrot Top began working with a duo called the Handsome Family in 1995 by releasing *Odessa*, which had been recorded at Kingsize with Trumfio and Hagler, on CD. Brett and Rennie Sparks had self-released two cassettes, playing what the Italian music chronicler Pierro Scaruffi calls "solemn alt-country infused with a cruel sense of urban alienation." There's a stripped-back and ghostly quality to their music, drawing on the vocal harmonies of the Carter Family and Louvin Brothers, the murder ballad tradition of American country and folk music, Brett Spark's personal experiences with bipolar disorder, and the musical experimentation going on around them in Chicago. Ian Aitch described the 1998 album *Through the Trees* as "the darkest recording to come out of the U.S. this side of death metal." The Handsome Family became the second tent-pole of their label, quickly gaining an audience in and outside of Chicago and ultimately releasing nine albums on the label.

8

london was ridiculous

1997

> At that moment in time in Chicago, there was a lot of really creative shit going on. It was mixing of all these different scenes. I just thought that that was normal, that's what people did in music, but that doesn't happen everywhere.
>
> —*Casey Rice*

By 1997 Urge Overkill and Smashing Pumpkins were each in stasis, and Liz Phair was emmeshed in recording her third album. Veruca Salt had followed a similar path in recording their second album, with sessions taking place in Maui, Hawaii, and additional recording in Chicago and Vancouver under the guidance of the experienced producer Bob Rock, who had worked with Aerosmith, Metallica, Bon Jovi, Mötley Crüe, and other corporate/arena acts. The resulting album, *Eight Arms to Hold You* (a title cribbed from the working title of the Beatles' *Help* movie), is glossy and bombastic. It also peaked at number 55 on the *Billboard* Top 200 charts, although the single "Volcano Girls" did better on the radio, charting in the Top Ten on the Modern Radio and Mainstream Rock charts. Fissures within the band began to show when drummer Jim Shapiro left after recording finished. Nina Gordon quit in early 1998, depriving Veruca Salt of the key songwriting and performing dynamic between her and Louise Post. Gordon admits on the band's website bio, "It was drugs and cheating and all that junk, and the two of us not talking about what was really going on." The great hopes of the Chicago alt-rock scene had all stalled by 1998. The slew of Chicago bands signed by the majors in their wake barely made ripples in the worlds of radio play and retail sales.

Curious music fans were being provided with a wider and wider selection of music to purchase. The "World Music" label had been applied haphazardly to almost any non-North American artist, but the use of it did indicate a growing presence in the marketplace. Steve Ratter describes working at Rhino Records in Los Angeles, where "almost every week we were getting things like Serge Gainsbourg reissues, Buena Vista Social Club, Los Zafiros, the African invasion, etc. It just seemed like that [world music] was searching for and found a whole new, hungry audience."

The members of Tortoise were especially interested in the Brazilian singer-songwriter Tom Zé, backing him on his first North American tour in 1998. Zé had been a member of the dissident tropicalia movement in Brazil in the late '60s and early '70s, along with Jorge Ben, Gal Costa, Gilberto Gil, Caetano Veloso, and the group Os Mutantes. The latter were also a major influence on Stereolab, with an idiosyncratic mix of psychedelic rock, Brazilian rhythms, and political activism against the military dictatorship in their home country that resonated with the English band's musical sensibilities and ideological priorities. Kurt Cobain had asked Os Mutantes to reunite in 1993, to no avail. Plenty of Americans discovered the band's records via imports of Polydor European pressings that Cargo and other distributors brought into the country. By 1996 the Omplatten label had reissued the first three Os Mutantes albums, and the musician David Byrne had released a compilation album on his Luaka Bop label.

Between November 1996 and November 1997, Tortoise were recording their third full-length album at John McEntire's SOMA studio in Chicago. Guitarist Jeff Parker had been fully absorbed into the band, and the resulting album, *TNT*, showed a wider instrumental palette than *Millions Now Living*, beginning with the drum and guitar interplay of the title cut. Chicago jazz musicians Rob Mazurek and Sara P. Smith contributed cornet and trombone, respectively, to the recording, which also featured bassoon and cello. Electronics were subtly mixed into the tracks, but the overt digital splicing of "Djed" did not make a reappearance.

In December 1996, John Corbett reported in the *Chicago Reader* on a quartet in town playing a "massive, merciless beat—bass and drums in hard pursuit of groove" topped with guitars casting "nets of fizzling, distorted, reverbed sound, peppered with little peeping loops and other assorted whizbangs." The band was Frontier, and they often played behind a fog machine-strobe light rig that produced murk, making band members hard to distinguish. One thing was certain: drummer Michael Tsoulos started out from a keen appreciation of reggae drumming and was soon able to replicate the interlocking percussion of drum 'n bass behind the walls of feedback. The first two Frontier albums were issued on a short-lived label called Tug-o-War run by Empty Bottle head honcho Bruce Finkelman. In 2000 the band had a Sunday night residency at the bar, and a discography consisting of four albums and three EPs that ran a stylistic gamut from pure feedback drones to dance beats, as well as numerous self-produced cassettes. Frontier had a limited but enthusiastic set of scenester and musician fans, but their "general reluctance to jump through the hoops rock bands are supposed to" prevented any bigger fanbase from growing, even when the Austin-based Emperor Jones label, with international distribution via Touch & Go, released their fourth album—which happened to be a recording of guitars leaned up against amps and set to feedback. Perhaps not the best introduction for a wider audience.

Connections were being made, projects were being undertaken, and it seemed like strands of musical DNA were combining and reproducing themselves in a nourishing petri dish called Chicago. The influence of Chicago musicians and labels began extending across the Atlantic. Thrill Jockey was able to license releases from the German and Austrian electronic avant-garde with records from Oval, Mouse on Mars, and Microstoria. If any record sums up the international exchange that was going on at the time, it's *Dots and Loops* by Stereolab—released in the fall of 1997. The album was recorded with members of Tortoise and Chicago jazz musicians David Max Crawford, Paul Mertens, Ross Reid, and Jeb Bishop all contributing tracks at John McEntire's SOMA studio in Chicago. In December 1996, Ken Vandermark traveled to Stockholm to record with the AALY Trio for an album on the Swedish Silkheart label. Silkheart had documented some of the music coming out of the southside of Chicago from the Ethnic Heritage Ensemble and Ernest Dawkins's New Horizons Ensemble, as well as a Hal Russell–Joel Futterman Quartet session. Cargo Chicago alumnus Bruno Johnson started the Okka Disk label in 1994 to document the work of Chicago saxophonist Fred Anderson. By 1995, Okka Disk was working with the Swedish saxophonist Mats Gustafsson, who in turn became a regular visitor to the Chicago improvising community.

David Grubbs's collaboration with Jim O'Rourke as Gastr del Sol had begun when, as Grubbs puts it, "We played together in a sludgy improvised jam session. Then he volunteered to be the tape editor/musique concrète auteur for what became Gastr del Sol's *Twenty Songs Less* EP, he and I started playing material from *The Serpentine Similar* and writing new stuff, and it snowballed from there."

Gastr del Sol released four albums and four EPs between 1993 and 1998, culminating in *Camofleur*. Drummer John McEntire was the third active member of the band and contributed his engineering skills and studio. A host of Chicago musicians contributed to the album, layering the instrumental canvas with trombone, cornet, clarinet, French horn, violin, and viola. The record ably mixes experimental textures with folkish, pop-song structures. Joshua Klein noted in *A.V. Club* that some songs "seem to reflect a new cosmopolitan slant," while "Gastr del Sol retains much of its identity thanks to Grubbs' poetic lyrics, linear guitar drones, and languid piano playing." Jim O'Rourke summed up the considerable strengths of Gastr del Sol in a 2018 interview: "There's a lot of so-called 'avant-garde' pop and rock music and I absolutely fucking hate that stuff. It treats the other forms of music as sprinkles that you put on top of things. It's not genuinely integrated into the song writing, it's not integrated into your choice of instruments. But I think what we did was absolutely genuine and was really an honest, true integration of those things, consciously."

Drag City manufactured Dexter's Cigar, a label run by Grubbs and O'Rourke and focused on reissuing lost avant rock, jazz, and electronic masterpieces as well as Grubbs's crucial pre-Bastro hardcore band Squirrel Bait, which had two members who went on to found Slint—Brian McMahan and Britt Walford. Grubbs, O'Rourke, and John McEntire also played and recorded in a revived version of the oddball '60s psychedelic band the Red Krayola and worked with the multimedia artist Stephen Prina. The creative partnership between O'Rourke and Grubbs ended with the release of *Camofleur*. O'Rourke moved to New York City to join Sonic Youth in 1999.

A vocational shift had happened at kranky. By 1996, Joel and I had both left our jobs at Cargo. Joel was able to draw a small salary from the label, which he supplemented by tending bar, and I went to work in the warehouse at Facets Multimedia. We were free of the restrictions of exclusive distribution through Cargo. We kept connected with our friends and colleagues there and were also able to work more closely with the distributors we had built relationships with such as Revolver in San Francisco. The label could sell all our releases to a number of distributors at one price, which helped to make kranky releases more evenly priced in record stores. However, we would have to look a little harder for new bands.

Joel and I were fans of a trio from Duluth, Minnesota, called Low from the time Andrew Beaujon had urged Joel to see them open for his band Eggs at the Empty Bottle in 1994. Low was made up of a guitarist, bassist, and drummer who played using brushes and a simple kit made up of a tom, snare drum, and cymbal. Their slow, deliberate music drew attention to every musical gesture that the group made. Low used silence to great effect, as guitarist-singer Alan Sparhawk told a college newspaper in 1997: "I think there's such a potent emptiness between two events . . . That emptiness between two events is just as important as the events themselves and when you strip time down and focus on it, it can be a very powerful and versatile thing."

Low and kranky had made an early connection when the label advertised in Sparhawk's fanzine *This Town Needs A . . .* Low released three albums and an EP via a label called Vernon Yard, which was manufactured by the major label Virgin and distributed by the heavyweight, quasi-indie Caroline Records distributor. Joel and I would have loved to work with the band, but they were connected to a label that was seemingly better financed and possessed more resources than kranky. After three full-length albums and multiple tours, Low had built an audience and profile, selling more records than some other bands on Vernon Yard who were given higher promotional budgets. But in 1997, Virgin decided to close down the label. Low had been dropped and found themselves without a record label. They were a veteran touring outfit, booked by Tom Windish, with national tours and European shows under their collective belt, spending most of their time "on the road, as usual," as a promotional postcard put it. Joel and I were astonished that another label didn't snap them up immediately. We asked if they would be interested in recording a few songs and offered a modest recording budget. Low accepted and decided to record at home in Duluth. Those recordings were released as a twelve-inch EP and CD called *Songs for a Dead Pilot* in October 1997. Our astonishment continued when bigger labels *still* didn't snap the band up, and kranky was able to release a double album from Low called *Secret Name* in April 1999. At the suggestion of the band, kranky hired a publicity firm called Autotonic to promote the album. Dan Mackta and Vicki Wheeler worked out of Memphis, Tennessee, and having them handle radio and press promotion in coordination with the band's touring boosted Low's profile and sales, as it allowed me to focus on providing venues and local stores on the tour route with promo materials. I could also devote more of my time to working on other kranky releases.

The connection with Low brought another artist to kranky, a singer-songwriter from Toledo, Ohio, named Jessica Bailiff. Her relationship with kranky began via her interactions with Low, whom she had met at a show in Detroit. Jessica had sent recordings she made with Alan Sparhawk to kranky at his suggestion. "When I signed with kranky," she says, "Joel asked if I wanted to use the original four-track recordings I'd sent, or if I wanted to go record somewhere. I knew I wanted to re-record much of what I'd done, plus some new songs. I called Al for advice . . . I told Al I actually wanted to record with him. I was the first 'band' to record at their 20° Below home studio."

That debut recording, *Even in Silence*, was released in June 1998 and was followed by *Hour of the Trace* in 1999, also recorded at 20° Below, and a self-titled album in 2002 recorded at home. Chris Dahlen reviewed *Jessica Bailiff* for *Pitchfork*, writing, "With good songs and inventive arrangements, she made the album taut and precise, turning simple elements into well-realized mood pieces." Bailiff's music, often tagged as "slowcore," found a supportive audience in Europe: "Tours were usually built around one good offer, and every time I broke even or came home with a little bit. There just wasn't a culture for providing hospitality to touring bands in the US like there was in Europe. There was a lot more funding for the arts. But also, there were people that put on shows independently or as collectives, not making anything off the evening, paying for it all out of their pockets, just wanting to bring bands they liked to their town. I felt a kinship with a lot of the bands, promoters, and audience members I met overseas."

A small "music first" network had spread out across the Atlantic, powered by like-minded people. From the perspective of bands, record labels, and promoters operating in more lucrative levels, they may have appeared to be more of a social than commercial effort. Those thin strands were numerous, however.

Ned Raggett summarized Bailiff's work like this: "From her first records in the last gasp of the 1990s, the Toledo, Ohio, songwriter Jessica Bailiff carved out her own space. She's collaborated with Dave Pearce of Flying Saucer Attack, and is, in one sense his U.S. equivalent. Though both touch on slowcore and shoegaze, they are impossible to pin down, playing with any number of other bands; both make songs that range from short piano pieces to 20-minute feedback driven monsters." If she lived in Chicago, would Bailiff have a higher profile as an artist? Joel and I often suggested as much to her. I'd argue that at least she would have had more opportunities to perform and, perhaps, connect with like-minded musicians to perform and tour with.

TAPE HISS MAKES ME HAPPY

From the time we heard *Music for Nitrous Oxide*, the first release from the Austin, Texas, duo Stars of the Lid, Joel and I wanted to sign the band to kranky. The duo had met, as Adam Wiltzie recalled for *XLR8R* magazine in 2003, at the stereo: "When you're at a party in 1990 and you attempt to put on Erik Satie, and everyone just scowls at you—Brian simply smiled." Brian McBride and Adam Wiltzie had passed four-track recordings back and forth between August 1993 and September 1994, "puttering around" and creating grainy drones. McBride recalls one early session: "One of the first times we actually sort of practiced in the same room was at my tiny little duplex in Austin—704b. With some mushrooms in our veins, we both watched the final ending to *Twin Peaks* and then Adam went into my bedroom, and I stayed in my living room, and we got our drone on." The duo's mutual obsessions with director David Lynch would become a hallmark of their work.

Wiltzie fills in the details of how the first CD came out: "I suppose there is a charm in the caveman way those early releases were captured on those little cassette recorders. My four-track recorder was probably the only article of value that I never hocked for money. Everything was captured on those little archaic devices. Brian had a radio show, he mixed four-track tape bits and bobs in and out of records with found samples, and anything else he could find. We were constantly making cassette mixes of his radio show stuff with all of the guitar drones I was making in my house." The tapes circulated, and the duo connected with Rob Foreman, who ran a label called Sedimental. Foreman persuaded McBride and Wiltzie to condense their work into the seventy-minute maximum compact discs could accommodate.

Track titles like "Swell Song" and "Tape Hiss Makes Me Happy" tell you everything you need to know about the band's aesthetic. We were smitten. Joel kept bringing in the CD to Cargo, and the sales staff kept shipping them out. Sedimental released a twelve-inch EP called *Gravitational Pull vs. the Desire for an Aquatic Life* in an edition of 709 white vinyl in the summer of 1996. Joel and I shared a few pints of ale that year with Adam Wiltzie at the Gingerman Tavern in Wrigleyville while he was in town manning the front-of-house sound system for the contempo-psych band Mercury Rev.

Cargo sold all one thousand *Music for Nitrous Oxide* CDs. Wiltzie says, "I was grateful to say the least. I had caught wind that Joel was just starting a label and put out the first Labradford record. (Still one of my favorite bands past or present.) So, when I was almost finished with the core of what would become *The Ballasted Orchestra*, we happened to be passing through the Windy City, so I called him on the phone and said, 'Mr. kranky, do you like tacos?' Our mutual admiration was formed on this evening, and we enjoy spicy food together still, to this day."

A plan was set in motion for the duo to record for kranky after the group's obligations to Sedimental were fulfilled. We couldn't have been happier, as Joel and I both wanted to work with Stars of the Lid as soon as we heard their first CD. Wiltzie tries to untangle the threads of the duo's process of constant recording and mixing: "Exact dates were all a bit blurry, as the *Gravitational Pull* record was sort of sandwiched in with *Nitrous Oxide*, so there were songs that were around in that period, for example "The Artificial Pine Arch Song" [from *The Ballasted Orchestra*], which we recorded back in the spring of '95 as that is the date that is still marked on that cassette tape. By the time we [Wiltzie, Leoschke, and Adams] met in '96 it was finished, so it was only letting go of the final mixes on the DAT tape."

Digital audio tape recorders (DATs, or ADATs) became popular in the mid-'90s for recording bands live, and Adam Wiltzie had borrowed one from an Austin record label. He had found work mixing live sound.

As Brian McBride describes the duo's methods: "Both of us were making bits and pieces on our four-track recorders around maybe '94-'95. 'The Artificial Pine Arch Song' was an outgrowth of the two of us practicing together in the same room. I recorded it on my four-track and of course I played around with the pitch and brought it to Adam. This obviously was our first record on kranky and we were more than excited to be a part of the label. I came up with the record's title, which arguably gave a name to the idea that we were recording underwater music."

In March 1997 the double album *The Ballasted Orchestra* was released on kranky. Mike Shanley wrote in *Discorder*, the magazine run by CiTR radio station at the University of British Columbia, "Adam Wiltzie and Brian McBride, armed with nothing but their guitars and maybe a few effects or samplers, create something symphonic, with long tones that rise up and spin around each other. In their hands, even empty space becomes as much a part of a song . . ." Wiltzie and McBride proceeded to tour, with compatriot Luke Savisky using four film projectors to bathe the band in color and motion. Savisky took found film and library stock to create a constantly changing, improvised light environment. Luke Savisky is, in many ways, the invisible third member of the band, and has, as Wiltzie puts it, "been doing visuals since the very first concert." Brian McBride describes how Savisky gradually became a regular touring member of the group as the visual component of the live Stars of the Lid experience became more defined: "If we'd perform in Austin either opening for a kranky band or having a record release party, he would provide his visual tricks. Sometimes we just played in darkness with a couple of glow sticks thrown on the stage." Savisky started touring with the band "between '97 and '99 . . . we were traveling with all these heavy projectors and his loops and projectors could often break. So, he'd spend hours at every show fixing things . . . there were definitely many spectacular shows, visual shows especially with these almost three-dimensional-looking trees slowly moving across the stage. I always said that Luke's layers essentially provided both something for us to lose ourselves and to play to, which was an extremely great addition."

This guaranteed that what Bill Meyer called a "vertiginous swirl of sound and sight" which changed from night to night would be the hallmark of live performances for Stars of the Lid. As Bill Meyer confirms to this day, "They were a hell of a psychedelic band for a while there when it was the two of them, with the visual and sonic experience." In October 1997, kranky manufactured a compact-disc version of *Gravitational Pull vs. the Desire for an Aquatic Life.*

Magnog's busy performance schedule had prevented any recording sessions. We suggested selecting some music from the original group recording the band sent us on cassette as an interim release. As Jeff Reilly from the band puts it, the double-CD release *More Weather* is "a compilation of stuff we had done on four-track before we recorded the first album, along with some solo noise tracks I recorded to create bridges between the various tracks. It included some of our earliest stuff along with something we recorded right around the time of the first album." Writing for *AllMusic*, Ned Raggett describes the album as "the product of a fine band that knew what it wanted to do and did it well . . . it's clear enough the group enjoyed improvisation in general, but also knew when to stop if nothing more would come of it or needed to be said . . . there are some truly monstrous performances."

SO, WATCH YOUR MAIL

Once kranky became an established label, we began to receive demos in the mail. People and bands mailed recordings to the label in hopes of getting kranky to sign them. There were many, many submissions from people who had no idea of what the label released and couldn't be bothered to try even basic research. Magical thinking exists. But Joel and I decided to listen to everything that arrived, even if a tape could only survive for ten seconds of listening before it was yanked out. Once we left Cargo and access to the latest releases, paying attention to incoming mail became more important. It paid off.

In August 1997, a package from Canada arrived in the kranky post office box. It was from a band in Montreal called godspeed you black emperor! They were looking for a show in Chicago that September. Joel got the package, listened to the cassette that was enclosed, and duplicated it. The album, entitled *F#A#∞*, had just been released in an edition of five hundred LPs as the debut release on a label called Constellation. Then Joel called me up, telling me he had something I needed to listen to. Patti Schmidt from the CBC radio program *Brave New Waves* in Montreal had told me about a band playing underground shows in the city in front of films. I got over to Joel's house after work, took the tape home, and listened. As soon as it was over, I called Joel back. We both agreed to do whatever we could to help the band out. I called Sue Miller at Lounge Ax, and she kindly added godspeed to a show headlined by the New York free-jazz drummer William Hooker in September.

David Bryant, a guitarist in godspeed, mailed the cassette as part of an effort to arrange shows using a musicians' self-help manual called *Book Your Own Fuckin' Life*. As he recalls: "We recorded *F#A#∞* in the spring of '97, duped a bunch of copies on cassette and started booking our first tour. We couldn't find a show in Chicago and were aware of kranky. I think we mailed a cassette using the kranky address from a Roy Montgomery record. The vinyl came out in August of '97 and we hit the road. We had no ulterior motive in mailing that cassette. We needed a show to plug a hole in the routing. I don't think any of us imagined a future beyond that tour."

It took one listen to *F#A#∞* to convince me to agree with Joel that godspeed you black emperor! should be on kranky. The opening monologue on the album, with a laconic voice somewhere between Harry Dean Stanton and Robert Mitchum saying, "The car's on fire and there's no driver at the wheel . . ." sets a mood for the record that never falters. Joel and I were both fans of Savage Republic, a Los Angeles band that mixed Middle Eastern-influenced electric guitars with metal percussion and ritualized performance, and many elements of the godspeed sound reminded us of them. The mix of violin, cello, upright bass, two drum kits, and guitars led us to believe that godspeed you black emperor! had an arsenal at their disposal that could be deployed in many effective ways. The performance we saw in Chicago was visceral and immediate, widening the sound of the album and impressing us with the band's obvious devotion to performing. David Bryant remembers that the Lounge Ax show was the first performance for the band through a club sound system. "It was the first time we played a show through a P.A. Up until that point it was just cranked amps and two loud drummers. I remember clearly, debating with the sound person on the merits of switching the P.A. off. He was super sweet with us though . . . gentle . . . and convinced us somehow. I have no idea how it all sounded in the room."

In many ways I was reminded of a band on Touch & Go: the Butthole Surfers, who also at one time had two drummers, and put an emphasis on live, multimedia performance with a commitment to traveling and playing live. Devotion is what it took;

that first godspeed tour was cobbled together, with the band often camping out as they moved around.

Bryant has many stories from that godspeed odyssey across the East Coast. "Mauro had his car, and we had a 1973 Dodge Tradesman 'family wagon' van which was our main vehicle. We burned through two water pumps, one of which we replaced on the street in front of Joel's house. I remember Chicago fondly for its cheap used auto parts. Replacing a water pump on a '73 Dodge Tradesman is a nightmare, there's very little room to work and you have to remove a symphony of bolts/belts/parts just to get to it. Steph, who was playing violin on that tour, was a decent mechanic and did most of the heavy lifting. We finished just before load in and Steph was completely covered in oil for the show."

You could make a movie. "In Rhinecliff, New York, we played this old railway hotel and stayed at a campsite nearby where we recorded music on an old Marantz cassette recorder. The motor was dying so you could hear the clunk of it through the built-in microphone and the speed oscillating. We also recorded the Blaise Bailey rant with that Marantz on the street outside the club in Providence, Rhode Island. In Long Branch, New Jersey, the family wagon was pulled over and drug dogs were dispatched. A heightened state of paranoia was kicking in at that point and we were stalked by an angry truck driver because we misused our CB radio in the van. In Arlington, Virginia, we played the Galaxy Hut and kept blowing the power. Carter from Labradford came out and gave me an old silver Morley wah pedal I still use."

There were not many people in the Lounge Ax watching the nine-person band that was the first act on a four-band bill. One of them was a former coworker of mine named JulieAnn "Jam" Tidy. She was working at Southern Records in London, and on vacation visiting Chicago. A Touch & Go band called Storm and

Stress were also on the bill that night, and JulieAnn wanted to catch the show: "I arrived at Lounge Ax early and saw the stage full of musicians but hardly anyone else in the venue. I remember being floored—absolutely mesmerized. I sat cross-legged on the floor in the middle of the room, eyes closed and head in my hands immersing myself in the steadily building waves of sound. When they finished, I don't think I ever ran to a merchandise table so fast in my life. Upon purchasing two copies of the *F#A#∞* LP, I bumped into Bruce, who told me that kranky had just signed godspeed for the CD rights. Since the day before Southern and kranky had agreed to a European distribution deal this meant that Southern would be doing the distribution."

Having worked with her, I knew that JulieAnn was a non-stop proponent when a band impressed her. "When I returned to London, I played godspeed to everyone who would listen and key distributors quickly shared my enthusiasm—but everyone agreed we first *had* to book a UK/European tour (which was quite a tall order considering they would need thirteen people and two vans). Unfortunately, tour promoters scoffed at the idea. But Dirk Hugsam in Germany was willing to drop everything to take it on and booked a six-week tour."

The secure, thorough European distribution that Joel and I had long sought came into existence. At Southern I was able to renew acquaintances with Allison Schnackenberg, a label manager I had worked with when I was at Touch & Go, and John Loder, the founder of Southern and a sound engineer who had a central role in the English punk movement in the '80s through his work with bands such as Crass, Rudimentary Peni, and Subhumans.

As pleased as Joel and I were to gain a stable European distribution deal, we also understood that kranky had a relatively low profile in the United Kingdom and Europe. We agreed to a proposal from Southern to manufacture a compilation CD of tracks from kranky releases cleverly entitled *kompilation*, and priced less than a CD single, as an introduction to the label and artists for British and European listeners. It was intended to be a loss leader, with plenty of promotional copies for the distributors in each European nation that Southern worked with, as well as stores, press, and radio. As JulieAnn notes, "John Loder was always impressed with labels that had good business sense and were confident enough to stand behind their product with ample promotional materials and touring. The fact that kranky was willing to do the CD at an extremely low price gained John's full support of the label. The distributors loved *kompilation*, especially as there were ample promo copies, and with a release date just before the godspeed tour the timing was perfect. It was great working with Bruce and Joel because of their no-nonsense approach, professionalism, and their unbridled belief in the music they were doing."

The CD was sequenced to open with "Dead Flag Blues" by godspeed you black emperor! to preview the upcoming CD release, along with tracks from Bowery Electric, Jessamine, Low, Magnog, Windy & Carl, Stars of the Lid, and other kranky releases.

Constellation Records in Montreal had also signed an exclusive distribution agreement with Southern. Southern "delayed Constellation's distribution of other titles and the *F#A#∞* LP to the EU/UK market to coincide with press for the godspeed European tour. Constellation was completely unknown," JulieAnn recalls. The role of the late Dirk Hugsam in taking on godspeed you black emperor! as clients can't be understated. Constellation paid tribute on Facebook: "Through sheer passion, enthusiasm and force of will, he figured out a way to bring over this unwieldy 9-piece group (and their three 16mm film projectors) for a first European tour . . . against all economic and logistical odds." The release of the *kompilation* sampler CD, the godspeed you black emperor! European tour, and distribution of the kranky and Constellation catalogs were beneficial to all involved and an example of the difference that coordinated, effective distribution could make. Constellation sold *F#A#∞* LPs and were able to grow their roster and catalog. For kranky, the ongoing relationship with an established distribution partner meant a greater profile in major markets. In my case, I was able to work closely with my Southern colleagues on kranky releases while concentrating more on US promotion.

The process of touring the United Kingdom for godspeed you black emperor! was far from smooth and brought its own stresses when the band reached the capital. The group's wariness of rock-star celebrity ran smack into the sensationalism and hype cycles of the English weekly music press. Bryant remembers it vividly: "London was ridiculous. At the Garage when we started playing, this wall of white light exploded from the front row: tabloid photographers. I couldn't see my guitar, couldn't play really. It was a total spectacle. We were sitting on fucking chairs! There was nothing to photograph. The insatiable black fucking hole of UK music tabloids at that time was depressing. Battle lines were drawn."

All of this paparazzi-ish action was for a band making their first appearance in London supporting a debut album jointly released by two obscure record labels. Years later, Simon Reynolds ably described the high self-regard and entitlement of the weeklies in *Pitchfork*: "Free from top-down interference, financially buoyant, loyally supported by a huge readership looking to be guided and enlightened, and covering a beat that was the indisputable center of contemporary culture, but also a prism through which one could examine politics or other art forms like film and fiction, the British rock press understandably developed a healthy collective ego—to put it mildly. This self-belief, which applied to each paper on the institutional level but also endowed certain individual writers with a messianic streak, was a self-fulfilling confidence trick. Act like you have the power to steer music in a righteous direction and you can make others believe; soon enough you are steering it."

In the future godspeed would exert more control over when and how their concerts would be covered, especially by the big weeklies, *New Musical Express* (or *NME*) and *Melody Maker*. The attractiveness of the band to the weeklies gave godspeed the leverage needed to dictate at least some terms of coverage. In the future, there would be no flashbulb ambushes.

Mark Nelson from Labradford had been recording on his own under the name Pan•American, releasing a two-song cassette on the small Richmond, Virginia, label Tenderette that Nelson describes today as "seriously under the influence of Henry Mancini and John Barry." Like Lawrence Chandler of Bowery Electric, Nelson had been experimenting with newly affordable sampling technology, in his case the Ensoniq ASR10 sampling keyboard. While working at a record store, Nelson had found that the dub reggae records reissued by the Blood & Fire and Pressure Sounds labels were "tearing the lid off a lot of things for me" and wanted to integrate similar rhythms into compositions, an idea that was "clearly not going to float" in Labradford. He had done some recording at Sound of Music Studios in Richmond, aided by guest appearances by percussionists Chris Gallo and Jim Thompson, and Peter Neff on hammered dulcimer. In the summer of 1997 Nelson moved to Chicago and began working on completing the debut Pan•American record at home.

In 1996, Stars of the Lid had opened for Labradford for a show in Austin, Texas. The Virginians stayed at Adam Wiltzie's house, and the two bands became friends. In 1997, Wiltzie asked the trio if Labradford would like to collaborate with Stars of the Lid for a twelve-inch EP series the Austin-based Trance Syndicate label was releasing called *The Kahanek Incident*. Each group mixed material from the other into a new composition. Bobby Donne created Labradford's track "Texas" using "Cantus: In

Memory of Warren Wiltzie" from *Gravitational Pull vs. the Desire for an Aquatic Life* and "Music for Twin Peaks Episode #30 Part II" and "24 Inch Cymbal" from the vinyl version of *The Ballasted Orchestra*. In turn, Stars of the Lid utilized "Pico," "Battered," and "The Cipher" from *Labradford* and "Disremembering" from *Prazision* to create *Virginia*. This interaction between the two bands continued, with Adam Wiltzie traveling to Europe to mix sound for Labradford in October 1997. After working on *The Kahanek Incident*, Donne suggested more musical collaboration with Wiltzie. The two began trading tapes in the mail, and in May 2000 Donne spent a week with Wiltzie recording at his home studio. What resulted was the *Aix Em Klemm* album kranky released in October 2000.

This was also the year that Andrew Fenchel began presenting shows in Chicago under the Lampo umbrella. As the organization's website puts it: "Rather than making programming decisions around tour schedules, we invite selected artists to create and perform new work for Lampo, and then we help them realize their vision. By design, Lampo produces few projects annually, focusing attention on each one, and making each a distinct experience for the artists and their audience." The series moved around a few places in town, including churches, eventually settling for a good while at a venue called 6Odum for most of the early 2000s. Each show was a special event, and no kranky-connected artists appeared until Dean Roberts played with Chicago percussionists Michael Zerang and Jim Baker and then Glen, Kotche in 2000. Or rather, kranky and Dean Roberts connected after the show. The same happened when Keith Fullerton Whitman and Greg Davis performed together. Lampo hosted many kranky-adjacent musicians working in long-form composition and legendary predecessors to the scene like Phill Niblock. And the concert series drew international attention to Chicago as a place where an audience for adventurous fringe music was ready and waiting to support visitors.

More music arrived in the kranky post office box from James Plotkin and Mark Spybey. Plotkin had been operating on the margins of extreme heavy metal since he had been a member of a band called Old Lady Drivers in 1987, venturing into more abstract musical forms like noise and guitar-based ambient music and playing in bands like avant-garde saxophonist John Zorn's Painkiller and the heavy metal dub band Scorn. Joel and I had both enjoyed a seven-inch single called "Swimming Against" and a CD of solo guitar music called *A Strange, Perplexing*. Plotkin remembers that he had been making loop- and drone-based music for some time: "My earliest ambient, or loop-based recordings were actually done using alto saxophone and trumpet. One day I was riding my bike and found a Delalab delay rack in a dumpster. I had no idea what it did, but I took it home and managed to hook it up to a mic and the four-track. It half-worked and would basically modulate the hell out of any loop you made like a broken tape deck."

Plotkin and Spybey met at a performance in New York in the summer of 1996, where they improvised together underneath the Brooklyn Bridge. Spybey had recorded under the name Dead Voices on Air and was a contributing member of Zoviet France, the mysterious collective whose atmospheric, intricately packaged record albums in the '80s had been a key influence on Joel and me and many kranky artists. Spybey more poetically describes the group as "Music for eyes. Strummers, blowers and beaters. Mixed like concrete. Ethnological forgery of sorts, but well intentioned." James Plotkin remembers, "I think we may have started the recording together, when he was in New York for the show, and continued it afterward." Spybey says, "I was actually introduced to James via a guy who worked for Invisible Records, Josh Diebel. I was asked to fill in at the Anchorage Festival for another Invisible band who had to pull out. I didn't want to do it by myself, so I'd made contact with James. It was an incredible venue. James really is a great improvising guitarist and we enjoyed playing together so we decided to make an album." The process replicated the collaborations musicians were carrying out across the international underground, where nontraditional music venues and performances threw musicians together and record labels were available to release what was produced.

Brent Gutzeit had been performing and recording in Tokyo and later in Chicago in a trio called TV Pow. The group used computers augmented by acoustic instruments and Gutzeit's handmade instruments. They also established links with many Japanese musicians and experimental and noise musicians worldwide. By late 1995 he was living in Chicago and working at Reckless Records, where Joel would put in work hours from time to time. Gutzeit describes how he came to be the first Chicago-based musician on kranky: "I met James Plotkin in Tokyo at a K.K. Null / Jim O'Rourke show. I was living there at the time and Plotkin was on tour. We really hit it off. I gave Plotkin my address and said let's do a mail project. A few months later he sent me a few tracks of guitar stuff, I took those tracks and mixed them along with some of my own sound on a borrowed Tascam four-track and sent it back to him. He remixed those tracks and sent them back to me. We ended up doing that back and forth for about four or five years."

One day at Reckless, Joel told Gutzeit that kranky was preparing a release by Mark Spybey and James Plotkin. Gutzeit mentioned his work with Plotkin and shared "a CDR or maybe it was a tape."

James Plotkin remembers, "I had a handful of kranky releases and knew of bands like Labradford and Bowery Electric—I've always enjoyed that style of slower, unfolding music in general. I was more than happy to have releases on the label, and it was a completely positive experience, which is something you rarely end up with in this business." When Joel made contact, Plotkin told him that the Plotkin-Gutzeit album needed a little fine-tuning. As he says, "We each had two passes and then I did the final mix. It took a while, as it did when projects were tape-based and through the mail." Plotkin passed along the Spybey collaboration, called *A Peripheral Blur*. We decided to release both recordings as CDs, beginning with the Plotkin-Spybey album in November 1998 and the Plotkin-Gutzeit CD, *Mosquito Dream*, in May 1999.

The Plotkin-Spybey recordings were characterized by a unique sound source. Mark Spybey used toys. He says, "I believe that by utilizing things like children's toys, that a.) the playing field is leveled, that we are all given access to making music regardless of acquired skill (which I believe can result in dull or technical music) and that b.) it can result in the creation of intuitive, interesting sounds. Less is often more. I pretty much did all of my work on a four-track cassette tape machine, with contact microphones, one effect unit and a bunch of toys."

Rolk Semprebon wrote in *Anodyne* magazine, "Guitars and toy sounds are processed into totally unrecognizable drones, then layered to create strange ambient soundscapes that achieve a fine balance between intricate and minimal. The title is apt, as there is always a sense that something not quite there is at the periphery of what one is hearing."

The Plotkin-Gutzeit album is also well-named, "one mysterious zoneout of a listen," as Ned Raggett put it. The CD folder artwork says simply, "Guitar deconstructions 1994–1998, designed for low-level listening. *Mosquito Dream* is alive with the hum of sounds that 'no longer resemble their source instruments.'" Chris Twomey wrote in the Canadian magazine *Exclaim!* that "these six deep droning tracks . . . will have your speakers shaking." Both CDs exemplified how affordable home recording equipment gave musicians more time to work on music, unburdened by having to pay for studio time and able to spend the hours they needed to record, edit, trade, record, and edit again. The time eaten up in mailing recordings back and forth via mail evaporated when high-speed Internet became commonplace.

The quantity and quality of cross-referencing musical collaboration in Chicago was increasing exponentially. In the fall of 1997, Jesus Lizard guitarist Duane Denison and drummer Jim Kimball released their third album, *Neutrons*, as DK3 (or the Denison-Kimball Trio) on the Touch & Go side label Quarterstick Records with Ken Vandermark on reeds. In the *Chicago Tribune*, Greg Kot wrote, "The album touches on jazz improvisation, movie-soundtrack texture, rock aggression and avant-garde experimentation without fully embracing any of those genres," noting, "The trio is emblematic of an emerging gray-area of music in the Chicago underground."

In 1997 the British Irdial-Discs label released a four-CD set called *The Conet Project*. The CDs were recordings of numbers stations, the shortwave radio stations of unconfirmed origin used by various nations' intelligence services to transmit coded messages to secret agents. The album is a great example of the outer range of sound recordings getting serious attention at the time. They flew off the Cargo shelves. "Conet" was a mishearing of one of the words on the recordings: the Czech word "konec," or "end" in English.

At the end of 2000, Wilco had completed preparatory recordings for their fourth studio album. A documentary entitled *I am Trying to Break Your Heart* was filmed about the completion of the album and the simultaneous drama around the departure of band members, beginning with drummer Ken Coomer. Michael Krassner of the Boxhead Ensemble, etc. had introduced Jeff Tweedy to Glenn Kotche, and the two performed with Jim O'Rourke under the name Loose Fur in May 2000, eventually recording together. Kotche joined Wilco in 2001 and provided the band with rhythmic flexibility and a spectrum of percussive textures beyond the standard drum kit. As the documentary displays in awkward detail, Tweedy brought on O'Rourke to mix the recordings and dismissed his band partner and audio engineer Jay Bennett.

In 2002, Wilco released *Yankee Foxtrot Motel*, an album which took its title from a numbers transmission on *The Conet Project* and used material from the CD set on two tracks. The cover artwork features the quintessentially Chicago image of the Marina City apartment buildings. There had been considerable back-and-forth over which label would release the album. After some reshuffling of the organizational chart at Warner and the elimination of Reprise Records, Wilco were dropped and negotiated to get the rights to *Yankee Foxtrot Motel* themselves, which was released via another Warners label, Nonesuch, and ultimately sold around 590,000 copies. Was this the point at which Chicago's underground avant-garde connected with guitar rock in the ultimate ouroboros? The publicity surrounding *Yankee Foxtrot Motel* and the movie indicated how Wilco had become *the* Chicago band for many people who didn't necessarily follow the comings and goings of the city's underground scene but were looking for some adventurousness in their rock music. The band and Jeff Tweedy as a solo performer toured and recorded constantly. And it didn't hurt that the profiles of Smashing Pumpkins and Liz Phair had receded.

From 1996 to 1997, the Chicago music scene and record labels had been ludicrously productive. Drag City had released approximately thirty-eight LPs and EPs in that time, not counting numerous seven-inch singles. Thrill Jockey had issued around twenty-four albums and EPs plus twelve-inch singles. Touch & Go had seventeen album credits during the same period, and kranky issued fifteen long-players. Our label was self-funded, and as its part-time employees, Joel and I worked intensely when we had free time. It seemed to us that releasing six to eight albums in a year was the ceiling for the label financially and aesthetically. The arrival of Low and godspeed you black emperor! brought greater sales, and greater need for tour support.

We were putting recordings by Stars of the Lid into production, and Labradford were musically productive. We had plenty to do working with bands from Montreal, Duluth, Austin, and Richmond, and didn't consider working with any Chicago bands or musicians until Brent Gutzeit handed Joel a cassette when they shared a shift at Reckless. A pile of promo CDs, mailing envelopes, shipping tape, and tubs became a permanent feature of my living room as I hauled them up and down the stairs to and from my second-floor apartment. And there were always shows to go to. On any given Saturday night, I had my choice from a multitude of bars and clubs where I was guaranteed to run into any number of people I knew. I could work the room on behalf of the label. I enjoyed living at a remove from Wicker Park and the congregation of movers and shakers there. As I later explained to my girlfriend Annie Feldmeier in an email, I didn't want to live where I would be "surrounded by indie rockers." But it came at a price: getting home from the Empty Bottle via the bus was time-consuming, inconvenient, and sometimes scary. I began looking for a car.

9 an audience hungry to hear what would happen next

1998

In many ways what follows is a typical Chicago story that illustrates how the music scene prospered in nooks and crannies across the city. Richard and Kevin Syska had been running a coffeehouse called Nervous Center on Lincoln Avenue in the northside Lincoln Square neighborhood beginning in 1995. By 1997 they had cleaned up the basement and started hosting shows. Ken Vandermark, who had been hosting performances at a small theater farther south on Lincoln called Lunar Cabaret, where he booked Roy Montgomery's first Chicago appearance, took up Richard Syska's invitation to book a weekly series at Nervous Center. Peter Margasak wrote about what had ensued over three years: "Before long the Nervous Center had become a key venue for the city's experimental music scene, providing valuable stage time for the young free-jazz players who were flocking here as well as an intimate venue in which to witness and interact with European heavies and touring American artists. It also hosted the first shows in Mike Javor's '/bin' electronic-music series. Though spaces like 6Odum, Deadtech, Lula

Cafe, and Myopic Books host similar shows on occasion, the Nervous Center is by far the most consistent of the bunch."

By 2000, the economic growth along the 4600 North block of Lincoln Avenue and a series of tax issues had combined to force the Syskas to close. This ebb and flow of available performance spaces reflected both the inventiveness of musicians and their supporters in creating venues and the gentrification of the city. To top it off, in the 1990s, Chicago city government constantly put a thumb on the scales via arcane regulations and tax preferences to favor big music promoters and real estate developers.

The smaller venues offered an experience that was different than jostling through crowded rock clubs. You could bring in a nonalcoholic drink, or buy a cup of coffee, and sit down and focus on listening. Decoupled from the consumption of alcohol, these spaces had a different feel. The promoters were differently motivated. Whether it was high-energy free jazz, abstract electronics, or long-in-developing drones, many musicians needed places to play beyond the Lounge Ax or Empty Bottle, and sometimes there were spaces and organizations that accommodated them.

The best feature of alternative venues like theaters, the basements of coffee houses, and churches was that they were smoke-free. The dangling cigarette has been the epitome of cool for the rock 'n roll performer and audience member alike for a long time. It's hard to believe more than a decade after Chicago banned indoor cigarette smoking in 2005, but I often came home after a night out with my clothes reeking from a combination of sweat and tobacco. And beer, which obviously had been spilled on me by someone else. The Lounge Ax or Empty Bottle could fill up with cigarette smoke quickly. A hot summer night would make shows doubly gross. People would head out between sets to escape the smoke, even on the coldest nights. I established a laundry regimen then that lasts to this day: wash clothes for the weekend on Friday morning and then wash the sweaty, smoky remains on Monday. Ron Mather confided that he adopted a similar obsession, concerned that the stink of the clothes he wore to hardcore and metal shows would seep into the rest of his wardrobe if not immediately cleansed.

The math had worked out in many ways for Chicago's musicians, at least those on the northside, who could play some variation of rock music and align themselves with independent labels. The number of recording studios had increased significantly since the late 1980s. Any of these studios was capable of recording music for release on a major label. As we've seen, in the mid-1990s there were talent scouts aplenty circulating through the clubs and record stores in Chicago. In 1997, Steve Albini had moved his studio out of his house and relocated to a custom-built two-studio complex. Idful had spun off SOMA, and Kingsize was busy. At Loose Booty, Brendan Burke had mixed and cleaned up a number of recordings for Roy Montgomery, one set of which kranky released as *Temple IV* in 1995, recorded numerous Ken Vandermark projects, and recorded part of the debut Wickerman album for the Hollywood label, a subsidiary of Universal. The latter band featured two of my coworkers at Cargo.

The London-based Reckless Records had opened a store in Lincoln Park in 1989 and expanded into Wicker Park in 1994. Musician and Reckless clerk Brent Gutzeit notes that the store played "an important part of the music scene, it not only provided jobs for musicians, but provided a meeting place for musicians and music lovers to interact on a personal level. Reckless is responsible for the formation of a lot of bands." In May 1995 my former Kaleidoscope colleague, Charlie Edwards, opened the Quaker Goes Deaf close by a second Reckless store in Wicker Park on North Avenue. There were numerous other stores in the city and near suburbs, but these stores located at major intersections by train stations and bus lines in two dense neighborhoods were focal points. Michael Krassner worked for 2nd Hand Tunes, a small chain with several locations on the northside of Chicago and Evanston: "I primarily bounced between the Clark Street location and the Lincoln store. There were a lot of great stores in that neighborhood back then like Reckless, Hi-Fi, Dusty Grooves, and others. Each store had their own ethos and covered certain niches."

Two active clubs, Lounge Ax and the Empty Bottle, were booking multi-band shows at least six nights a week, specialized in underground music of all stripes, and could accommodate about three hundred people each. A constantly expanding and contracting group of smaller venues hosted more esoteric acts. Metro held about twelve hundred people for bands with larger draws and often put local bands on bills supporting touring groups. There were occasional shows in nontraditional venues like the ornate public library that was converted into the Chicago Cultural Center, or on-campus spaces in Hyde Park or Evanston.

Chicago had three free-form college radio stations in WNUR, WHPK, and WZRD operating out of Northwestern University, the University of Chicago, and Northeastern Illinois University, respectively. Each had specialty shows focused on punk or heavy metal or reggae or electronic music, and live shows where bands could play in the studio. Johnny Mars would regularly trawl the Cargo warehouse looking for new records to play on the mainstream-ish station WXRT, where he would spice up a set by playing some left-of-center music or the latest single from the United Kingdom.

The infrastructure was solid. All the organizations listed, with the exception of the radio stations, also provided gainful employment for musicians and music enthusiasts. The radio stations provided airtime for music enthusiasts like the writer and impresario John Corbett and trained cohorts of students that would enter the music workforce in Chicago.

Chicago had its versions of the free alternative newspapers that had sprouted in the 1960s across the United States. Collectively they had stepped into the void of entertainment and cultural coverage that daily papers ignored. There were two weeklies that covered underground music and had wide enough circulation to make a measurable impact. The *Chicago Reader*, founded in 1971 and the most prominent, was a must-have for finding concert and movie listings in the days before the Internet. Bill Wyman's interests in the rising, would-be stars of the Chicago scene drew attention and inspired pushback. Wyman's musical interests were given away by the title of his column: "Hitsville." In defense of his viewpoint, Wyman has written, "I didn't think groups should get brownie points for being local. Music was music, and I held local acts to the same standard I did national ones." Wyman's role as an editor meant that this ethos was also applied to other writers who proposed or "pitched" record reviews or bands for coverage. Bill Meyer recalls how Wyman dismissed one of his pitches, saying, "Oh, that's nice, but we don't want too much of that Tim Adams music," referring to the owner of the popular Ajax Records mail-order service. Those of us who saw the *Reader*'s ad sheets and understood how much money local clubs and record stores were spending to advertise bills made up of mostly local musicians can be forgiven if we were not impressed with this attitude. Labels would often join local or chain record stores in co-op ads. A label would provide free goods as its contribution toward the expense of a record store advertisement. It was one way to alert people to upcoming shows, or in-store appearances. Although we didn't do this much at kranky, we did it enough to know that ads in the *Reader* were not cheap and that clubs like Lounge Ax or Empty Bottle and record stores like Reckless were spending significant money there every week. By 1986 it was estimated that the *Reader* made about $6.7 million yearly in revenue. All of that came from classifieds and display ads. The abstract principle of separation of editorial and advertising functions at newspapers didn't mean much from our perspective. It was strongly felt by many that the Chicago music community deserved more and better coverage from the *Chicago Reader*.

That did happen eventually. Wyman, managing editor Alison True, and editor-in-chief Michael Lenehan collectively decided in 1993 to invite Peter Margasak, then publishing a wide-ranging fanzine called *Butt Rag*, to contribute music reviews. A Margasak column called "Spot Check" followed, and by 1995 he was a full-time writer at the weekly. Margasak's column evolved into "Post No Bills" and topped the weekly music listings section. In July 1996, Kiki Yablon came to the *Reader* as music editor, and the quantity of coverage gradually improved as more space was given to music. The *Reader* had always emphasized quality writing in all its coverage. Bill Meyer recalls that True and then Yablon were "really rigorous. It was like a graduate course in writing." Writers like Monica Kendrick, beginning in 1996, and Meyer from 1992 onward, had more column space for reviews and previews in the paper, which worked to the benefit of kranky and other independent labels in town as a wider range of music got covered.

NewCity was a relative latecomer, founded in 1986 by Brian and Jan Hieggelke. It was streamlined compared to the *Reader* and was a launching pad for the work of underground cartoonist Chris Ware. Music coverage was confined to one column a week, but music critic Ben Kim often took notice of peripheral music like the sort kranky released and wrote about it in print. It came out a day earlier than the *Reader*, which, along with an easier-to-access size, often made *NewCity* the weekly I'd pick up for movie and music listings. *NewCity* also published a yearly feature ranking who they thought were the most important music-related personages in the city. Each yearly summary would begin with an apologia for restricting the rankings, as if the editorial staff were kidnapped and forced to write the feature. Which was supported, of course, by full-page ads from various major labels congratulating their winners. Cheesy though it was, the yearly list did emphasize Chicago's central place in the music business firmament.

Even the daily papers were covering interesting music. Greg Kot began writing for the *Tribune* in 1990 and Jim DeRogatis started at the *Sun-Times* in 1993. Both took an active interest in the local scene and in bands coming through town. I showed a little tough love to DeRogatis when he called to ask for a free copy of the first Labradford record. Two hours earlier that day Joel and I had been eating lunch at Jim's Grill while dissecting DeRogatis's review of a live show by Heart with some consternation. I asked him to give Labradford some coverage before I put him on the mailing list for free CDs. He recalls our first phone conversation when I told him that he would have to prove his worthiness: "That's cool. I can always get rid of my third copy of the Stone Temple Pilots. I'll trade that in. I came from this world (of fanzines and independent labels). I'm having to cover Britney Spears and Bruce Springsteen, and Labradford and I got no problem with that. There's a lot of bad things about being a daily newspaper critic like having to review a Britney Spears concert. But the freedom that could come with writing record reviews for Sunday and it's got to be Bruce Springsteen, but I am also putting in kranky, or Thrill Jockey, or Bloodshot releases, because I'm interested in everything."

As Bill Meyer, who came to write for the *Chicago Tribune*, notes, "I can remember Greg Kot writing about Peter Jefferson and Alistair Galbraith in 1993 when they first came here. Greg was engaging that stuff with the same seriousness as what he wrote about Michael Jackson." Kot came to music writing from a background in newspaper journalism, which informed his commitment to cover what he saw as newsworthy musical happenings in Chicago.

EVERYBODY WAS JAMMING WITH EACH OTHER

There was something about the Chicago music scene that is harder to quantify, but definitely existed: an attitude of mutual support and aid. When I worked at Kaleidoscope, my coworkers were in bands like Eleventh Dream Day and the Jesus Lizard. At Cargo, many of the employees were in bands and would show up at each other's shows to lend support. This was, to some extent, an inheritance from the early days of the hardcore punk rock circuit, when bands had to depend on each other to organize and pull off shows. I had seen the ethos in action when I roadied for Laughing Hyenas and saw how they coordinated with the Milwaukee band Die Kreuzen to perform together in weekend shows across the Midwest. This do-it-yourself, or DIY, approach worked for sound engineers like Steve Albini and John McEntire who had begun as musicians. As David Trumfio puts it, "Touring and meeting other people on a similar path was very important to keeping my focus. Being a musician is and was essential to being a successful engineer and/or producer in my opinion. You have to have that perspective to know how to relate to the people you're recording." As groups returned to Chicago from touring, they offered reciprocal aid to bands they played with in other cities. Tortoise provided space in their loft to Stereolab, and Carter Brown from Labradford sold equipment to Douglas McCombs from Tortoise. In Chicago, musicians performed and recorded together, crossing over genre boundaries to interact. Tom Windish summarizes it by saying, "It wasn't like the Touch & Go people couldn't be friends with the Drag City people or the Wax Trax! people couldn't be friends with the Bloodshot people." Brent Gutzeit, who came to Chicago from Kalamazoo, Michigan, in late 1995, describes the scene: "Everybody was jamming with each other. Jazz dudes playing alongside experimental / noise musicians, punk kids and no wave folks. Ken Vandermark was setting up improv and jazz shows at the Bop-Shop and Hot House. Michael Zerang set up shows at Lunar Cabaret. Fireside Bowl had punk shows as well as experimental stuff. Lounge Ax always had great rock shows. Empty Bottle used to have a lot of great shows. I set up jazz and experimental shows at Roby's on Division. Then there was Fred Anderson's Velvet Lounge down on the southside. There were underground venues like ODUM, Milk of Burgundy, and Magnatroid where the no wave and experimental bands would play. Even smaller independent cafés like the Nervous Center in Lincoln Square and Lula Cafe in Logan Square hosted experimental shows. There was no pressure to be a 'rock star' and nobody had big egos. There was a lot of crossover in band members, which influenced rock bands to venture into the outer peripheries of music, which provided musical growth in the 'rock' scene."

Ken Vandermark breaks down the resources and people who made Chicago such an exciting city to be in: "A combination of creative factors fell into place in Chicago during the mid-'90s that was unique to any city I've seen before or since. A large number of innovative musicians, working in different genres, were living very close to each other. Key players had been developing their ideas for years, and many were roughly the same age—from their late twenties to early thirties. A number of adventurous music journalists, also in the same age group, were starting to get published in established Chicago periodicals. People who ran the venues who presented the cutting-edge music were of this generation too. Music listings for more avant-garde material were getting posted effectively online. All of this activity coalesced at the same time, without any one individual 'controlling' it. And there was an audience hungry to hear what would happen next, night after night."

Bill Meyer sees this cooperative spirit from the independent scene of the mid-1990s in present-day Chicago: "I describe it as an act of collective will. This thing exists because it does not exist in this way, anywhere else in the world. What we have now are people who really want to get together. They will rehearse each other's pieces and they will be in each other's bands. They don't resent each other's successes. If you go to New York, there's a lot of people doing things, but there's also a lot more hierarchy involved. You don't have that here. And I think that to some extent, the Touch & Go aesthetic imported over into the people who came after Ken Vandermark and were very attentive to that kind of thing."

In Chicago, 1998 was a year of significant releases from Tortoise, Gastr del Sol, and the Touch & Go edition of the Dirty Three's *Ocean Songs*. The latter was an Australian band made up of violinist Warren Ellis, drummer Jim White, and guitarist Mick Turner. Their fourth album was recorded in Chicago by Steve Albini and is one of the most accurately titled ever. *Ocean Songs* ebbs and flows with the trio's interplay and became very popular with rock fans who may have been familiar with the Touch & Go label but were otherwise unenthusiastic about the new bands in Chicago. In performance, the Dirty Three were dynamic, with Ellis being particularly charismatic. White moved to the city and contributed to the Boxhead Ensemble and numerous recording sessions. Drag City released Gastr del Sol's *Camofleur*, solo records from Grubbs, and a triple-LP/double-CD compilation of Stereolab tracks called *Aluminum Tunes*. Thrill Jockey were channeling the Tortoise *TNT* album through Touch & Go Distribution.

The Chicago scene was producing an incredible range of music. Lisa Bralts-Kelly observes that unlike earlier in the decade, when groups moved to Seattle to make it as grunge stars, "Nobody came to Chicago to sound like Smashing Pumpkins or Liz Phair." And unlike centers of the "industry" like New York City and Los Angeles, prone to waves of hype that focused on a few bands, as occurred with the Strokes beginning in 2001, a multitude of Chicago bands could develop, connect with supportive labels, and build an audience.

In August 1998, Minty Fresh Records released the second album, *Plano*, from the Aluminum Group, a band organized around Frank and John Navin. Gail O'Hara would later describe the brothers in *Chick Factor* fanzine as "two foxy fags from Chicago with a penchant for soft rock, Mies, and Prada." The brothers named their band after a line of postwar modernist furniture designed by Charles and Ray Eames, and the album is named after the Illinois town where modernist architect Mies van der Rohe built his famous Farnsworth House, featured on the cover artwork. Recorded by David Trumfio and Mike Hagler, with guest appearances from Chicago musicians Sally Timms, Liz Conant, and Susan Voelz, *Plano* was one in a series of arch and artful albums that, as the *Advocate* put it, merged "the smooth retro romance of easy listening with the uneasy futurism of avant-garde rock." The Aluminum Group would go on to record albums with Jim O'Rourke and John Herndon engineering and collaborate with members of Tortoise and the Sea and Cake. Informed by the Navin brothers' queerness and sense of style, the Aluminum Group stood out in a scene of straight guys clad in flannel, Carhartt jackets, and work boots.

The trip that Braden King had taken to Alaska resulted in a documentary film, codirected with photographer Laura Moya, called *Dutch Harbor: Where the Sea Breaks Its Back*, released in 1998. Michael Krassner describes the process of creating the soundtrack for the film in the summer of 1996 with a group of musicians that came to be called the Boxhead Ensemble: "My coworker at 2nd Hand Tunes Scott Rutherford put on the new Gastr del Sol record *Upgrade and Afterlife*. This was EXACTLY what I was looking for, knocked the wind out of me. At the time I never had heard anything like it, cold and beautiful. Unsentimental music. Austere."

Krassner started contacting musicians, beginning with David Grubbs and Jim O'Rourke and roping in guitarist Charles Kim and Ken Vandermark. His friend Kurt Kellison of Atavistic

Records connected Krassner to Rick Rizzo and Douglas McCombs from Eleventh Dream Day. The assembled group recorded the soundtrack to the film in less than a day, combining and recombining into different groupings while the film was projected on the side of the studio wall. Krassner sees that July 1996 session as a mile marker: "Surprisingly, most of the musicians had never played with each other up to that point. I think the Chicago music scene was just at the precipice of really breaking down the walls and exploring and mixing up all genres."

The Boxhead Ensemble expanded to include their Truckstop comrade Joe Ferguson, plus David Grubbs, Charles Kim, Douglas McCombs, Jim O'Rourke, David Pavkovic, Rick Rizzo, and Ken Vandermark for the purpose of improvising music to accompany film showings. The resulting soundtrack, including a contribution from Will Oldham called "Ebb's Folly," was released on a CD by Atavistic in 1997. The Fiftieth International Film Festival describes *Dutch Harbor* as an "atmospheric black-and-white documentary that consciously moved away from the usual documentary form" where "music provides a major contribution to the unusual and icy mood of the film."

Braden King notes, "I met or initially encountered a lot of the musicians who ended up on the *Dutch Harbor* soundtrack through my involvement with Atavistic and Touch & Go but also through our friends at the other studios—Idful, Kingsize. It all felt very noncompetitive and open." The Boxhead Ensemble became an ongoing project, touring the United States and Europe to accompany film screenings with a rotating lineup. King and Astria Suparak eventually co-curated a program of existing and new short films created specifically for the Ensemble to perform alongside. Michael Krassner describes the touring group as "a really different animal. I have no idea whose idea it was to tour with the film. *Dutch Harbor* and its soundtrack garnered some attention, primarily due to all the attention the Chicago scene was getting at the time. By then the music was becoming wilder, with more of a focus on American folk music and less of a modern classical feel. It was a complete mess but a lot of fun."

The attention these performances and screenings received across the country and in Europe may have inspired the creation of a reality television show set in Dutch Harbor called *Deadliest Catch*. The program has been hosted by the Discovery Channel for sixteen years since 2005.

Cornetist Rob Mazurek had been the locus of several groups playing under the Chicago Underground heading. Drummer Chad Taylor and Mazurek made up the Chicago Underground Duo, bassist Noel Kupersmith rounded out the Chicago Underground Trio, Jeff Parker added guitar to make up the Chicago Underground Quartet, and the Chicago Underground Orchestra with bassist Chris Lopes and trombonist Sara P. Smith added to the combination. The larger group scored a set on the summer 1997 Chicago Jazz Fest main stage and released a CD called *Playground* on the Delmark label in February 1998. Later that year Thrill Jockey issued a CD by the Duo recorded at WNUR, the Lunar Cabaret, and the loft of ace film projectionist James Bond, and a Trio recording came out on Delmark in early 1999. Mazurek was working with "two very interesting labels" simultaneously: "I think audiences were somewhat similar because like the musicians, the listeners and critics were also right there together wanting to experience some new sonic alchemy. Delmark has a more traditional feel perhaps, but they were also seminal figures in bringing early AACM and other avant-garde musics to the people. Thrill Jockey is more from the experimental rock/electronic music side with forays into free jazz and other genres. Both were important conduits for the music."

In February, Drag City released the final Gastr del Sol album, *Camofleur*. It demonstrated the range of collaborators and instrumental voices that David Grubbs and Jim O'Rourke could call on, including Chicago-based improvisational jazz musicians Jeb Bishop on trombone, Ken Vandermark on saxophone, Rob

Mazurek on trumpet, drummer Steve Butters, and vocals by an enchanting country singer discovered by Drag City named Edith Frost. Austrian electronicist Markus Popp, aka Oval, added his manipulative skills. Grubbs and O'Rourke had been performing and recording constantly since 1994. As Grubbs puts it, "Jim exuded confidence as an improviser, and we learned a huge amount from him. It also blew my mind when we started playing with folks like Mats Gustafsson; it really took me some time to understand that he and others with jazz and free-improvisation backgrounds were genuinely interested in what we were doing. I think that I had a sense of improvisation as this kind of no-turning-back practice: why would they be interested in a group that still primarily played written material?"

The use of melodic repetition in *Camofleur* paralleled what Labradford had developed beginning with their self-titled album in 1996. Both groups were incorporating varied instrumental voices, although Labradford were not interested in improvisation in the same way as Gastr del Sol, and were less likely to cut and splice tape together. What Labradford had been doing was balancing precise sounds and melodies with immersive and overwhelming drones, while Gastr del Sol incorporated rhythmic elements. Both groups were pushing the boundaries of the song structurally and texturally.

Early in the year kranky released the debut, self-titled Pan•American album. A *Puncture* magazine review noted that the album's "coiled, conserved energy dub rhythms don't obscure the delicacy and expressiveness of the underlying structure. While radiant, liquid guitar motifs trace delicate patterns across the surface, the adaptive and limber rhythm tracks add necessary tension and cohesion." Mark Nelson moved from Richmond to Chicago shortly after the album was released.

Once he had settled in Chicago, Nelson was able to play out locally as well as interact with local musicians and engineers. Within a few years he had recorded a second Pan•American album with the aid of mixing by Casey Rice and guest performances by Rob Mazurek on cornet and vocals from Alan Sparhawk and Mimi Parker of Low. As Mazurek describes his role in the "360 Business / 360 Bypass" album sessions, "I remember very pleasant experiences with Mark Nelson and Casey Rice making that recording . . . laid back and cool . . . free. Everything I made back then was with the intention of projecting my own sound at the time. If someone was crazy enough to ask me to do something, I would tell them, 'I will give you all I have, but I will give you me, not something already perceived in your head' . . . and it worked out well I think." A number of split-single and single releases from Pan•American also began appearing on labels from across North America and Europe.

In September 1998, kranky released the third and final album from Jessamine, prophetically entitled *Don't Stay Too Long*. Access to their own studio, Magnetic Park, and a decreased touring schedule allowed the band to tighten up their songs. Years later, writer Willcoma described album tracks on the Tiny Mix Tapes website as "a cold hard diamond, wrapped in miles of black silk. Call this space-funk prog, or whatever you want."

SOMETIMES, JUST DRIFTING ALONG . . .

The term "Label Supremo" fits Paul Smith to a tee. Assisted by Pat Naylor, he had crowbarred the entry of American post-hardcore noise bands Big Black, Sonic Youth, and the Butthole Surfers into the English underground's consciousness in the mid- and late '80s. His attention fell on Labradford in the mid-'90s after hearing some tracks from *A Stable Reference* on Donal Dineen's *Here Comes the Night* radio program in Ireland.

At that point in time, kranky releases were exported to the United Kingdom by Cargo Chicago and other American distributors, and the label did not have an exclusive distribution agreement with anyone overseas. The licensing arrangement with Flying Nun had come to an end with the demise of the label's London office. The original kranky-Labradford contract had been limited to two albums, and all subsequent agreements were based on a handshake. So, just as kranky did by contracting with godspeed you black emperor! to press CDs, Paul Smith saw an opportunity and took it. Labradford and kranky would continue working together in the North American market. Joel and I saw a higher profile for Labradford in Europe and the United Kingdom, especially in the weekly English press that had an influence on many Americans, as being good for sales in North America. Blast First also arranged to issue the first two Pan•American albums.

The group had agreed to have Blast First distribute their third, self-titled album. But touring the United Kingdom had been difficult for Labradford. Paul Smith came up with an idea: "I was working a good bit with David Sefton, then head of contemporary music at London's prestigious Southbank Centre. He was broadly of my musical generation and equally importantly had, like myself, a 'northern' mind-set of chippyness toward any establishment. He was keen, nay driven, to present 'rock' music in the setting of one of London's leading 'culture-bunkers.' In 1998 he generously let me try out a *Labradford's First Annual Festival of Drifting*.

"The band were open to any idea that didn't involve six weeks in a tour van. The 'drifting' bit was a suitable adjective, descriptive of the band's musical effect, but once attached to a repositioning of the 1966 Situationist 'cowboy' graphic (which was on my radar as it had been more recently folded into Malcolm McClaren/Vivienne Westwood's punk ethos) gave the whole notion a bit more edge, and just as importantly kept us all away from any kind of New Age-ness."

A performance by Bang on a Can of Brian Eno's *Music for Airports* was included to pass the Southbank Centre's sniff test.

Smith's comments regarding the classical music world and ambient music accurately describe one of the challenges of the time in promoting music that straddled so many categories. Suffice it to say that Labradford playing at the Southbank Centre was a foot in the door. As was a show at a disused synagogue in Whitechapel, East London, where the trio played with "no electricity, just candlelight and history," as the *NME* observed. The opening was too narrow in space and time for the reluctant Virginians to force their way in. But the door would open a bit more for Stars of the Lid as their music gradually incorporated a wider sound palette and the duo worked to gain access to a greater variety of performance venues, especially in Europe.

I made the trip to London for that first Drifting Festival, taking the opportunity to meet with colleagues at Southern Records and then basking in the presence of Brian Eno himself at the Southbank Centre. Backstage, Eno told Labradford's Mark Nelson that his guitar playing was like "Duane Eddy playing Erik Satie." Eno didn't bother to stick around to see the band's actual performance, however. I had more fun quaffing a few after the show with Labradford, Smith, noise musician Russell Haswell, and a personal idol: Bruce Gilbert, guitar player for art punk pioneers Wire. A day or so later I ran into Jim O'Rourke at an after-hours bar run out of a Turkish snookers club. Misty, ale-colored memories.

The year 1998 proved to be one marked by successes that would eventually enable the kranky owners to work full-time on the label. In 2019, *The Current* public radio program website detailed how, by 1999, CD sales had reached their peak, with people "buying the highest proportion of a single format of music that had ever been tracked before. The compact disc was not only the most popular format, but for a brief period of time it was the *only* format people were purchasing." On the underground level, vinyl was still selling, but CDs were the bread and butter for most labels.

By the late '90s, many of the challenges that came with the smaller packaging for CDs were overcome. Sheila Sachs designed album art for many Chicago labels and describes the shift to CDs: "It was a difficult transition for the designer going from twelve inches down to four—a lot less impact! I think it took a while for everyone to adjust—and then the CD packaging really flourished." Joel and graphic designer Craig McCaffrey worked with our CD manufacturer on cardboard envelope-styled CD booklets so that many kranky CDs were not packaged in plastic jewel boxes. This gave more flexibility to designers and had the added bonus of saving the label money on shipping. The layout was so successful that the CD plant offered it as a packaging option for their other clients.

At kranky, we had the good fortune of adding Low to the label roster. They brought a significant audience with them and a devotion to touring that expanded their fanbase. Labradford were at their creative peak. Stars of the Lid were working on what would become their magnum opus. The addition of one band to the roster turbo-boosted label sales and ultimately meant that Joel and I could make kranky our full-time vocation.

Newly signed godspeed you black emperor! had authorized a CD version of *F#A#∞* as the first album in a two-album deal. They revisited the material and recorded more with Daryl Smith at Chemical Sound in Toronto. The CD, with a new song called "Providence" and some songs reordered from the original LP to use the CD's extended length to best effect, was released in June 1998 to immediate acclaim. My trip to London included a stop at Southern Records, which carried Dischord and Touch & Go Records titles and distributed them via a division called Southern Records Distribution to Europe and the United Kingdom. Having witnessed the first godspeed concert in Chicago, JulieAnn (Jam) Tidy had returned to London spreading her unalloyed enthusiasm about what she had seen and heard to her English colleagues. Southern and kranky had made a distribution agreement for every title excluding the Labradford albums that Flying Nun UK had previously licensed from kranky. Eventually, Southern would pick up the first two Labradford albums when Flying Nun, being absorbed with their own problems, made no effort to keep them.

WE WERE PROUD AND SHY MOTHERFUCKERS, AND WE ENGAGED WITH THE WORLD THUSLY

As we prepared godspeed's *F#A#∞* CD for release, I had a discussion with the band about how I would go about promoting their record. This was my customary process that included arranging a publicity photo, talking about the recording and how it would be represented in a band biography and press release, and seeing if an artist had any supporters in the press or college radio that they wanted to make certain would get a pre-release, promotional CD. godspeed you black emperor! had a very specific set of requirements. They did not want a press photo of the full group, relenting after my pleading by providing a hazy shot of an undetermined group of people walking down train tracks. The band would not do any interviews. In 2012, godspeed you! black emperor outlined their rationale behind this approach to the *Guardian*: "We started making this noise together when we were young and broke—the only thing we knew for sure was that professional music-writers seemed hopelessly out of touch and nobody gave a shit about the shit we loved. We knew that there were other people out there who felt the same way, and we wanted to bypass what we saw as unnecessary hurdles and find those people on our own. We were proud and shy motherfuckers, and we engaged with the world thusly. Meaning we decided no singer, no leader, no interviews, no press photos. We played sitting down and projected movies on top of us. No rock poses."

The band's perspective made sense to me. They were an instrumental collective, making musical and business decisions as a group. Joel and I had operated kranky as a music and artists first label, and we agreed to promote the CD as the band wanted. We were going to do things the band's way as much as we could. Over the course of my experience promoting music at Touch & Go and kranky, I had experienced more than a little frustration trying to pry band photos from musicians or pestering musicians to follow up on interview requests. A photo of people, any people really, suited my purposes. The process of promoting music is a playground for the passive-aggressive, with many an opportunity for heel dragging and prevaricating by musicians who really don't want to promote themselves for whatever reason. I respected godspeed for stating what they would not do up front. And I had a suspicion.

Just as they had told Joel and me when we first agreed to release their music on CD, godspeed you black emperor! began touring North America in 1998. Between the two of us, Low's booking agent Tom Windish got a copy of the CD accompanied by some strong recommendations. The band opened a Montreal show for indie rock barometer Sonic Youth in May, undertook an East Coast tour in August and September, and devoted October to opening for Low. Windish had come around. Picking up an opening spot with a larger band is a strategy many bands have adopted as a way of exposing themselves to a large audience. There are many examples in rock lore of it backfiring. That would not be the case for godspeed. The two bands often performed Low's "Do You Know How to Waltz?" together. As we suspected, opening for Low and performing in front of people who would listen with open minds was a perfect setting for a relatively unknown nine-person band from Montreal. The audiences were impressed, and the word spread. The October 10 performance at Schubas in Chicago had a long waiting line before doors opened, a new thing for Joel and me to witness as the owners of the label working with both bands. Tom Windish was at the show with Bernie Bahrmasel, an astute observer of the Chicago music scene, who recalls to Windish, "We were at the show at Schubas when they opened for Low and I loved them and told you they would be bigger than Tortoise . . . I remember you thinking I was overblowing it with praise . . . but you liked them as well." The night's Low performance concluded with a thirty-minute joint performance by the two bands.

In November godspeed crossed the Atlantic to play more shows in the United Kingdom and Europe. The staff at Southern Records and their partners in Europe had more chances to see what the fuss was about. An English booking agent named Barry Hogan quickly agreed to work with the band.

godspeed were getting plenty of attention despite the lack of interviews in magazines and the absence of an official, staged publicity photo. For one thing, the sheer size of a nine-person band on stage was a bit of a novelty for indie rock audiences. The lineup had stabilized into one of Effrim Menuck, Mike Moya, and Dave Bryant on guitars, Marco Pezzente and Thierry Amar on bass guitars, drummers Adrian Girt and Bruce Cawdron, violinist Sophie Trudeau, and Norsola Johnson on cello. As a performing unit, they could not be ignored, with wave after wave of drums and strings building crescendos that were as powerful as any heavy metal band. The people who attended a godspeed you black emperor! performance knew who the band was by the end of the show. As I suspected, as people raved about the band's performances, the interest of writers and publications in the band grew exponentially. Being denied direct contact with the band via interviews made godspeed that much more alluring. This was especially true in England, where the band compelled writers from the powerful weekly papers to show up on time for their shows to claim their free tickets at the box office, or risk losing them to any punter who was willing to show up and pay for them. The effect was Pavlovian.

In March 2020, Mark Richardson revisited *F#A#∞* in an extended review for *Pitchfork*: "Godspeed's avoidance of the trappings of the music industry only enhanced their prophetic aura in the year after the release of *F#A#∞*. They issued no photos, sold no t-shirts, and gave very few interviews. Given all the mysteries surrounding the record itself, and the openness to interpretation of the mostly instrumental music, that contextual void left a lot of room for the imagination."

In November 1998 the group descended on the BBC's Maida Vale Studios to record a performance for John Peel's radio program. As was their custom, they assigned working titles to the tracks that were still works in progress: "Hung Over as the Queen in Maida Vale: Monheim," "Chart #3," and "Steve Reich." A year later the band named a piece on their live sets "Gorecki" after the Third Symphony, *Symphony of Sorrowful Songs*, by the Polish composer Henryk Górecki. The 1992 recording of the symphony by the London Sinfonietta and soprano Dawn Upshaw had been an international best-seller, and godspeed were not the only kranky band to have copies on their shelves. As Mark Nelson says, the recording was "a big gateway drug for indie people to classical music."

Live sessions on the John Peel program were a marker for a band, not only as an opportunity to broadcast their music across the United Kingdom and points beyond, but also to receive the seal of approval from one of the preeminent tastemakers of the international underground. John Peel kept a keen eye on the up-and-comers. Over thirty-seven years virtually any band or artist worth naming recorded for Peel, from Elton John in 1968 to Nirvana in 1989. Bands would usually record and mix three songs in the course of a day. Labradford had played a session in 1996, Bowery Electric in 1997, and Low would play four sessions from 1999 to 2013. The godspeed you black emperor! session aired in January 1999.

In the fall of 1995, Stars of the Lid were on tour opening for an Austin band called Bedhead. They were approached by a painter named Jon McCafferty, who told the duo that he often listened to their music while painting. McCafferty contributed a painting to cover art by alt-rock titans R.E.M. A long-distance collaboration ensued, with McCafferty recording himself painting and Adam Wiltzie incorporating the resulting sounds into Stars of the Lid compositions. The resulting album was titled *Per Aspera Ad Astra*, attributed to Stars of the Lid and Jon McCafferty and released on kranky in November 1998. As the band put it in the liner notes on the inside of the gatefold cover, which featured a McCafferty painting with the title embossed into the cardboard CD sleeve and LP jacket: "The merging of color and sound is something we've thought about quite often. Why should the visual artist be confined to the packaging while the 'musician' is in charge of the rest—especially when both dimensions may reflect back into each other."

In addition to Adam Wiltzie and Brian McBride, Sara Nelson contributed cello to the recordings. Steve Ciabattoni wrote in the *CMJ New Music Report*, "The humming harmony of cellos on 'Anchor States: Part One' provides the boldest strokes; but elsewhere the soft blurs of sound suggest ultra-slow-motion close-ups of a brush thick with paint sliding across a virgin canvas." In addition to the principals' guitars, tapes, and synthesizers, Stars of the Lid were exploring more instrumental options. Brian McBride believes that "it was just in us. I spent the majority of my childhood life listening to my father playing his classical music through the walls of my bedroom. I think I've always had these muted diver's tones within me." This would eventually result in the integration of string sections and horns into Stars of the Lid recordings and performances and the band becoming connected with the nascent "neoclassical" musical genre.

MEANWHILE, ON YOUR COMPUTER . . .

Paypal launched in the fall of 1998. There were parallel advances in bank transfer via the Internet. Up to that point, wire transfers had been expensive and time-consuming. The spread of Internet access brought with it the ability to send money around the world quickly and relatively inexpensively from your desktop. Trips to the bank to arrange overseas payments became a thing of the past. There would be no more reliance on money orders or cashier's checks for verified payment, no concern about foreign currencies, and no more worries about when or if the troubled Chicago postal system could get a check delivered to the right place at the right time—or at all. Sales were such that kranky's royalty payments to godspeed you black emperor! were pretty hefty. Delivering them via bank transfer took away a few worries.

There was another Internet-related development in 1998 that would affect kranky, the music scene in Chicago, and the greater market for music. The online bookseller Amazon.com announced that they would begin to sell compact discs at 30 to 40 percent under the prices seen in retail stores. It would be a blow to the independent record stores that kranky and other independent labels relied on, just as Amazon's rise had hurt independent bookstores. Leslie Ransom describes the view from Touch & Go Distribution: "We were witnessing the rise of the Internet for sales. As those online outlets grew in influence, they started pressing for more and more deals and discounts if they were going to carry and support our releases." Labels and distributors were stuck between the rock of their desire to sell more CDs, and the hard place of cuts to profit margins that discounting necessitated. The more discerning label and distributor operators had a sneaking suspicion that large sales to online retailers would eventually come back as returns just as they often had with record store chains. Ransom accurately describes the view from Chicago when she says, "We were the outsiders. All the major-label folks were based in New York and LA. We were pragmatic, possibly to a fault. We questioned every discount someone wanted."

10 both ends fixed

1999

In the fall of 1999, Labradford and godspeed you black emperor! toured the United States together. It was a unique pairing that, given the presence of a nine-person band, came with logistical challenges, as Bobby Donne of Labradford notes: "godspeed you black emperor! was very kind to us, and it seemed (to me) to be a good fit for both parties. They were starting to really blow up then so most, if not all, of the gigs were sold out. But they fucking sound checked FOREVER! You could not get them to quicken up the sound check time." I was hearing stories from bemused and/or frustrated onlookers at the shows. The Canadian band seemingly poured out of their tour vehicle and were persnickety as all get-out in checking sound levels before each performance. Given the size and instrumental lineup of the band, and the variable quality of sound systems and condescension of the mostly male staff that their female soundperson had to deal with at the clubs they played, it was understandable.

Labradford were supporting their fourth album, *Mi Media Naranja*. It had been recorded in Richmond with contributions from Chris Johnson on violin and Ulysses Kirksey on cello, with Carter Brown picking up Fender Rhodes electric piano and Mark Nelson adding slide guitar. The band expressed their frustration with the conventions of song titling by designating each track on the album a letter or two: S, G, WR, C, I, V, and P. Stephen Thompson praised the album's "moody, epic, film-score vibe" in *A.V. Club*, and he was not alone in expressing critical approval. As Carter Brown puts it, "Labradford was always moving forward."

Brown also remembers that godspeed you black emperor! "opened for us and we very quickly realized that for logistics, and for a lot of reasons, they needed to headline." Just as Jessamine and Magnog had shared stages together, and Low and godspeed had performed together live, members of godspeed would join Labradford in performance. "They started playing on 'Pico,' a song on *Mi Media Naranja*. And we started playing that and I forget who started, maybe Norsola Johnson started a violin part and then there was like a little subtle drum part. That was just a little treat, and we never told anyone what to play, it was all an organic addition to the song and made it really special."

Despite the personal and artistic connections between the bands, crossing the country alongside godspeed turned out to be frustrating for Labradford. It underlined their weariness with touring, as Mark Nelson details: "I liked everyone in that band without exception—but that was an extremely difficult tour, and I would say clearly the end was near for Labradford after that. We had already had issues playing live. We had started the tour as 'co-headliners' but after about three shows it became blindingly obvious that 85–90 percent of the audience was there for godspeed you black emperor! That was disheartening to say the least."

It had been, as Carter Brown puts it, "a lot of time and a lot of miles." With Brown having moved to Washington, DC, in the summer of 1996, Bobby Donne remaining in Richmond, and Mark Nelson relocated in Chicago, coordination became complicated for the band. Much of Labradford's personal and musical dynamics were forged in long practice sessions in Richmond with cigarette and beer breaks for discussion. It had been a trying tour for them that brought a sense of futility with it. Multiweek US tours would become a thing of the past. Labradford shifted to becoming more of a recording and less of a performing unit from that point forward. The trio's turn to recording produced a great run of albums. *Mi Media Naranja* was followed by *E luxo so* in the summer of 1999. Joined by Peter Neff on hammered dulcimer and string players Chris Johnson, Craig Markva, Jamie Evans, and Jonathan Morken, Labradford expressed new depths that straddled the electronic avant-garde and the rough-hewn folk music traditions of their native Virginia. Tomas Palermo wrote in *XLR8R* that Labradford had "refined their sound, improving with each effort while not making their previous works obsolete . . . electronic-dub and cut-ups appear . . . grounding the album in future dreams as much as their music's wood frame-house timelessness. An ambiguous desolation runs through this album, songs that evoke longing and waiting through long winters or hot summers. But even in their darkness Labradford are far from pretentious, another reason why they qualify as America's best underground band of the Nineties."

Growing increasingly weary of the conventions around titling songs, the group simply listed album credits as track names. So, for example, the first track on the album is "Recorded and mixed at Sound of Music, Richmond, Va." As Mark Nelson explained in an interview, "We got the idea that song titles were really more an element of the design of the LP sleeve than any discreet message about the music. So that's why we did it like that—we tried to incorporate it into the graphics."

Keith Fullerton Whitman remembers where he first came across Labradford in a record store in Ridgewood, New Jersey: "Aside from the typically wizened owner, there was a younger guy that would be in every second or third time that seemed especially on top of it. He handed me the original marbled Green 2LP of *Prazision* and of course I was instantly hooked; with the aesthetic, sure, but mostly the pace of it. I was ready. I followed the label fervently from then on, it was all in heavy rotation for me, especially Stars of the Lid, Windy & Carl, Roy Montgomery, Jessamine . . ."

Whitman began releasing music and eventually performed with Labradford in New York: "I was fairly shocked when Mark got in touch about opening for them at the Leonard Street Knitting Factory when they came through. Total dream-fantasy moment. Amazing concert, so languorous and hazy. Björk showed up with the Matmos guys, the whole thing, very important night in the personal scheme of things."

Touring was a triumphant undertaking for godspeed you black emperor! It was indisputable that the band was on the rise. Even with the time-space challenges of moving a nine-person band, projectionist, and sound person around North America and Europe, they seemed energized by playing live. Audiences would emerge from a performance as if from a wind tunnel. Attendance grew and the CDs flowed forth from the kranky shelves. The band took time off at the end of the year and worked on recording two pieces that became an EP called *Slow Riot for New Zero Kanada*, released on CD by kranky and vinyl by Constellation. Both were packaged in striking and mysterious covers featuring copper-embossed Hebrew letters on a black background. The opening of the CD booklet was reversed from the usual right-hand side to accommodate the reading direction of the cover text: "Tohu va-Vohu," meaning "unformed and void," and found in the Book of Genesis in the Old Testament of the Bible and Torah. The recording the group made in Providence on their first tour of Blaise Bailey Finnegan ranting about a speeding ticket and then heatedly reciting the lyrics of the heavy metal band Iron Maiden's "Virus," which he claims on the recording as his own original poem, was incorporated into the track "BBF3." The band acquired a larger, but no more reliable, vehicle for touring, as David Bryant recounts: "At that point we were traveling in an old half school bus (that also broke down a lot) and had to be towed to the Schubas show in Chicago. The tow-truck driver let us all stay in the bus while it rode down the highway on a flatbed truck. We had to keep our heads down so the cops wouldn't see." The two consecutive shows were overwhelmingly supported. David Bryant remembers, "The tow-truck pulled up in front of Schubas very late and there was a huge line of people waiting to get let in. I remember feeling anxious about the size of that line. Maybe that is when things started to feel differently for me? Things were changing somehow."

The greater world was taking notice, as witnessed by the *New York Times*: "Although godspeed's music incorporates improvisation, it certainly isn't jazz; although it relies largely on rock's instruments and vocabulary, it's not rock, either. It's the first music I've heard in a long time to make me feel that new, vernacular musical languages are slowly working themselves out." The *Washington Post* compared two kranky releases of that year: "Portions of godspeed you black emperor's *Slow Riot for New Zero Kanada* resemble (Labradford's) *E luxo so*, although this Montreal group favors harsher timbres than its Richmond counterpart. Beguilingly enigmatic enough to have been labeled 'the last great band of the century' by Britain's trend-hungry *New Musical Express*, gybe! tends to gradually amplify from its pastoral passages to epic crescendos."

The popularity of the group inspired some interesting scenarios. The brokerage house Merrill Lynch dangled a considerable amount of money in front of godspeed to use their music in a television commercial. The offer was refused. The band acceded to an interview request for a cover story in *NME*, on the condition that they didn't have to pose for a photograph. The crafty Brits worked in a live photo on the cover to accompany the band's emailed responses to questions from writer John Robinson. The group collectively voiced their assessment of the situation well:

"Nobody owes us anything, we know that; we don't actively pursue interviews or media exposure, BUT, when we're asked, we reserve the right to define our own terms and boundaries . . . to us, this is the most obvious thing in the world." It was interesting for Joel and me to see how many people in and out of the underground responded to a band that more often than not simply ignored what was defined as success.

We were doing well thanks to the increased sales Low and godspeed brought kranky. Joel was able to work from home. My innate caution led me to reduce my hours at Facets and slowly transition to working full-time for kranky, and Joel continued to pick up shifts at Reckless or the Gingerman Tavern. We each operated out-of-office in our apartments.

The central place of Chicago in the indie rock firmament was confirmed in 1999 when Ryan Schreiber moved to town from Minneapolis, bringing his *Pitchfork* with him. Over time the website would grow into a maker and breaker of musicians' dreams.

11 after this they chose silence 2000–2002

And this time I can swear I hear a hint of a chuckle.

—*Jim DeRogatis*

The initial years of the twenty-first century were "bounteous indeed" for kranky, as I wrote to my girlfriend Annie Feldmeier. "All of this is due to the remarkable success of godspeed you black emperor! and Low. It's at the point where we have solid back catalogue sales and sales just keep coming in. Cash flow at long last." We had to spend down at the end of the fiscal year in June 2001 with a tax payment due on July 15, buying office supplies to the point where I ended up with eight printer cartridges. I continued by noting, "When Joel and I started we had very distinct notions of all the things we didn't want to do. The biggest gas about being where we are now is to think about all the things kranky doesn't have to do that other labels do and realize that we still have the level of independence that we do. It still amazes me that so many people are attached to so many vestiges of the music business that really don't have a thing to do with selling records." There were no kranky showcases at music conferences like SXSW. We were wary of giving out discounts to get chain-store sales. Advertisements were few and far between.

Low had recorded several Christmas songs, and kranky funded production of their Christmas CD, distributing it in 2000. The Gap used their version of "Little Drummer Boy" on a television commercial, netting the band some cash for a new van, health insurance, and raising their profile. Tom Windish found them a Japanese booking agent, and an American tour had Low playing at six-hundred-plus-capacity venues in big cities.

In October, godspeed headlined a show at the Metro in Chicago as part of a year-long tour across the United Kingdom, Ireland, Japan, and North America. "The whole godspeed juggernaut is amazing to watch right now," I wrote. The guest list at the Metro had one hundred names on it, fifteen of which I had submitted from kranky. The other eighty-five folks were all Chicago press, radio, and retail folks on the "standard" Metro list who were suddenly interested in the band.

In London, booking agent Barry Hogan began working on a festival named after the Velvet Underground song "All Tomorrow's Parties." The idea, inspired by an event hosted by the Scottish group Belle & Sebastian at an English holiday camp, was to have a band select some groups they wanted to play with. This came to be called "curating" as the language of museum and cultural studies slowly infiltrated underground rock. It was ironic given that most of the artists involved were not yet welcome in the white cubes of highbrow cultural institutions. The enthusiasm of fandom was becoming distasteful across the upper tiers of the underground scene. Differentiation had to be established. I surmised that "picking your favorite bands" was too passé to use, as it carried the implication of a troubling equality between would-be tastemakers and fans. Or a reminder to some that they started as fans and not all-knowing guardians of the Rainbow Bridge.

Bands and fans stayed multiple nights in apartments, or "chalets" as they were called, at the Pontin's resort along the seaside in East Sussex. The Scottish band Mogwai headlined the first festival in June 2000, where kranky artists Labradford, Pan•American, and godspeed you black emperor! all performed. There was a distinctive Chicago presence in the first three editions of ATP, with "curation" provided by Tortoise in 2001 and Shellac in 2002, and Chicago artists the Eternals, the Fred Anderson Trio, the Sea and Cake, U.S. Maple, Dianogah, Robbie Fulks, P.W. Long, the Lonesome Organist, Plush, and Wilco all playing. Touch & Go Records was represented by Arcwelder, Flour, Calexico, P.W. Long, Rachel's, Shipping News, Silkworm, the New Year, and Shannon Wright. These lineups not only reflected a mutual admiration society between underground bands, but also the commercial and artistic heft of Chicago bands and record labels. As Josh Madell from New York City's Other Music store puts it: "There can be little doubt that Chicago in the 1990s and early 2000s was the cutting-edge music scene in the US. These artists and labels were offering a different take on indie music, it was not just personal and approachable, the hallmarks of indie rock, but it was also diverse, bringing together jazz, noise, modern classical, global, and experimental sounds, and creating something forward-looking out of all of that history. For me, someone always interested in what is happening now and next in underground music, 1990s Chicago was one of the most exciting places in the world."

The festival was an instantaneous success. Following the pattern that repeats itself in the music business with depressing regularity, the All Tomorrow's Parties concert series spawned a record label in 2001, expansion of the festival into the United States, Iceland, and Australia, a second festival called "I'll Be Your Mirror," collaborations with the Pitchfork and Primavera music festivals, and a third festival called "Don't Look Back." The latter, of course, was *all about* looking backward, with bands covering their old albums in their entirety. Expansion led to the inevitable collapse in 2016. Naturally, bands were left holding the bag on airline tickets and the other expenses they accrued to perform far from home. In years to come, the language of grant applications, academia, and museum labels would pervade underground music intellectually in parallel with a growth in festivals. The two trends brought serious economic forces to bear on musicians' creative processes. But in the triumphal moments of the early twenty-first century, the onset of festivals showcasing the best of underground were seen as a welcome alternative to the big summer themed festivals like Ozzfest or the Warped tour. What could go wrong when the cool people were doing the "curating"?

The Chicago music scene made an appearance on the silver screen. *High Fidelity* opened across the country in March 2000. Based on the book by Nick Hornby set in London, the movie had been filmed in Chicago in the spring of 1999 at locations varying from Lane Tech High School to the Lounge Ax. The star and cowriter John Cusak and writer D. V. DeVincentis grew up in Evanston and knew a lot of people in the music scene. Liz Phair auditioned for a role. *High Fidelity* featured some Chicago underground musicians in bit parts, a goodly portion of the soundtrack came from Drag City artists, and the record collection of Drag City owner Dan Koretzky made a cameo. Joel Leoschke and I were bemused by and remote from the filming. Neither of us had read the book. We both lived above the hipster equator roughly marked by North Avenue. The Rainbo Club at the epicenter of that world was not our chosen hang spot, so the opportunities for Joel and me to see and be seen were limited. As were the opportunities to "represent." Which was fine by us.

DISCRETE ENTROPY

Sometime in the spring of 2000 Joel was preparing to move and came across a box of demos sent to kranky. Even with our commitment to listen to everything that came in the mail, the unsolicited submissions piled up. He had no idea how long that box had been sitting there. Joel pulled out a package from Vancouver. Scott Morgan had been drumming and playing guitars in bands around Vancouver from high school through his graduation from Simon Fraser University in 1996. One of these bands was Destroyer, which had a guitarist named Nicolas Bragg. Bragg also led a band called Blaise Pascal, which Joel and I entertained the notion of working with when we were at Cargo. As Morgan recalls, "The idea to send something to kranky came from my friend Nic Bragg, who managed one of Vancouver's most prominent independent record stores called Zulu Records. I had a copy of Labradford's *Mi Media Naranja* that I had bought at Zulu and was vaguely familiar with the label. I sent kranky and a few other labels the demo and kranky were the only ones that responded."

The demo was a self-released CD called *A New Demonstration of Thermodynamic Tendencies*. Morgan worked under the name loscil, a portmanteau of the terms "loop" and "oscillate" taken from the Csound computing system he used to compose and record. In college, Morgan studied computer and electroacoustic music and continued working on electronic music after graduation, often performing at a friend's theater. Morgan explains, "loscil technically got its live start as part of a series I curated along with two close friends called the Multiplex Grand. It was held at a local experimental cinema called the Blinding Light. I was experimenting with some early loscil AV stuff—music with reactive visuals."

He also worked as a sound designer for video games. From 1998 to 1999, Morgan applied himself to the CD that eventually ended up in the kranky P.O. box. Morgan worked with low-key rhythm in ways that were reminiscent of the strains of minimalist techno coming out of Detroit and Cologne, Germany, at the time, while layering his own vaporous melodies above and through the listening field. We were impressed with what we heard. Once again, extended connections made at Cargo came into play. Joel made a call to Zulu Records, where he had a contact working at the store's in-house record label, to do some background research. Having obtained a positive character reference on the phone, Joel followed up with a call to Scott Morgan, and the deed was done.

The title of the self-released CD reflects an organizing theme of thermodynamics inspired by a physics textbook Morgan found in a used bookstore. The music and song titles were refined and applied to the debut loscil CD that kranky released in fall 2001 called *Triple Point*. All but one track from the demo made it onto the CD. One reviewer at the *Portland Mercury* noted, "The titles of the songs essentially describe what the music sounds like; 'Pressure,' for instance, sounds exactly like a group of beakers bubbling with condensation, or fissures in the earth breathing out vapor." Andy Kellman summarized what appeared to be a contradiction at the time: "Having been released by kranky—their logo probably won't be able to attract the attention of experimental techno fans who remain loyal to a few select labels and choose not to venture outside of that tiny realm."

Fortunately, plenty of music fans took notice of the CD. Stars of the Lid were impressed enough to ask loscil to open for their European tour. Morgan says, "It was my first solo touring experience and it was a little crazy but super fun." Scott Morgan would continue to apply a thematic approach to loscil recordings, with the immediate follow-up *Submers* being devoted to submarines and utilizing mutated samples of orchestral recordings.

I WOULD MAKE SOME TACOS, WE WOULD BUY A MAGNUM OF RED WINE, TURN ON THE FOUR-TRACK, AND START RECORDING PHRASES

Adam Wiltzie and Brian McBride had been working on a new Stars of the Lid album since 1997. The resulting work became a CD entitled *Avec Laudenum* released on the Belgian Sub Rosa label in 1999, which kranky reissued in 2002. Brian McBride recalls how that transitional recording was made in 1997, with Wiltzie having moved to Brussels: "Adam did a bulk of the recording with me only adding some different parts in the middle of the record. But I thought the first piece ("The Atomium, Parts One, Two and Three") had this perfect build to it. And to be honest, it seemed like the bulk of this record by Adam just oozed out of him."

The duo each constantly recorded at home, making it hard to pinpoint when "sessions" for any Stars of the Lid album began and ended. It was an intentionally time-consuming process. As McBride later put it in *Rolling Stone* in 2015, the duo concocted "a plan . . . [to] release something longer that would give people something more extensive to chew on."

The process of trading music back and forth between the two had gradually begun to include recordings of strings and horns. As Brian McBride recalls, "I was in Chicago, and back in those days we used to send DAT tapes to each other in the mail. Being so separated was kind of a good thing because it gave us both time to either think through or ruminate about what the other person had done and be a little more attentive and deliberate with what to do next." As the scope of the duo widened, so did the music. Although he states there was not a "conscious decision" to add instrumentation, Adam Wiltzie remembers how he worked with cellist Sarah Nelson, "a good friend and drinking buddy. . . . We would end up over at my shotgun shack, I would make some tacos, we would buy a magnum of red wine, turn on the four-track, and start recording phrases. I did not even use a click track back then, so sometimes I wonder how it all stayed together."

The product of this incremental process of addition ended up stretching over two compact discs and six sides of vinyl. *The Tired Sounds of Stars of the Lid* became the duo's breakthrough album, steadily enlarging the audience in a process remarkably akin to the deliberate, extended development of the music itself. Christopher Weingarten observed in the 2015 *Rolling Stone* article quoting McBride, "Sometime after the release of their sixth studio album, 2001's *The Tired Sounds of the Stars of the Lid*, Austin-borne drone duo Stars of the Lid quietly, patiently moved from obscurity into semi-obscurity. It didn't make too much of a ripple upon its release beyond raves from alt-leaning press, but it slowly spread. In the 14 years since, a generation of similarly evocative composers—Max Richter, Jóhann Jóhannsson, Ólafur Arnalds—have risen to prominence in Stars of the Lid's wake."

The group leavened the seriousness of the sprawling, atmospheric album with song titles like "Austin Texas Mental Hospital," "Gas Farming," "The Lonely People (Are Getting Lonelier)," a reference to Wiltzie's Chicago childhood in "A Love Song (for Cubs)," and the by-then-obligatory David Lynch reference, "Mulholland." Craig McCaffrey's cover design, complete with photos of McBride and Wiltzie each sleeping, is appropriately translucent and glowing in Rothko-esque shades of yellow and orange. Brian McBride told the *Austin Chronicle* in 2001, "I do think we're composers, there's some pretentiousness associated with that word, which I think is part of the reason we probably haven't embraced that for a long time, but that's really what's going on." "Joel and I both agree that Stars of the Lid are best described as contemporary composers," I wrote in an email in August that year. *The Tired Sounds* is expansive in every sense of the word and rewards extended listening. I recall that kranky received fan mail from a couple who played the music as the woman gave birth.

The duo proceeded to tour in support of the album, bolstered by Luke Savisky's film work. Scott Morgan / loscil supported a European tour in 2002 and recalls, "They had Luke Savisky doing live film looping and layering. Jaw-dropping stuff. He was pretty much a permanent member of the Stars of the Lid live act and his work was super inspirational. Seeing this definitely rejuvenated my interest in doing visuals, but it wasn't until many years later that I got back into it partly due to advances in software and projection technology."

McBride describes how Stars of the Lid expanded their touring lineup: "After recording *The Tired Sounds*, when we were beginning to figure things out for our second time to tour in Europe, I had suggested that we find a quartet or at least some string musicians. At that time, we weren't as connected with that side of the music world. So, we put an ad on Myspace and found ourselves a trio: Lucinda Chua, Noura Sanatian, and Ela Baruch. The tour became an exploration in understanding the way those string sounds should mix with our own tones. And it even produced a song or two that's never been released but made up on the road."

Wiltzie's time in Belgium doing sound engineering for bands had given the group entrée into performance spaces outside the usual circuit of rock clubs and bars. Stars of the Lid began to perform in cathedrals and theaters, where the combination of sights and sounds worked to their best advantage, and where attendees could sit and quietly absorb it all. Brian McBride says, "The decision to avoid rock clubs was a conscious attempt for us. Those places witness way too much music to really care. It's just a big ol' job most of them seem to hate. In consideration of wanting to have spaces that were more conducive to the sound that came out of amps, we wanted higher ceilings, greater natural reverb, and to take people out of their element. Surprisingly, it wasn't all that difficult to have promoters find a church to perform in."

Wiltzie notes, "Europe is of course ahead of the USA in terms of social funding for some venues. Barbican (in London) being one of them. This venue has a budget to repair and maintain equipment and pay sound and lighting staff a proper wage with benefits." American event bookers were slower to pick up on the potential of the band for non-rock venues. I made a fruitless attempt to convince a programming manager at the Atlanta Symphony Orchestra to arrange a Stars of the Lid appearance, for example. As the twenty-first century progressed, some adventurous booking agents had found venues like a planetarium in Calgary, Alberta, in 2002 and another in Champaign, Illinois, in 2008, to name two examples of the locations that became available for Stars of the Lid performances outside the usual nightclub circuit. Playing with a string section in turn opened up creative possibilities for the core duo, and a contradictory renewed appreciation for electric guitar from Brian McBride: "When we went on tour and performed, we started hearing rumblings from the crowd saying, 'I can't believe they pulled it off.' Which I hope refers to capturing something about the original pieces and not just droning in D. But that definitely helped us to realize that classical musicians could help re-create parts of our records. For me, I was playing around with new samplers and recording strings and muting them in the distance. You can only use just your guitar for tones for so long. Scratch that, you actually can't use it enough."

Over time, the popularity of Stars of the Lid grew as *The Tired Sounds* slowly and surely sold more copies. The band took six years to record a follow-up album, but somehow the absence of recordings made the group more popular. Adam Wiltzie says, "I remember after *Tired Sounds* came out there was the usual couple reviews here and there, and it did not even sell a thousand copies, until a few years later suddenly Joel sent over a statement, and in six months it had sold three thousand-plus copies, and it continued to keep selling and we are almost twenty years later, and it keeps selling in the physical format. I have no idea what caused SOTL to be classified the way it has become so revered. It is as if the concept of 'do nothing for as long as possible' actually is a business model for success."

Scarcity really did create demand.

FEEDBACK ZWEI

In Boston, Keith Fullerton Whitman had been experimenting with processing guitars through a computer in real time. He opened some shows for indie rock bands Damon and Naomi and Yo La Tengo, the latter being "a very high-profile gig given the relative a-commerciality of the sounds produced." Whitman's three-inch CD got into the hands of a label called Apartment B, which released a CD called *21:30 for acoustic guitar . . .* in early 2000. Whitman played some shows opening for Labradford, who urged him to pass along the CD to kranky. It was an easy call for Joel and me, and we asked if Keith would want to release some of his guitar pieces with us. As Keith describes the recording process, "After you guys got in touch, I took it extremely seriously, and spent the greater part of 2002 working on it, building patches in Max-MSP to do exactly what I needed them to. It would be a week of recording, then a week of building and refinement. I think the whole album-cycle was three years, from conceptualizing to recording to release to touring."

The turn into a new century brought entry into the Japanese market for kranky. We were contracted by P-Vine, a label that had started out by specializing in rhythm 'n blues reissues. P-Vine took notice of the American underground and gradually began licensing newer music from American and British labels, including Drag City and Thrill Jockey. The godspeed you black emperor! albums were the first titles P-Vine manufactured in Japan, and the label imported other kranky titles to sell alongside the recordings they licensed for production. In addition to releasing albums in Japan, P-Vine sold to stores in Taiwan and Hong Kong. Our location in Chicago meant that kranky could consolidate our shipments to P-Vine with those from other labels at the Touch & Go warehouse to keep shipping costs low for all the labels involved. Once again, being in Chicago had made distribution easier for kranky. Joel had asked for an advance payment against royalties when kranky signed the deal for the godspeed albums, which our Japanese partners quickly recouped. The Low albums followed.

In February 2000, godspeed you black emperor! spent nine days in Toronto with Daryl Smith at Chemical Sound recording what would become their second full-length album and the last released on compact disc by kranky: *Lift Your Skinny Fists Like Antennas to Heaven*. It turned out to be a double-CD set when released in October 2000.

The third, and final, Festival of Drifting took place in June 2000 at five venues across the United Kingdom. The concert series experienced diminishing returns over time, neither picking up momentum nor showcasing Labradford to full effect. Being part of a package tour, even surrounded by musically sympathetic acts, had run its course for the band. As Mark Nelson observes, "I think it's fair to fundamentally want the music to stand apart and on its own." The three members of Labradford met in Chicago that July to record their sixth album with Steve Albini at his Electrical Audio studio. Unlike the previous three albums, this session consisted of the basic trio with Carter Brown on organ, synthesizers, and electric piano, Mark Nelson playing guitar, and Bobby Donne using four- and six-string bass guitars. The group had decided to record with Albini, as Donne confirms, "after listening to *Secret Name* by Low," which had been recorded in November 1998 at Electrical

Audio and released in 1999 on kranky. The completed album, called *fixed:context*, was released in February 2001 on kranky in North America and Blast First in the United Kingdom and Europe. It would turn out to be the final Labradford recording. Mark Nelson's remembrance of the recording process indicates why: "It was an effort to get out of our usual ways and try something different. I think that it worked okay—the problem was really that the material wasn't there. We hadn't developed it enough and so that record feels about 60 percent realized to me. Steve was great personally, but not what we needed in that moment. It would have been great in retrospect to work with a traditional producer who might have pushed or challenged us. We were a band that needed direction and a little push, and we went to the guy whose whole thing is to let the band be the band they are. Fucking crazy when you think about it."

If *fixed:context* was the result of a creative stalemate or underdevelopment, reviewers and listeners didn't seem to notice. Andy Kellman wrote in *AllMusic*, "The addition and subtraction of its graceful layers ebb and flow, shifting like harm-free plate tectonics. Like the best ambient music, it's solemn and deceptively melodic." The album earned a rare 8.0 score on a scale of 10 on the taste-making/confirming *Pitchfork* website, with Mark Richardson writing, "Each time I played it, *fixed:context* burrowed just a little deeper in my brain and I now hum the simple themes constantly, even when the record is nowhere in sight."

Joel and I could each tell from our conversations with Mark Nelson and Carter Brown that Labradford had lost something as a band. Geographic separation had ended the rehearsal sessions where they worked out their differences over cigarettes and beer. The chemistry that drove the original duo had dissipated. There was a finality to the album.

As Mark Richardson tweeted in March 2021: "Listening to the final Labradford album . . . their whole run was stripping their music down further with each record, so it makes sense after this they chose silence."

By 2000 godspeed you black emperor! was playing multi-night stands in larger cities like London, San Francisco, and New York, where they headlined a benefit for the Anthology Film Archives in August and returned for three more shows in December. The group played their first Japanese shows in November 2000 in Tokyo, returning for more performances in later 2001. Brent S. Sirota rated *Lift Your Skinny Fists Like Antennas to Heaven* a 9.0 out of 10 on *Pitchfork*, even mentioning a "Labradford-like introduction of repetitive guitar and subtle chimes" on the track "Broken Windows, Locks of Love Part III." If you are persuaded by the wisdom of crowds, as of the writing of this book, 26,560 reviewers on the Rate Your Music website give the album a 4.6 out of a possible 5.0 grade.

Other than going to shows or shopping for records, I didn't spend much time in the neighborhoods radiating around what Joel and I sarcastically called "Ground Zero": the intersection of Milwaukee, North, and Damen Avenues. The Rainbo, favored as it was by so many movers and shakers in the scene, always felt like someone else's clubhouse to me. At some time in the late '80s, a friend at Wax Trax! took me to a small, dark bar on Dickens called Danny's Tavern that suited me much better. Dark, with candlelit alcoves in what must have been an apartment at some point, Danny's was a great place to meet someone when I happened to be in the vicinity, and as the years passed and two turntables and a mixer appeared, Joel and I would DJ there occasionally.

In 1992 a bar called the Hopleaf opened within walking distance from my apartment and became my go-to spot. I often met up with Joel, or Paul Hieger, a Cargo coworker who lived nearby, and could be reasonably confident on any given night that I would be running into Brendan Burke or Ken Vandermark, who lived in the neighborhood. Bruno Johnson, who ran the Okka Disk free-jazz label, tended bar there too. Every now and then Ken would bring visiting musicians in. I found the growth of craft breweries and distilleries to be an interesting parallel to that of independent record labels, and the Hopleaf had a prodigious selection. I never did get to any of those Drag City New Year's Eve parties.

HELLO VIENNA

Kevin Drumm had been active in the Chicago music scene first in a Touch & Go-influenced trio called Bull, featuring the former Big Black bass guitarist Dave Riley, and then improvising on prepared or tabletop guitar. The latter is a technique that involves placing an electric guitar flat on a table and coaxing sounds out with various clips, screwdrivers, and other unorthodox aids. The English guitarist Keith Rowe had pioneered the practice in the 1960s with the group AMM. In addition to his own recording projects, Drumm appeared on albums by Chicagoans Gastr del Sol, Ken Vandermark, Brent Gutzeit, and in concert and on record with a variety of improvisational bigwigs. Drumm had gradually added laptop computer and analog synthesizers to his sonic arsenal, and from 2000 to 2001 worked on what is probably the most accurately titled album of all time, *Sheer Hellish Miasma*. Released in May of 2002 on the Austrian Mego label, it was well described on the *Dusted* website as a work where "Mass and density are the only consistent criteria . . . it would be difficult to distinguish one instrument from another in the mix, and near impossible to extract any single component, so deeply interwoven is the disc's resonance."

The release via an Austrian label illustrates how connections between Chicago musicians and labels and forward-looking electronic musicians and labels around the world had grown by the new century. Thrill Jockey Records had released albums from the Austrian Markus Popp, who recorded and performed as Oval, the German duo Mouse on Mars in the late 1990s, Takemura Nobukazu from Osaka, Japan, beginning in 1999, and the Austrian trio Radian in 2002. On the kranky side, Mark Nelson's Pan•American project released music via labels in Belgium and Italy, and Nelson collaborated with the German visual artist Thomas Demand on a twelve-inch EP and photograph set. Jessica Bailiff and David Pearce from Flying Saucer Attack established a long-distance collaborative project they called clearhorizon.

By 2002 the kranky-Low relationship had become especially productive. The *Things We Lost in the Fire* and *Secret Name* albums had each been recorded in Chicago with Steve Albini at Electrical Audio studios and featured expanded instrumentation, with strings and keyboards augmenting the trio's melodies. Low toured North America and Europe extensively and visited Australia for the first time in February 2002. Joel and I balked at the Australian promoter's request for $900 to support advertising for the tour. It was more than we had spent to that point on advertising *Secret Name* worldwide.

For their third album for kranky, *Trust*, the trio handed over the final mixdown of recordings to Tchad Blake, an experienced producer who had worked with Peter Gabriel's RealWorld label and artists like Tom Waits, Los Lobos, and a band called Soul Coughing that Low had toured with. Backing vocals were supplied on two songs by Gerry Beckley, a member of the '70s soft-rock band America. In May 2002 I emailed Annie Feldmeier my observation that the final product was "a more expansive sound, a development and not necessarily just another Low album." As Mark Nelson observed, Low put themselves in the position to get new perspectives and input on their recording process.

NO, WE'RE NOT DONE WITH IT

Though the opportunities to record and perform music outside the borders of guitar-centered indie rock had widened, the barriers of sexism and racial segregation remained. At kranky, Joel and I each worked two jobs for about seven years before the label became self-supporting, seldom having time to look beyond the immediate needs of the day. We were heterosexual white males, from the suburbs, living on the north side of Chicago. As music fans we would attend jazz performances at Fred Anderson's Velvet Lounge, where musicians from across the city drew together in the South Loop, or go to jazz performances in Hyde Park, but we made no efforts to connect with musicians or record labels on the south and west sides of the city for business purposes.

Looking back on the times, Greg Kot speculates, "Chicago has become more integrated musically in recent years, but in the '80s and '90s, house and hip-hop remained cut off from what was happening on the northside." There were isolated cases such as Thrill Jockey releasing collaborative work between Tortoise and house music pioneer Derrick Carter, albums by the hip-hop duo All Natural, or kranky working with Lichens, the project of the African American musician Robert A. A. Lowe. In the latter case, Joel and I met Lowe when he worked at the Empty Bottle, which hardly counts as leaping any geographic or social barriers.

If you happened to stay up late at night watching Chicago public-access TV, you might have caught a glimpse of the new dance music forming on the westside called "footwork." Like house music, the scene evolved in an abandoned space. In this case, competitive dancing and parties took place in an empty kindergarten that became known as the Underground Track Factory. Composed electronically to accompany dancers moving at five steps per second, footwork shared frantic snares, clave triplets, and sub-bass with jungle, and cut-up samples of jazz and rhythm-and-blues. The first single to emerge was RP Boo's "Baby Come On" in 1997. For most of us on the northside, discovery came either by chance on cable or much later via compilations that started coming out on the UK Planet Mu label in 2010. That's how segregated Chicago as a city was and is.

Time and money were and are serious restraints for musicians and record-label employees who often had to balance creative and "real world" jobs. Those restraints existed on the north and south sides of Chicago alike. Building channels of communication and collaboration across spatial and genre divides was most often set aside in favor of the pursuit of closer, more immediate opportunities.

These structural issues in the business of music were matched by the day-to-day experiences of women musicians. Dawn Smithson can tell stories, and things haven't changed much since she played bass and sang in Jessamine. "I can give you the stock responses: Got told I play pretty *good* for a *girl* by some people I thought were way more progressive than that, countless men shocked when I rolled in with a bass and even more shocked that I knew how to play it well, followed around at Guitar Center and American Music constantly being asked if I needed help, mansplained to when I found what I wanted (I would never ask anyone working at the stores, I would ask my friends first and come in prepared), men trying to tell me how to set up my own equipment etc." The process was similar when it came to Jessamine interviews: "No one really ever asked me anything in interviews. Rex was obviously the point person because he was the one making contact with people most of the time and he was the one who could spin yarns about influences, but I had a lot to say and had very much to do with how our band sounded and it often felt like I was overlooked."

Martha Schwendener, who played bass in Bowery Electric and had begun a career as an art critic, has depressingly similar stories: "One I've recounted the most is when I was carrying my amp head into a club and someone said to me, 'You shouldn't be carrying your boyfriend's equipment.' When it was Lawrence [Chandler] and me working, it was a clear division of labor and we fought, but we respected each other's talents and contributions. Once when we were touring, we were DJing and it was suggested (by members of our crowd) that I should step aside and let the boys DJ. Once we were out with the music critic Sasha Frere-Jones and Dave Allen from Gang of Four was at the table—one of my real favorite bands as a kid—and Sasha said someone played 'like a girl.' He was embarrassed and immediately corrected himself—that is, after I pointed it out."

Now, working as an art critic, Schwendener's experiences with sexism haven't changed. "I once said to Roberta Smith, my senior colleague at the *New York Times*, 'I thought we were done with this' (she's seen extraordinary sexism over the years). 'No,' she said, 'We're not done with it.'"

Schwendener and Smithson each played bass, anchoring and powering two intensely rhythmic bands, yet faced dismissive attitudes from the minute they walked in the door of a club. Smithson tells one story that summarizes the pains and rewards for her: "There were other times when I don't think people realized the bass was coming from a 'girl' because they didn't see me. We played at a café in San Luis Obispo and we really killed. When we were loading out, I walked by two guys sitting inside and one of them said, "Are you the bass player?" and I said yeah, and he said something like "You really rocked! Reminded me of Zeppelin!" I don't think they were into our music exactly, but they specifically liked the bass and had no idea what my gender was until they saw me loading out, so it was completely unbiased. One of the things about people not thinking that women can play (or more specifically compose) great music, is that there is always this thing in the back of your mind wondering if you're just a show pony and if you were a man, people wouldn't give you the time of day. It's a great way to fall deep into self-doubt."

Leslie Ransom recalls the obstacles she faced as director of sales at Touch & Go: "When I started, I was replacing another woman in the position. Initially, I had to run every decision past Corey Rusk. I don't think that was because I was a woman, but rather that he was loath to relinquish control over his label. Touch & Go had a lot of great strong women in positions of responsibility. In the world outside of Touch & Go, I did have to work harder to be heard. I think the biggest challenge was being seen as a 'real' music person rather than someone's girlfriend or being there to go home with a band member. Within the Chicago scene, there was less because we knew each other. Chicago also had folks like Sue Miller and Julia Adams at Lounge Ax who had real power."

Leslie faced condescension related to where and for whom she worked that was a little harder to pin down. "If I went to see big retailers or distributors outside of my usual circle, the challenge of being heard over my male counterparts was more complicated. I was from Chicago and an indie label AND I was a girl. So, I often got the impression people thought I didn't know how things worked. How much of that was sexism as opposed to elitism is hard to gauge."

Jessica Bailiff faced barriers based on her location in Toledo, Ohio, as well as her gender; she found it was "harder to book my own shows here as there was little interest and little to no pay when there was."

MEANWHILE, ON YOUR COMPUTER . . .

Of course, by 2002 networking had become vastly easier than it was in 1993. Upgrades in technology had made connecting and exchanging information via the Internet much easier. The slow adoption of Adobe's PDF format sped up when the portable text and image files became visible on web browsers. By 1999 it became the accepted file format for information exchange on the Internet. The speed and specificity of email had radically improved, and with broadband, musicians could trade sound files easily, aiding collaboration. We all know by now that the blade was two-sided: sharing sound files also became easier for consumers, and sales figures for CDs and LPs plummeted accordingly.

STUBBORN TINY LIGHTS VS. CLUSTERING DARKNESS

In the fall of 2001, godspeed you black emperor! was free from the agreement with kranky to release their albums on compact disc. But the band was not done with Chicago. They began recording with Steve Albini at Electrical Audio. A slew of Chicago's improvising musicians appeared on the track "Rockets Fall on Rocket Falls," including Geof Bradfield on bass clarinet, Rob Mazurek on trumpet, double bassist Josh Abrams, and on clarinet, Matana Roberts, who would go on in the new century to record a series of stunning albums for the Constellation label. After mixing it at their Montreal Hotel2Tango studio in the winter and with mastering by John Loder and Steve Rooke in London, the band moved an exclamation point in their name, changing from godspeed you black emperor! to godspeed you! black emperor, and released *Yanqui U.X.O* as a CD and double LP in November 2002.

That year a feature film called *28 Days Later* used a track from *F#A#∞* called "East Hastings" to portray the empty streets of London in a post-apocalyptic, zombie-infested world. The director, Danny Boyle, told the *Guardian* how he talked the band into letting him use their music on the film soundtrack: "They were very clear about how unlikely it was that they would give us permission to use it. But we kept at them. We went up to Newcastle to meet them when they were on tour . . . We took them out to dinner—well, it was scampi and chips, or vegetarian scampi and chips—anyway, they were lovely people. They asked to see the whole film, we showed them the whole film, and they gave us permission. I couldn't believe it, really!"

By the beginning of the new century, it was obvious that the major labels had moved on from Chicago. The success of the Strokes and Interpol in New York, and the rise of LCD Soundsystem and the related DFA label had drawn attention Manhattan-wards. The White Stripes began a climb to prominence and sports stadium omnipresence with their third album, *White Blood Cells*.

A quartet called OK Go had begun to work, and I mean work, in Chicago around 1998, plastering eye-catching posters around town, opening for bands coming through town, playing at live performances of the NPR radio program *This American Life*, and opening for the world's cleverest band, They Might Be Giants, on a national tour. Eventually an album they recorded with Dave Trumfio served as the root material, with some new songs featuring studio drummers, on OK Go's self-titled debut album on Capitol Records, released in September 2002. The group played a crisp, sprightly variation on indie guitar rock with a sprinkling of electronics. The album did reasonably well for a debut, making the lower rungs of the *Billboard* radio charts. Things really took off after a smartly choreographed video for the song "Here It Goes Again" on their second album became a viral sensation online. OK Go were the last Chicago rock band to emerge from the 1990s, get a major-label deal, and reach a measure of widespread success. Their savvy use of Internet-based marketing played no small part in this.

The slow rise of Chicago hip-hop to national attention that began with Common's *Resurrection* and Da Brat's platinum *Funkdafied* in 1994 accelerated as Kanye West made the move from producer to recording artist. When it came to Chicago, major-label scouts had a new (to them) hip-hop scene to focus on in which the payoffs were much larger and immediate than they had been with indie rock bands.

The feeding frenzy had passed, and there had been changes in the independent music business landscape in Chicago. Cargo Distribution's Chicago office had closed in 1998, "wracked . . . by deepening cash-flow problems," as *Billboard* put it. No one who had worked there was surprised. Patrick Monaghan had slowly been widening the number of record labels distributed via Carrot Top Records, and eventually opened the CTD distribution company. Reckless Records continued to prosper, opening satellite stores in Evanston and downtown Chicago. A mail-order operation specializing in new and used funky music of all kinds from jazz to world music called Dusty Groove established itself as a collectors' mail-order favorite beginning in 1996 and then full-fledged retail store by 2001.

The geography of the music scene had shifted by the onset of the new century. The original focal point in Lincoln Park and Old Town had shifted in the 1990s to an area roughly encompassing Wicker Park, Bucktown, and Ukrainian Village to the south. More and more musicians were moving farther west toward Garfield Park or south to Pilsen. The latter was slowly gentrifying from a predominantly Mexican American neighborhood as art galleries became established there. Near-downtown neighborhoods Printer's Row and River North began to attract residents as mayor Richard Daley's efforts to encourage gracious condominium living downtown bore fruit. Across the northside and down to Wicker Park itself, apartment buildings were being converted to condos. In an email to Annie Feldmeier in August 2001, I waxed poetic about running an errand five miles west to Pulaski and Wrightwood, and seeing "actual factories, lots of single-family homes" and "no Starbucks, no condos, fewer cars, like Chicago when I first moved here."

> Your website indicated that they were available in black. If that has changed and you have them in say grey heather with light blue printing or maybe a hooded sweatshirt in leaf green with white ink (like the ones worn by youth swim teams) I'll take one of those.
>
> —note from kranky T-shirt mail order, 2001

At kranky, 2002 had been especially notable, highlighted by the release of Low's *Trust*, the second loscil CD *Submers*, Keith Fullerton Whitman's debut on the imprint Playthroughs, and a reissue of a Stars of the Lid 1999 Belgian release, *Avec Laudenum*. Having strong catalog sellers from Low, godspeed you! black emperor, and Labradford and the steady sales growth of *Tired Sounds of Stars of the Lid* not only allowed Joel and me to work full-time at the label but also allowed us to take chances on some new bands like Out Hud, Christmas Decorations, Rex Ritter, Andy Brown's post-Jessamine band Fontanelle, and two solo projects from Fontanelle members called Nudge and Strategy. A long-standing desire to work with the Houston band Charalambides came to fruition when kranky reissued *Unknown Spin*, which originally had been released as a CD-R in a pressing of three hundred. As the website *Raven Sings the Blues* so aptly put it, "Charalambides exist in a kind of ephemeral limbo between psych, folk, drone and experimental songform." Their first album recorded specifically for kranky, *Joy Shapes*, remains one of the label's most intense listens, described in the same review as "tremendously thought-provoking and vastly troubled." Take a look at the *Pitchfork* Top 50 Albums of 2002 list and you will find Chicago-based artists Neko Case, Kevin Drumm (*Sheer Hellish Miasma*), the Fire Show, and Wilco (*Yankee Hotel Foxtrot*) and releases from Chicago labels Touch & Go, Bloodshot, Perishable, and even kranky. The kranky release was Keith Fullerton Whitman's *Playthroughs*, a recording of "extremely skeletal sinewave-resonances" that got critical acclaim and "hit like thunderclap," according to the artist.

The influence and profiles of more experimental Chicago bands like those along the Tortoise axis had peaked by the early 2000s. In his *Pitchfork* year-end review, Rob Mitchum was insightful in saying, "It's possible 2002 will be looked back on as the Year the Indie Kids Started Dancing Again." Critical attention focused on bands like the Rapture and LCD Soundsystem, and the groups recording for the associated DFA label made music cribbed from '80s post-punk, German electronic pulses from the '70s, and house music. The more specialized, avant-focused 2002 Brainwashed Reader's Poll listed kranky titles from Low, Keith Fullerton Whitman, Out Hud, and Pan•American. It was obvious that straightforward indie guitar rock was just one flavor of many available to listeners and concertgoers, and no longer set the pace for or defined underground music. In Chicago, a bar in the northside Roscoe Village neighborhood called the Hungry Brain had been hosting shows by a new generational cohort of free-jazz and improvising musicians starting in 2001. That scene not only reloaded itself, so to speak, but began to interact more with musicians from the city's southside.

The tireless performance and recording pace Weasel Walter set for himself and, as he puts it on his website, the work "forging alliances" and "creating unprecedented bridge between free jazz/improvised music and the Chicago rock club scene" had ripples across the United States. Genres like prog (or "progressive") rock, no wave, noise, and free jazz were being fractured and recombined by groups such as Wolf Eyes, Erase Errata, Lake of Dracula, Lightning Bolt, and others. Walter coined the genre name "brutal prog" on the "avant-progressive" listserv in 2000 to define the highly composed, intricate, and urgent music his long-standing Flying Luttenbachers group was making. It's one genre name among many, but brutal prog does illustrate the cross-fertilization that radiated outward from Chicago early in the twenty-first century. Weasel Walter moved to Oakland, California, in 2003, where he hooked up with Bay Area bands and kept up a variety of bands, projects, and collaborations.

Bloodshot Records celebrated their fifth anniversary in 2000 and by then had gained success with Chicago-based artists like Robbie Fulks, Kelly Hogan, the Waco Brothers, and others playing energized country and country-derived music. This in turn motivated well-known artists from out of town to work with the label. The label's best-known artist, Neko Case, had a background playing with Vancouver indie bands like Cub and, more prominently, the New Pornographers before producing her own take on country music with her 1997 album *The Virginian*. In 2000 she moved to Chicago and was tending bar at the Hideout; by 2009 she was based in Vermont and working with the Anti label, and her album *Middle Cyclone* had debuted at number 3 on the *Billboard* Top 200 chart.

The power and techniques of the drone and the crescendo had been absorbed into the extreme edges of heavy metal. In the summer of 2003, the heavy atmospheric duo SUNN O))), made up of guitarists Stephen O'Malley and former Engine Kid Greg Anderson, came to Chicago to play at the Empty Bottle, bringing Rex Ritter from Jessamine along to add bowel-vibrating moog tones. I picked them up at their hotel downtown and took them to Jim's Grill for lunch with Joel. O'Malley and Anderson had also started a quartet called Khanate with James Plotkin that explored slower-than-Sabbath pacing and long tones.

Thrill Jockey entered the new century releasing a wide variety of recordings from groups across the world. The label's Chicago-based bands were spinning off a variety of solo albums and regroupings from members of Tortoise and the Sea and Cake. The fourth Tortoise album, *Standards*, got a respectful but slightly salty response, as epitomized in this *A.V. Club* review: "As always, the band is poised between capturing a momentary, malleable inspiration and shaping that moment into some timeless anthem, and as always, it chooses to dither and delay, settling for a sometimes pleasant, sometimes maddening, almost always stimulating exploration of atmospherics." The giddy gushing by critics that accompanied *Millions Now Living* was a thing of the past, although the band retained a sizable audience. Thrill Jockey had taken on a shape-shifting artist named Bobby Conn, who John Corbett wrote was adept at "layering his view with tons of cultural and musical references," and whose "citations freely combine the ridiculous and the sublime," often with the aid of avant-garde players such as Julie Pomerleau, Ernst Karel, and Fred Lonberg-Holm. This kind of collaboration, established in the city in the 1990s, was a permanent feature of the Chicago underground music scene going forward and would continue to draw in new cadres of musicians from near and far.

Keith Whitman had observed the Chicago scene from a distance, working at the Forced Exposure warehouse and booking shows in suburban Cambridge, Massachusetts. "There's a certain myopia, especially acute in Indie Rock at the time, that just wasn't there in the music that was coming out of Chicago then," says Whitman. He eventually investigated in person. "I desperately wanted to see it all first-hand, and when I finally did it did not disappoint. I met Casey Rice, and when I was invited to come out for a gig at the Empty Bottle, I stayed with him. I talked to Kevin Drumm for maybe thirty seconds, and the next day we went to the Gene Siskel Theater to see *Persona*; this was far away from the ways that people were in my life at that point. I think this is at the core of what made it all so viable; not just the bleeding of the edges of genre and ideology, but a palpable willingness and desire to keep working, keep busy, try it from all angles. I never got the feeling that anyone there took a day off, but it was then possible for hundreds of musicians to live exclusively off of their musical endeavors in Chicago; a world away from where we are right now."

Although kranky worked with a relatively small number of Chicago-based musicians, the label benefited from the fermentation happening around us. Brian McBride from Stars of the Lid and Mark Nelson from Labradford had moved to the city. There were venues available for kranky bands to play in from the time Sue Miller added Labradford to an Archers of Loaf show at Lounge Ax in February 1994. The local press was well-informed and supportive—even if Peter Margasak did preview that first Chicago performance by adding the backhanded compliment, "By all means get there early to catch Labradford, but may I suggest bringing a cot."

THE CASE OF LABRADFORD

By late 2019, Labradford was described by the *Aquarium Drunkard* website as the "ground-breaking" group "whose slow-moving ambient soundscapes influenced a generation of slo-core, post-rock and electro-acoustic experimenters," and kranky as a label "which has since grown to define a cerebral sort of electronically enhanced drone music." I wouldn't argue with these assessments. Still, Mark Nelson hits on something when he notes that Labradford "never were out enough for *The Wire* magazine and were never straight enough for *Pitchfork*." That led to palpable frustration on my part as the guy trying to get the band the critical attention I thought they were due, and obviously for the band when Labradford was active. With the advantage of distance, I see that mixture of experimentation and accessibility as Labradford's core strength and the reason for their influence on the artists that followed them. This balance also contributed to the feeling of timelessness in the band's music. In making an Internet mix that included a Labradford track, the German producer and musician Christian Kleine noted, "I always find it interesting to listen to music where you cannot tell if it's thirty years old or yesterday." Stuart Braithwaite from the Scottish band Mogwai made a similar list for *The Guardian* in 2008, choosing the song "Streamlining." "This is just one of the most amazing songs I have ever heard," he says. "Totally dream-like. It's such a shame that Labradford aren't making music anymore. They were fantastic." In 2017, director Paolo Sorrentino chose the Labradford track "By Chris Johnston, Craig Markva, Jamie Evans" from *E luxo so* for a recurring role in the soundtrack to his HBO series *The Young Pope*, saying in an interview, "It's a piece of music I've been acquainted with for some time and that I'd also tried to introduce in previous films . . . It's a piece that simply hypnotizes me with its musical texture and simplicity. Plus, I love it when a piece of music is mostly unchanging and only features slight variations." The group even appears in the Oxford University Press's *Encyclopedia of Popular Music*.

James A. Hodgkinson submitted a thesis paper to the Department of Sociology at the University of Surrey in England in October 2000 called "An Unstable Reference," a play on the title of the second Labradford album, *A Stable Reference*. The scholar calls Labradford "a particularly significant and influential group" and devotes a chapter to "The Case of Labradford." Looking back on writing his thesis, and a contribution called "The Fanzine Discourse over Post-Rock" to the essay collection *Music Scenes: Local, Translocal, and Virtual*, Hodgkinson says, "The quality of Labradford is shown in that I listen to them still, despite having a record collection bursting at the seams with various drone/ambient/whatever you want to call it releases, some of it made after them, but much of it before. Quite often the writing about some new artist would be more exciting than the music itself when you finally got to hear it. But Labradford were always one of my favorites, from first listen to now."

Years later, Lucas Schleicher reminisced about discovering the group's third album *Labradford* as a teenager: "I remember trying to describe this to disinterested friends at fifteen and being perplexed by what they were doing. There were vocals, sort of, and it was ambient music, sort of, but there were rock instruments in the mix and melodies and nobody else I knew was working in such a unique way. Love this album, love the cover, love the loneliness and isolation it makes me feel just thinking about it. The sound of the Midwest spreading out in every direction forever."

As Brad Labonte noted in a *Dusted* review of the reissued *Prazision*, "Many seemingly disparate artists are currently mining this territory." You can see the impact Labradford made on the independent music scene every month on the digital retail and streaming site Bandcamp. Each month the site's "Bandcamp Daily" runs a "Best New Ambient Music on Bandcamp" summary featuring six to eight new releases, as a sample of the new music in the genre being released through the site. I could go on.

The focus of this book has been on Chicago, and how the kranky label developed amidst the music scene in the 1990s. The city has been a lodestar for popular music performance and a center of recording and distribution, drawing musicians from far and wide even before 1922, when Louis Armstrong followed his mentor, Joe "King" Oliver, from New Orleans to Chicago to perform in the Creole Jazz Band. Or when the WLS Radio *Barn Dance* program launched in 1924 and helped create a national audience for country music. Or when Thomas Andrew Dorsey came up with "gospel songs" to describe the combination of evangelical hymns, blues, and jazz music he was writing, and the publishing empire he created. Leave it to Rob Mazurek of Chicago Underground to sum up how the 1990s in Chicago were special for underground music:

"It was beautiful. You had clubs like Lunar Cabaret, our weekly sessions at the Green Mill, the Rainbo Club, Hideout,

Empty Bottle, Lounge Ax. A deep cross-pollination of ideas and styles was happening and continues happening to this day. But you must realize that this was always happening. Chicago has such a deep history. But it sure felt great to be in this environment at that time."

epilogue

specifically dissatisfied since 1993

On the evening of December 8, 2018, I walked down the aisle at Rockefeller Chapel at the University of Chicago to return to my seat. The first set had ended at one of three shows across the continent celebrating kranky's twenty-fifth anniversary. The sounds created by the musicians and the light show projected across the gothic nooks and crannies of the chapel interior made for a mesmerizing evening. Out of an old habit, I surveyed the audience and was gratified to see a sold-out show made up of many ages and nearly gender-balanced. I saw old friends, familiar faces, and many strangers. Brian Foote, my successor as the kranky promotions person, introduced me to the audience as I moved toward my seat. Does anybody really like being called out in church? Thankfully, most of the crowd was indifferent to Brian's gracious comments and to me. I felt the sensations of bodily displacement and expedited my progress back to my pew. When I spoke with Brian during another intermission, he informed me that the performances in Portland, Los Angeles, and New York were similarly attended.

I had sold my share of the label to Joel Leoschke thirteen years earlier. In 2014 Joel moved to Portland. A year later my wife and I left Chicago for Urbana, Illinois. When I visited the label warehouse to research this book, it was in a squat, single-story cinder block building that looked like it had been plucked from the suburbs surrounding O'Hare by the hand of some bemused god and dropped into the Pacific Northwest.

"Thrive" is not a word that Joel or I would ever use to describe kranky's status. Then and now I think we both possess cellular levels of diffidence about the music business. The label continues to discover artists and release their recordings, and revamp and reissue older ones. I have yet to see any music writers recognize the predominance of recent kranky releases from female and intersex artists.

The marketplace kranky operates in has changed much since 1993, battered by the advent of digital formats and the decimation of record stores, then shrunk by streaming, then experiencing a revival in the demand for vinyl and subsequent delays in vinyl production times, and (as of the time of this writing) hammered by a pandemic that has wreaked havoc on live performance and the network that sustained independent labels and artists. Joel and Brian carry on, and musicians eagerly join the label roster.

In Chicago, peers at Thrill Jockey, Drag City, and Bloodshot (to name a few) are on their feet despite all the shots the independent sector has taken in the new century. New independent labels have found space to develop in the city.

Chicago as a city has changed a lot in the last thirty years, and not always for the better. It remains a breeding ground for great music. On any given day I am prepared to argue with total strangers that it always will be.

acknowledgments

This book would not have been written without Annie Feldmeier Adams, who has always believed in the absolute necessity of telling this story and has always had unwavering faith that I was the person to tell it.

I am deeply indebted to Jessica Hopper and Casey Kittrel, who presented me with an opportunity and then patiently guided and challenged me through a process that began with a pitch and ended up with a book on the shelf. I'm grateful to the staff at the University of Texas Press for taking a chance on this project and shepherding it through to completion.

Joel Leoschke has provided material, intellectual, and social generosity throughout this process. One happy consequence of this undertaking was being able to shoot the breeze in the kranky warehouse as if a day hadn't passed between us. Here's to many more Founder's Dinners to come.

It was the privilege of my professional life to represent and advocate for the work of the musicians on the kranky roster for fifteen years. Thanks to Carter Brown and Mark Nelson for stepping off the ledge with Joel Leoschke and me, and to all the musicians who put their trust in the label. This book is not only shaped by the interviews so many provided so amiably, but also by many conversations over the years.

Working at a record label by necessity involves putting on blinders and focusing on the tasks at hand, so I am thankful that so many people in so many places took the time to help expand my perspective on music making in Chicago and beyond. Special thanks to Lisa Bralts-Kelly, a good neighbor and guide as I looked back. And to Patrick Monaghan, who could answer the question, "Did you see what I saw?"

I'm glad that the collective efforts of the Discogs community created a deep well of information that I could utilize. I'm grateful to Jacob Walter for suggesting that I put a bit more of myself into the book. My thanks to Dan Mackta at Qobuz, because there were times when only Renaissance lute jams would do the trick. The staff of the upper level at the University of Illinois Undergraduate Library were welcoming and friendly to the "independent scholar" in their midst. I regret that a pandemic kept me from completing my work there.

Thank you for the good times, Chicago. You're an effervescent, goofy, clumsy, and brutal beast.

author's notes

I began researching the material in this book in the fall of 2019. I was able to travel to Portland, Oregon, in October that year to meet in person with Joel Leoschke and rifle through the kranky archives. Andy Brown and Rex Ritter shared their Jessamine recollections, and a conversation with Scot Rutherford, a keen observer of events and music in Chicago and beyond, was illuminating.

I visited Toledo, Ohio, and Dearborn, Michigan, that year to meet with Jessica Bailiff, Carl Hultgren, Mat Sweet, and Windy Weber. Those wide-ranging conversations provided direction and background for the book, and follow-up emails are used extensively within it.

I'm grateful to Carter Brown, Jim DeRogatis, Joel Mark, Mark Nelson, Casey Rice, and Tom Windish for taking the time to talk on the telephone, often at odd hours across oceans.

In-person conversations with Lisa Bralts-Kelly, Bill Meyer, and Bob Steltman filled in many blanks for me and inspired further inquiry.

I conducted email interviews with Bernie Bahrmasel, Andrew Beaujon, David Bryant, Michael Bullington, Brendan Burke, Lawrence Chandler, Paul Dickow, Bobby Donne, Chris Farmer, Mark Greenberg, David Grubbs, Brent Gutzeit, James Hodgkinson, Vivian Host, Peter Kember, Braden King, Greg Kot, Michael Krassner, Mark Lux, Josh Madell, Rob Mazurek, Brian McBride, Douglas McCombs, Phil McMullen, Gareth Mitchell,

Patrick Monaghan, Roy Montgomery, Scott Morgan, Tomas Palermo, David Pearce, Kim Pieters, James Plotkin, Leslie Ransom, Ned Raggett, Adam Reach, Jeff Reilly, Simon Reynolds, Sheila Sachs, Martha Schwendener, Philip Sherburne, Paul Smith, Dawn Smithson, Mark Spybey, Peter Stapleton (RIP), Tim Stegall, JulieAnn "Jam" Tidy, David Trumfio, Ken Vandermark, Chuck van Zyl, Richard Walker, Keith Fullerton Whitman, Jon Whitney, Adam Wiltzie, and Brad Wood. All quotes in the book from those individuals not directly attributed in published writing are from these conversations and interviews.

This book refers to many musicians and recordings. Here is some information for anyone interested in further exploration: the *Chicago Reader* online archives at chicagoreader.com provided much background material and the opportunity to revisit the writing of John Corbett, Monica Kendrick, Peter Margasak, and Bill Meyer—all of whom wrote extensively and insightfully about the music scene in the city and Chicago's musical exchanges with the greater world. I recommend them to anyone interested in digging deeper.

Simon Reynolds maintains archives of his writing projects centered at blissout.blogspot.com. You can trace the origins of the post-rock genre and delve into Reynolds's work at English music weeklies, magazines, newspapers, and the books he's published. I may not agree with him all the time, but his writing is well-organized and argued and fun to mentally debate with.

The Wire also archives past articles and reviews for subscribers online at thewire.co.uk. The English magazine emerged in the early '90s as the go-to source for those interested in obscure, weird, and/or cutting-edge music from all angles. As such, it gets inevitable pushback as elitist or the like. There are few music magazines even being published these days, much less any covering a wide range of "new" music. Funnily enough, as I compile these notes, kranky artist Grouper is on the cover of the September 2021 issue. That only took twenty-eight years.

The *Ptolemaic Terrascope* is on the web at terrascope.co.uk. Their list of Top 100 Albums is a great introduction to their "thing," along with archives of past issues and interviews that go back to the first issue in 1989. There is also a detailed list of all the Terrastock festivals to be found there. Andrew Young attends to the website. Although the print magazine ceased publication in 2005, Phil McMullen occasionally publishes *Terrascopaedia* on letterpress. Find out more at www.ptolemaic.org.

Jon Whitney and company have kept brainwashed.com operating since 1996, reviewing and sampling recordings, as well as maintaining webpages for Jessica Bailiff, Bowery Electric, godspeed you! black emperor, Labradford, Pan•American, Stars of the Lid, Windy & Carl, and numerous non-kranky artists including Tortoise. These and the archive of Reader's Polls give insight into what people were listening to and writing about then and now. Since the beginning, *Brainwashed* has been a labor of love and an invaluable resource.

If details like catalog numbers and the like are of interest to you, look no further than Discogs.com. The hive mind of contributors has compiled all the information you need to track down when, where, and by whom recordings were made and released into the world.

index